DONALD G. JACKSON
SOLDIER OF CINEMA

SCOTT SHAW

BUDDHA ROSE PUBLICATIONS

Donald G. Jackson: Soldier of Cinema
Copyright 2020 By Scott Shaw
www.scottshaw.com
All Rights Reserved

Cover Photographs of Donald G. Jackson
By Scott Shaw
Copyright © 2002 All Rights Reserved.

This book contains material protected under International and Federal Copyright Laws and Treaties. Any unauthorized reprint or use of this material is prohibited. No part of this book may be reproduced or transmitted in any form or by any means, electronic or mechanical, including photocopying, recording, or by any information storage and retrieval system without express written permission from the author or publisher.

First Edition 2020

ISBN 10: 1-949251-22-5
ISBN 13: 978-1-949251-22-7

Library of Congress Control Number: 2020932389

Printed in the United States of America
10 9 8 7 6 5 4 3 2

DONALD G. JACKSON
SOLDIER OF CINEMA

Table of Contents

Introduction — 9

PART I: *In His Own Words* — 17
- Mission Statement — 19
- Welcome to the Endless Gray Ribbon — 22
- RWB — 28
- The Seven Steps of Zen Filmmaking — 32
- RevDonaldo's Quick History of Zen Filmmaking — 34
- Raw Energy — 38
- One Shot Sam Bluegrass Party — 39
- The New Church of Zen Entertainment — 41
- Palomino Club — 42
- Guns of El Chupacabra Study Guide — 47
- Donald G. Jackson Filmography — 51
- DGJ Newsgroup Postings — 57
- Soldier of Cinema: The Gospel of Revdonaldo — 97

PART II: *The Films and The Filmmaking* — 117
- Making The Roller Blade Seven — 119
- Roller Blade Seven: *The Story of the Production* — 141
- Max Hell Frog Warrior: *The History and the Evolution* — 165
- Max Hell Frog Warrior: *The Story of the Production* — 171

The Saga of Guns of El Chupacabra *and the Art of Zen Filmmaking*	191
Guns of El Chupacabra *The Story of the Production*	203
Making The Rock n' Roll Cops	220
The Rock n' Roll Cops *The Story of the Production*	233
Donald G. Jackson and The Demon Lover	264
PART III: *Asked and Answered*	269
Donald G. Jackson: The Final Interview	271
Max Hell Frog Warrior: The Facts and The Fiction	309
The High Priest of Zen Filmmaking	340
Big Sister 2000 and Women in Prison Films	349
Donald G. Jackson: The Filmmaker and The Filmmaking	353
Donald G. Jackson: Small Town Roots	361
Donald G. Jackson and Demon Lover Diary	365
PART IV: *Tidbits*	371
I'm an Artist Goddamn it!	373
The Personality of Philosophy	375
Everybody Wants Something from Me but Nobody Ever Gives Me Anything	377
Zen Filmmaking: The Good, The Bad, and The People That Don't Know What the Fuck They're Talking About	379
The Same Yet Different	383

Honoring People's Wishes and What You Can Do About What You Can Do	386
Stirring the Pot	389
Zen Filmmaking: SS vs. DGJ	392
Knowing What You Don't Know	394
Conclusion	**397**
Appendix	**399**

Introduction

Fade In:

Every now and then you meet someone and they change the trajectory of your life. The meeting is only one part of this equation, however, the second part is what you do with what you have gained from this meeting. Certainly, this is the case with my meeting Donald G. Jackson.

Donald G. Jackson and I created a new style of filmmaking, *Zen Filmmaking*. *Zen Filmmaking* amalgamated the freedom-based cinematic mindset that we both possessed. It embraced our love for Samurai, Hong Kong, Spaghetti Western, and the Art House Cinema that grew out of the subculture of the 1960s. It drew upon my years of involvement with Eastern Meditative Thought and the Martial Arts and Donald G. Jackson's love for all things Bushido. Though I was the one who formalized and wrote extensively about this system of cinema, had Donald G. Jackson and I not met and together formulated the foundation for this method, *Zen Filmmaking* would assuredly have not been created. Thus, I can be certain that our meeting changed both of our lives.

Don, as I will refer to him from this point forward, came up in the era when movies were shot on film. This was an expensive process. Not nearly as cheap as it has become today when people can win awards for films that they have created entirely on their iPhone. He used to say, *"Making movies is the easy part, getting the money to make movies is the hard part."* It was a different age and time. This too was the case when Don and I first began working together; film was the name of the game. And, filmmaking was not cheap.

By the end of our first completed production as a team, *The Roller Blade Seven,* the Video Revolution had begun to take hold. Times were changing. In fact, on the very last day of actual production of *The Roller Blade Seven* we rented two Canon video cameras and we shot footage that, years later, after Don's passing, I edited and released as the first *Zen Documentary, Interview: The Roller Blade Seven Documentary.*

As the Video Revolution took hold, both Don and I began to shoot some but not all of our movies on video. Though Don never lived to see the Digital Revolution, by the later days of Don's life the time of shooting movies solely on film was behind us. We both lived through this transition and I believe we played, at least a small part, in ushering in this new era.

As I have long stated, Don was a complicated, very temperamental guy. He had a lot of inner demons including intense anger control issues, obsessive-compulsive disorder, and I believe an undiagnosed case of bipolar disorder. He had, as I would title it, *"The Elvis Complex,"* He really felt he was the center of the universe. All this led to his life and his legacy becoming defined as both an appreciated and a hated filmmaker. All of which will be detailed in the later pages of this book.

Once upon a time, movies that Don made were shown in drive-in theaters and played on late night TV. As we all understand, drive-in theaters are long gone and his movies have long ago faded from public view on TV. As the years have gone by, however, I have watched as interest in his movies has both faded and in other ways been revitalized. His known films such as *Hell Comes to Frogtown, Roller Blade Warriors, The Roller Blade Seven,* and *Max*

Hell Frog Warrior appear to hold a place in Cult Film History but most of his other movies have vanished from public knowledge. This is why it somewhat surprises me when I find people writing about Don.

There have been numerous on-line reviews written about his films over the years. Though not the first, recently there was a Film School Master's Thesis written about *Zen Filmmaking*. Though the focus of the thesis was concentrated primarily on myself, the author did include a discussion about Donald G. Jackson. There was also a book recently self-published about Donald G. Jackson. What the author of this book did was to scour and reference the articles and the interviews on my website, (scottshaw.com), that pertained to Don, and then draw conclusions about Don's life and his filmmaking career. Many of this author's declarations were, however, erroneous.

I certainly understand that if your film work is going to be presented to the public, this style of scrutiny cannot be avoided. But, being an academic, I find this method of life-chronicling writings disingenuous as none of these aforementioned people have contacted and discussed the actual facts of *Zen Filmmaking* or the life of Donald G. Jackson with me. This is the same with many of the others who have written about or discussed Don and I in audio or video productions.

These actions and others set me to thinking that it may be a good idea to go through my Donald G. Jackson and *Zen Filmmaking* archives, collect his writings, combine those with some of my writings that involved Don, and present them in one cohesive unit. Though I had never planned to compose a book like this, observing recent occurrences set me to make the decision to do so.

Don, himself, liked to write but other creative endeavors always seemed to take up his time, so his actual written output was minimal. He would tell me that he used to enjoy writing articles for the staple-bound fanzines of the 1960s and 1970s but that was long before the Computer Age so I believe most of those writings will be lost to the hands of time forever. He did, however, constantly carry a 6 X 9 notebook around with him. With an obsession, he noted every occurrence in his life: the time a person came into his office, the time they left, when he heard a song he liked on the radio, every new thought that he had, the time he arrived at a location, and even when he got in or out of his car. By the time of his death there had to be hundreds if not thousands of those notebooks.

I always thought that it would be a great experiment in poetry to take those writings and turn them into a book. *"The Obsessional Scribbles of Donald G. Jackson,"* I suggested to him as a title. But, scribbling was the problem. Virtually no one, not even Don, could read his writing.

There was one exception to this rule, however. After Don's passing his wife called me up in tears one day. She had found a notebook that detailed one of Don's liaisons with a starlet. Holding firm to the, *"Man Code,"* I just played along like I didn't know. But, that was the legacy Don left behind; he left a lot of damage in his wake.

Ultimately Janet, Don's wife, destroyed all of the notebooks. Thus, *The Obsessional Scribbles of Donald G. Jackson* are lost forever.

Don had encountered an enormous amount of medical debt due to his years of illness from leukemia. As we all know, this is not uncommon and illustrates a very flawed depiction of our American society; as sick people are not taken care of. This drove his wife towards bankruptcy after his passing. Hand-in-hand with this, just after his death, the landlord of the house Don had rented for over two decades, in Canoga Park, evicted Janet and Don's daughter, Marty.

Don was an obsessive collector. Perhaps better put, he was a hoarder. ...Though he was a very well organized hoarder. The walls of his home were literally lined with organized boxes full of everything from comic books, to videotapes, onto cassettes, LPs, and CDs, you name it...

Shortly before Don entered into the final stages of his life, he had rented two large dumpsters and filled them both with discarded items, such as years of movie memorabilia, costuming, and generalized junk. Plus, he had discovered eBay and had sold much of his filmmaking equipment and some of his vintage film magazines, posters, memorabilia, and even some of his beloved vintage comic books. Though this was the case, when Don's wife was faced with eviction, she had only thirty days to clear out all of the remaining items of which there was a lot. Like I told her, *"You need a year to do this,"* but all she had was one month.

Every few days Janet would call me up and I would drive over to the house, literally stuffing my car with items that had to be discarded. For example, I was given all of Don's massive VHS collection that I donated to *The Salvation Army.* ...He and I had different viewing preferences... Plus, I was given so much other stuff that I cannot even remember what it was.

I always felt terribly sorry for Janet and Marty after Don's passing. The man had made millions of dollars in the film industry and just blew every penny. Like I always said, even to his face, *"Don was the greatest squanderer of money I have ever met."* Yet, he did not own a home and by the time of his death, he did not even own a car. Not to mention, he left his family bankrupt. Thus, that is the legacy of Donald G. Jackson.

As is always the case with people who do or did not personally known an individual, they possess an idealized image of that person. In the documentary I promised Don that I would make about him as he lay in the final days of his life in his hospitable bed, *"Diary of a Michigan Migrant Film Worker,"* I show the true Donald G. Jackson and the process he, (and I), undertook in making his last feature film. A fan of his once asked me about some of the rage-driven chaotic behavior Don displayed in that film. As I told him, and as I say to you the reader, there were two films I could have made when choosing the footage for that documentary. One was the film I made, that hopefully did a good job of portraying the true Donald G. Jackson. The other would have been one that truly showed his dark side and the complete chaos that he created in every possible situation, for no other reason than something concocted within his own mind.

For those of you who wish to witness the true Donald G. Jackson, I recommend you watch that documentary, as it is very revealing. In the meantime, hopefully the words presented in this book will guide you to a deeper understanding of the man and the filmmaker.

Though I have attempted to present a few initial facts in this introduction, it is essential that I state here that this book is not a biography of Donald G. Jackson. What this book offers are the writings that Don, (himself), composed, and then the book will present essays I have written about my extensive dealings with the man.

This book begins with Don in his own words. These writing are presented with virtually no alterations in punctuation or formatting; just the most basic of spelling corrections. The book then progresses to the tales of our interactions, stories of our filmmaking, and interviews that discuss Donald G. Jackson both in his own words and mine. Finally, the book will present tidbits of information that the reader may find interesting and useful in understanding the man and the filmmaker.

This book is composed so that the reader or the researcher will be able to access a large amount of information about Donald G. Jackson all in one place in order to hopefully gain an insightful understanding about who and what Donald G. Jacksons actually was or was not. The writings presented in this book are based upon numerous resources. There are chapters from previously published books, magazine articles, interviews, web offerings, and blogs. Each will hopefully provide you with deeper insight into Donald G. Jackson.

Though some of the writings presented in this book may be found in other places, they are presented here as a one-stop location. Thus, for you film school students, historians, and other researchers who actually desire a formalized point of published academic reference, here is your instrument.

To be fair, aside from his own writings and the interview with Don presented in these pages, these writings are based upon my interpretation of the occurrences that took place in association with Donald G. Jackson. He may have had a completely different understanding about what took place. But, as I was arguably the person who knew him the best, at least in terms of his filmmaking, I believe these writings will provide the reader with a bird's eye view into who Donald G. Jackson actually was.

When Don was nearing the final stages of his life, he was very worried that his filmmaking legacy would be lost. He believed that his wife or his daughter would not possess the desire or the ability to complete his unfinished films and to keep his name and his movies in the public eye. At this point, he assigned all the rights, title, and interest to all of his films to me and he also gave me the many years of unedited footage that he had collected from his working solo and/or the two of us working as a team. From this, I edited and finished many of the movies that he had started. As I often say, *"This is why so many more of the movies Donald G. Jackson created were released after his passing than when he was alive."* In the years since his passing, though I never intentionally signed-up for the job, I have also been the one chosen to keep his name alive in the minds of those who are interested in independent cinema.

With all this being said, what you will find in the pages of this book are numerous writings detailing the life, the lifestyle, the thoughts, and the method of filmmaking employed by Donald G. Jackson. I trust as you read through these pages you will come to a clearer understanding of a man who devoted his entire life to the creation of independent cinema.

Scott Shaw
20 January 2020

PART I
IN HIS OWN WORDS

Mission Statement

I've been making independent films since the mid-60's. This site will share my creative experiences and offer an opportunity to view my Work including the films that are HARD TO FIND, OUT OF PRINT, UNRELEASED, NEW FEATURES, and WORKS-IN-PROGRESS. We'll FLASHBACK to making my first movie THE DEMON LOVER that was theatrically released by The TEXAS CHAINSAW MASSACRE distribution executives. You'll learn the truth about the A.F.I. sponsored shock-u-mentary DEMON LOVER DIARY and how a self-righteous high school drop-out with his college educated girl friend conspired to destroy my filmmaking dream and turn it into a nightmare.

DEMON LOVER DIARY would play for almost twenty years and win top awards at almost every film festival.

You'll learn why it will NEVER BE RELEASED ON VIDEO – plus How we got GUNNAR HANSEN, soon to become famous as LEATHERFACE, to make a guest appearance. Why the original artist of HOWARD THE DUCK acted in, and why rock star TED NUGENT, bailed from THE DEMON LOVER. Shot in 16mm for only three thousand dollars in cash.

We raised more money and blew it up to 35mm for theatrical release. The film played New York's Lyric Theater (where they shot a scene for TAXI DRIVER on 42nd Street and the Southern U.S. Drive-in Circuit.

THE DEMON LOVER inspired many others to get started making movies and influenced such hits as HALLOWEEN, THE EVIL DEAD, and FRIDAY THE 13TH.

Long before the WWF and RAW there was my Michigan-made wrestling-horror movie RINGSIDE IN HELL. After seeing Altman's NASHVILLE, this film evolved into a Country-rock docu-drama known as RINGSIDE then became a Rock n' Roll Wrestling film distributed by NEW WORLD VIDEO. I LIKE TO HURT PEOPLE quickly grossed ½ MILLION DOLLARS for the distributor, and allowed me to sell them site unseen - ROLLER BLADE. Futuristic Rebel Nuns on skates with magic butter-fly knives that would evolve into Sacred Samurai Swords.

I'll show you the best from thirty years of production photos and tell stories about my experiences working with JAMES CAMERON on TERMINATOR and his Spaghetti Western rock video REACH with BILL PAXTON's band MARTINI RANCH.

Photos and info working with the Academy Award Winning SKOTAK BROTHERS.

Filming in Michigan and moving to California for my ROGER CORMAN DAZE.

Shooting in the World's Largest film format IMAX/OMNIMAX.

Making ROLLER BLADE on my Visa card- shot silent with an old windup Bolex and Outdated reversal film stock.

Working without a script using a technique I'd come to recognize as Zen Filmmaking.

ROLLER BLADE would earn ONE MILLION DOLLARS for NEW WORLD VIDEO and result in the funding of HELL COMES TO FROGTOWN for 1.5 MILLION DOLLARS.

Later how I made RETURN TO FROGTOWN with SAG actors in ten days for only $180,000.

I'll offer Tons of photos and info on film work with JULIE STRAIN including the ROCKY HORROR PICTURE SHOW for the NEW MILLENNIUM - LINGERIE KICKBOXER.

Behind the Scenes with TRACI LORDS on SHOCK EM DEAD and why TRACI wasn't in RETURN TO FROGTOWN because the Executive Producer had no idea who she was and ROLLER BLADE SEVEN. even though her checks were signed.

CAMERA FOR HIRE shooting for FRED OLEN RAY and many others.

FILM TALENT and MUSIC DISCOVERIES.

IMPOSSIBLE TO FIND FILMS and ESOTERIC INFLUENCES that will never be seen again.

ZENDANCE. COM will feature the films of DONALD G. JACKSON and showcase new talent discoveries - Plus the Over-Looked and Under-rated.

You'll hear bands like COWBOY BUDDAH and WALDEN DAHL.

THE ZENDANCE MIME TROUPE will entertain you with THE ZENDANCE DANCERS.

I'll explain my 'CODE OF THE BUSHIDO' methods of living, working eating, drinking, and enjoying music and movies.

I'll post photos of me with famous folks and tell you great stories and working with the rich and famous.

Welcome to the Endless Gray Ribbon:

The road goes on forever, and the party never ends! I've been making films since the mid-60's. This site will share my creative experiences and offer an opportunity to view my Work including the films that are HARD TO FIND, OUT OF PRINT, UNRELEASED, NEW FEATURES and WORKS-IN-PROGRESS. We'll FLASHBACK to making my first feature film THE DEMON LOVER that was theatrically released by the TEXAS CHAINSAW MASSACRE distribution executives. You'll learn the truth about the A.F.I. sponsored Mock-U-Mentary DEMON LOVER DIARY and how a self-righteous high school drop-out with his college educated girlfriend conspired to destroy my filmmaking dream and turn it into a nightmare. DEMON LOVER DIARY

would play for more
than twenty years and
win top awards at
almost every important
film festival.
You'll learn why it will
NEVER-BE-RELEASED
on HOME VIDEO - Plus
How we got GUNNAR HANSEN
soon to be famous
as LEATHERFACE,
to make a guest appearance.
Why the original artist
of HOWARD THE DUCK
acted in, and why rock star
TED NUGENT, bailed from
THE DEMON LOVER.
Shot in 16mm
for only three thousand
dollars in cash, we
raised more money and
blew it up to 35mm
for theatrical release.
The film played
the famous Lyric Theater
on 42nd Street, where
they shot a scene
for TAXI DRIVER.
Our seven prints traveled
the Southern Drive-In
Circuit including Florida
and Texas.
THE DEMON LOVER
inspired many others to
start making films,
and influenced such hits

as HALLOWEEN, THE EVIL
DEAD, and FRIDAY THE 13TH.
Long before the WWF,
there was my Michigan-made
Wrestling-Horror Movie,
RINGSIDE IN HELL.
After seeing Altman's film,
NASHVILLE, my movie
evolved into a
Country-Rock, Docu-Drama
known as RINGSIDE.
After minor editing,
changing the music,
and giving it a new title -
I LIKE TO HURT PEOPLE
quickly grossed ½ MILLION
DOLLARS for New World Video.
This same distributor next
allowed me to sell them
site unseen - ROLLER BLADE.
Futuristic Rebel Nuns
on roller skates
with magic butter-fly
knives that would evolve
into sacred samurai swords.
I'll show you the best
from thirty years of
production photos and
tell stories about my
experiences working with
JAMES CAMERON on TERMINATOR,
and his Spaghetti Western
Rock Video - REACH,
with BILL PAXTON's band
MARTINI RANCH.
PHOTOS and info working

with the Academy Award
Winning SKOTAK BROTHERS.
Moving to California for
my ROGER CORMAN DAZE.
Shooting in the World's
Largest film format
IMAX/OMNIMAX.
Making ROLLER BLADE
on my Visa Card -
shot silent with an old
wind-up Bolex and
Outdated reversal film stock.
Working without a script
using a technique I'd come
to recognize as
ZenFilmMaking.
ROLLER BLADE would earn
ONE MILLION DOLLARS
for NEW WORLD VIDEO
and result in the
funding of
HELL COMES TO FROGTOWN
for a budget of
1.5 MILLION DOLLARS.
Later, how I made
RETURN TO FROGTOWN
with SAG actors
in ten days
for only $180,000.
I'll offer tons of
photos and info on
my film work with
JULIE STRAIN including
the ROCKY HORROR PICTURE
SHOW for the
New Millennium -

LINGERIE KICKBOXER.
Behind the Scenes with
TRACI LORDS on
SHOCK 'EM DEAD.
CAMERA FOR HIRE
Shooting Adventures with
FRED OLEN RAY
and many others.
Difficult and IMPOSSIBLE
to find strange underground
films that will
never be seen again.
The evolution of esoteric
influences into commercial
acceptance.
ZENDANCE. COM
will feature the
Film Works of
DONALD G. JACKSON
and Showcase New Film
and Music Talent
Discoveries - PLUS
the Over-Looked
and Under-Rated.
You'll hear great bands
like COWBOY BUDDAH
and WALDEN DAHL.
Enjoy entertainment from
THE ZENDANCE MIME TROUPE.
I'll explain my
CODE OF THE BUSHIDO
methods of living, working,
eating, and drinking rules.
Post photos of me with
celebrities and tell you

great stories about working
with the rich and famous.

RWB

Maverick Hollywood filmmaker, DONALD G. JACKSON has always broken the rules and gone against the trends, but this past summer JACKSON went on the air with a radio show broadcast on 99.3 FM - Radio Free Lenawee out of the Ann Arbor Michigan area.

The Saturday night show RED, WHITE & BLUEGRASS started up on June 9, 2001 playing JACKSON'S brand of folk, bluegrass, roots music, and alt. country to a small audience of dedicated listeners on what had primarily been a talk radio station.

Broadcast "live" in Michigan, the RWB as Jackson likes to call it - featured local bluegrass artists dropping by to sing in the studio, phone interviews, and CD's both old and new.

Since returning to Los Angeles, Jackson has started producing his show from a studio in Santa Ana working with FLETCHER HARRINGTON (lead singer of the band COWBOY BUDDHA). RWB continues to play great music from new artists that mainstream radio mostly ignores.

"I've found many great new performers from the pages of NO DEPRESSION MAGAZINE and on the alt. country site of MP3. Sometimes I'll find a song that is just so good I can't sleep! Plus as an added bonus, Jackson has been digging out tunes from his "rare vinyl" 45 and record album collection dating back to the 50's. And if that's not enough - he even plays folk music tapes he recorded on a reel to reel machine in the 60's of undiscovered bands that are gone, but not forgotten.

Sometimes FLETCHER HARRINGTON sings live.

RWB featured new songs from FLETCHER'S solo album "EYES ON FIRE AND KNUCKLES SORE" that has since been released to critical acclaim.

RWB offers commentary and jokes on an eclectic range of music.

When we start talking about "mountain music" - then we have to include the Hollywood Hills, and that opens up the show for music with no boundaries.

"We even play a bluegrass version of the BANANA BOAT song! And no place on Earth can you hear all the different versions of Jackson's favorite song of all time - LONG BLACK VEIL.

"I'm always adding new renditions - the latest being by HELLBETTY from Denmark." The O' BROTHER, WHERE ART THOU soundtrack was the main inspiration for finally starting my own radio show.

After the switchboard lit up when I started playing songs from it during breaks on the regular talk show, I realized I'd started something good.

"What made me feel great, on November 7th was to see was to see producer, T-Bone Burnett on stage accepting the award for Country Music album of the year. A few days later, I talked to T-Bone at SPACELAND in Silverlake. He was highly amused by the concept of my RWB radio show, but got sick while performing his new "art rock" music on stage and didn't get interviewed.

Larry Cordell's bluegrass version of MURDER ON MUSIC ROW was another song that inspired me to share my knowledge of music by producing a radio show. I'm thrilled that both my favorite songs of 2001 won top awards," said Jackson. RED, WHITE & BLUEGRASS is now expanding to the worldwide audience on the internet.

The RWB has featured interviews and special appearances by music performers including
HANK WILLIAMS III
THE DERAILERS JUNIOR BROWN
RAUL MALO
DAVE EDMUNDS
ROBBIE FULKS
DEL McCOURY
CARLA OLSON
SPLIT LIP RAYFIELD
AUSTIN LOUNGE LIZARDS
JUDY HENSKE
CHRIS HILLMAN
and others.

"We're just getting started" says Jackson who credits Michigan's Pastor Rick Strawcutter for first putting him on the air. "It's a Christian broadcasting station, and we kinda had to be careful about some of the music we played. Once in a while, I'd sneak in a RAMONES song just to see if anyone called the station to complain, and one day someone finally did – so we had to expand to the internet!"

Actually the FCC recently came in and raided the Michigan radio station and confiscated all the broadcasting equipment, but that's another story. So for now the RWB is "Safe At Home" on RadioCountry.Org. And the latest news is that Jackson, working for Lightsource Entertainment Network, has established a group of VIDEO DIGILANTES to show up and document various events across the country. The first project was in Chicago for the 60th Birthday Party of legendary folk singer – DWAIN STORY. DWAIN was a member of THE KNOBLICK UPPER 10,OOO who recorded for Mercury Records in the early 60's.

"Introduction" and "Workout" are the two best bluegrass albums in the history of the world - bar none!" says Jackson.

Later as a solo artist, DWAIN STORY often shared the stage with performers such as BOB DYLAN, PHIL OCHS, STEVE GOODMAN, RAMBLIN' JACK ELLIOT, CHLORIS NOELKE and many more.

A preview version of this Feb. 3, 2002 DWAIN STORY concert will be shown at the ZENDANCE FILM FESTIVAL in Joshua Tree, CA

RWB was originally broadcast on 99.3 FM outside Ann Arbor, MI.

Zendance.com has archived fifteen of these shows and they are available on Compact Disc.

The Seven Steps of Zen Filmmaking

1. SURVEY RESOURCES:
Research and make a list of available performers, locations, props, wardrobe, and vehicles for ready access.

2. EQUIPMENT CHECK:
Decide what camera to use and make certain everything is working including lights, etc.

3. THE ROUNDUP:
Once at the location, an important part of the Zen ritual is to 'lasso the energy'. Drive or walk around the area to survey the situation and get familiar with the environment.

4. ALLOW THE 'ZEN' ENERGY TO STRIKE:
You'll be able to create very special movies with what you've put together. Allow the Zen energy to strike. Take advantage of mistakes, unexpected events, accidents, unusual occurrences. And even those actor friends who didn't show up.

Using the Zen Filmmaking technique, the actors who come back the most end up being the stars of the movie.

It would be a waste of time to write a script in most cases when you are dealing with low budget. And there is no way following a script would be as much fun.

Always remember - having fun is what it's all about.

Zen Filmmaking allows 'spontaneous creation' and you'll be amazed at the results.

5. ALWAYS OFFER REWARDS:
Pay your cast and crew if possible, but always feed them well.
Know when to stop shooting.
Keep everyone happy so they'll enjoy filming and want to return.

6. STOCKPILE FOOTAGE:
Don't edit right away. Let the footage incubate into your thought process.
When you zen edit, you'll be amazed at the combinations and ideas you'll have. The film will take on a life all it's own.

7. PRESENT THE MOVIE:
Promote, distribute, do interviews, and get the word out. Many will want to see what you've accomplished.

RevDonaldo's Quick History of Zen Filmmaking

I've made movies with screenplays-
HELL COMES TO FROGTOWN,
KILL-KILL, OVERKILL!,
LAST IMPRESSION,
and many more.

The most fun I've had has been working with 'spontaneous creation' and doing Zen Filmmaking.

My first Zen film was EVE OF DESTRUCTION, a regular 8mm music video made in 1965.

I DONALD SUPERSTAR
And I DONALD SUPERSPY (66-67) followed shot in 16mm.

SPACE STATION WACO(68) was shot in Super 8 B&H Filmosound.

My first commercial feature film
THE DEMON LOVER (75)
was shot in 16mm and blown-up to 35mm for theatrical release.

We had a script to show investors, but most of the screenplay was abandoned in favor of Zen Filmmaking.

My second feature I LIKE TO HURT PEOPLE (78-80) was released straight-to-video and cable by New World.

This very first wrestling documentary feature was total Zen.

Not one word was ever written until a transcript was made for foreign sales by someone we hired to log the film, and transcribe the final product.

ROLLER BLADE (84)
was advertised as New World Pictures's First Made For Video Feature.

Screenwriter friend, Randy Frakes helped from time to time with certain key dialogue, but there was never a screenplay.

ROLLER BLADE WARRIORS (88) was a combination of screenplay and spontaneous creation.

The Zen process had the producers pretty scared because we were shooting in 35MM with SAG actors.

The movie still plays on USA Cable.

SCOTT SHAW joined me for the making of
ROLLER BLADE SEVEN
and
RETURN OF THE ROLLER BLADE SEVEN (91-92).

When actors would ask to see the script, our response was always the same. 'Scripts are for sissies! We don't need no stinkin' script.'

We're filmmakers, not book writers.

And besides, there's really only ONE STORY - THE GREATEST STORY EVER TOLD,
but that's a different subject.

IT'S SHOWTIME had scripted dialogue for some of our novice actors, but the pros like Andy Kaufman's TAXI buddy Jeff Conaway loved my spontaneous creation Zen style.

BIG SISTER 2000 (94)

had some key dialogue scripted for certain actors, but the best parts are Total Zen.

RAW ENERGY (95)
is a great example of Zen Magic at work.

Other films now out on Home Video including
ARMAGEDDON BOULEVARD
And
RIDE WITH THE DEVIL
serve as further examples of Zen.

SPEED-FLICK
has the following movies
in post-production for Home Video:
ROCK N' ROLL COPS
Produced by Donald G. Jackson
(with a vengeance!)
and Directed by Scott Shaw.

Other new films ready for final editing include such titles as
VAMPIRATES OF HOLLYWOOD,
MIMES- SILENT & DEADLY,
PAGING DOCTOR PRAISEWATER,

And
ONE SHOT SAM.

All textbook examples of Zen Filmmaking.

Raw Energy

I'd enjoyed Oliver Stone's movie NATURAL BORN KILLERS, and wanted to have some fun. A few friends were available to act. We had free locations, and my Canon L-2 Hi-8 Camera. I think we put together some magic because the film was very easy to make. We even took advantage of a carnival that we happened to pass by. The results of this stolen location are on the screen. We edited using a Sony Hi-8 deck to a Super VHS master. We next 'film-looked' as we bumped to Beta SP. During post, I used a new soundmixer who was rather impressed with my work - and thought he'd pay me a compliment. "Dude, these are great images. You're ready to start shooting on film." - I spent some time explaining to him that I've shot in every film format including regular 8mm, Super 8, 16, 35, and Omnimax/Imax. I shot on tape because I wanted to. It was both an artistic and financial choice. I knew a new age was coming when it would be considered respectable to work in formats other than film. Now it seems many artists are catching up. Long before BLAIR WITCH PROJECT, I'd shot an experimental Mockumentary called UFO:SECRET VIDEO(86) using a VHS Camcorder. We're in the process of digging this one out of our storage vaults for some minor fine tuning and new release as a SPEED-FLICK. Should be fun!

--RevDonaldo

Light Source Entertainment Journal Number One

ONE SHOT SAM BLUEGRASS CHRISTMAS PARTY

by Donald G. Jackson

Saturday December 19, 1998 at the world-famous ALLEY in North Hollywood was the scene of the 'underground' pop culture/folk music/independent filmmaker event of the year.

Hollywood International Multimedia Group, Hollywood Entertainment Network, Inc, and The Master of Light Institute presented an event that was filmed for inclusion a new motion picture entitled ONE SHOT SAM and a video special entitled THE NEW CHURCH OF ZEN ENTERTAINMENT.

Special bands included COWBOY BUDDHA promoting the music from the new movie RIDE WITH THE DEVIL and a fantastic bluegrass group - WALDEN DAHL.

In the loft watching and having fun was LARRY MURRAY from the Capitol recording group THE HEARTS AND FLOWERS. Larry was a writer for THE SMOTHERS BROTHERS, and JOHNNY CASH.

Making an entrance into the party with 'perfect timing' was JUDY and CRAIG. She was just in time for the opening sermon delivered by Revdonaldo in tribute to the legendary FUGS. Our press reporters caught JUDY HENSKE with two cameras and she was quizzed about everything from DAVE GUARD to PHIL OCHS. Acting as impromptu moderator was BOB MIZRAHI who is one of JUDY's biggest fans and who was a personal friend of DAVE GUARD. More important than the fact JUDY didn't answer any questions was the cosmic experience of being in the presence of the greatest female singer in history! Don't even ask to see this interview because the tape has already been sealed in a vault not to be opened until the year 2050. Standing in the radiant glow of JUDY HENSKE is reward enough for anyone who loves her and the wonderful music she creates. The questions will always be more important than the answers. God, if you're out there...if you're listening...Thank you for JUDY HENSKE! She continues to be an inspiration to every artist who hears her music. The vinyl albums I collected and played hundreds of times changed my life like no other music artist ever has. Meeting JUDY and being her friend is an experience for which I will always be forever grateful.

--Donald G. Jackson

The New Church of Zen Entertainment

Before Christmas of 1998, I rented the famous ALLEY rehearsal stage in North Hollywood for a Party to be documented on DV. Sort of my version of THE LAST WALTZ. meets DR. GENE SCOTT. Our 'Bands' included the BlueGrass stylings of WALDEN DAHL along with our stock music players COWBOY BUDDHA.

MIME GIRL, the Official Zendance Mascot was on hand along with the Zendance Go Go Girls.

Invited friends included the Legendary JUDY HENSKE, who has a new solo CD (and was once part of the Capitol Recording group DAVE GUARD AND THE WHISKEYHILL SINGERS) and LARRY MURRAY- (from one of my favorite music groups of all time, also on Capitol Records) THE HEARTS AND FLOWERS.

This historical documented event can be enjoyed in Part One of a soon-to-be-released production available only thru ZENDANCE.COM.

Other Church functions are scheduled to take place this year and will be part of our Gospel of Enlightenment thru Filmmaking.

--RevDonaldo

Palomino Club

It would be hard for me to describe my life without telling the story of the Palomino Club from 1971 to 1995(?) when it closed it's doors to the public. In an industrial part of North Hollywood, it was the watering hole for roofers, machine shop workers, studio people, aerospace workers from nearby Lockheed or Bendix, or anybody really. It was the bar for many LAPD North Hollywood Division officers. It was also a fine grill serving great steaks, burgers for lunch and dinner. The lunch menu was simple but very inexpensive, attracting crowds during the midday. Since it closed as a business, the building has been rented out frequently as a movie and TV setting. As a movie location, The Palomino is most famous for Any Which Way But Loose, but it has also been the location for many other movies and TV shoots since it closed. The first time I went in late 1971, I saw Doug Kershaw and it was a life changing experience. The intimately small room with it's low ceiling gave a feeling more like being in your own living room. The room's ambience was only one aspect of the club's unique appeal. It was a regular bar, a restaurant and The San Fernando Valley's trendiest/squarest nightclub. As a bar it's prices were as low as the next dive on Lankershim Blvd. Even before the sound system was upgraded in the '80s, the small sized room had good acoustics. The stars usually walked from the dressing rooms in the back to the stage through the crowd and anyone could just walk back to the dressing room to see if the performers were receiving visitors. Usually they did. The homey atmosphere of the Palomino made the artists feel comfortable greeting their fans before the show or between shows. In the early '70, the key to The Pal's success was the Thomas Brothers' style. Billy was the well-dressed manager who greeted the customers and handled most visible "out front" operations. Running the bar and overseeing the nightclub's operation, he was a generous, kind man who was genuinely interested in pleasing his customers in spite of the stress of operating a very busy, successful nightclub. Mr. Fortuna was the matre de in those days and the well-dressed urbane pair of Billy Thomas and Mr. Fortuna gave the honky-tonk roadhouse a professional air while the anxious crowd was seated for the evening's show. If Billy was the heart of the club, Tommy was the brains, Tommy handled the backroom; booking the acts, handling the artists and running the business end of the club, bar and kitchen from his tiny office. Tommy was not as generous as Billy nor as polite but his caustic wit was quite entertaining as long as you were not the target of his barbed observations. The "real" manager/employee-wrangler was Mikey; a gruff German who greeted you with "Yah-Yah!" and a string of obscenities in German. The "old" ('70s) bartenders Bobby, Jimmy Ellis and later ('80s) Big Steve, Little Gary or Woody were good people to know as they could grease almost any wheel inside the club, as long as you kept them well-lubricated. The waitresses were as sweet or as ornery as you can imagine. In the very early '70s, the club offered a Monday night (all you can eat) full buffet featuring real BBQ and prime rib for the insane price of $2 in addition to your admission. The club had a house band later called The Palomino Riders featuring many of the country music's best studio musicians. The legendary Thursday night Talent Contests were free and the kind of entertainment they provided was priceless, The Talent nights were another legend on their own merit. (Later in the late '80s and early '90s, Ronnie Mack's Barn Dance brought the Hollywood Hillbilly clubgoers up to North Hollywood for the "Roots Rock" scene.) Paying admission was not much of a consideration because sitting on the bar during the day were complimentary tickets to most shows and often for the BBQ! If the tickets were not visible, a simple request to Billy was all it took. I lived around the corner from The Palomino and it was on my way home from work so it was my local tavern. Hanging around there in the afternoon had another advantage besides "Double Hour" (a double "well" drink for the price of a single) from 4 to 6 p.m. That's when the soundchecks were usually held and were open to the crowd sitting around the bar. I remember Emmy Lou Harris, The Bellamy Brothers, Reba MacEntyre, Delbert McClinton and many others really putting on mini-concerts for the appreciative regulars drinking at the bar. After the soundcheck, the artists would often pull up a stool at the bar and relax. Around 1973, I first heard the buzz about this girl named Linda Ronstadt and seeing her early shows there was an incredible experience. Once I sat very close and as she would pull the mike away from her mouth to really push a song home, her voice soared over the band and house PA system, literally giving me goosepimples. One night Jackson Browne came from the audience to join her singing "Rock Me On The Water," magnificently to put it mildly. One night she opened the set singing "That'll Be The Day" reading the lyrics off a piece of paper. After the song she said something like "We just learned that yesterday, sorry it's so rough!" She ended that show singing "You're No Good" and it was the first time I'd ever heard her sing it. I was almost devastated by her power and vocal authority; probably the best show-stopper I ever saw. I can't go into a list of all the talent I saw there, or this will become a book. The sheer number of great acts I saw there makes it hard to single them out. Some regulars were Hoyt Axton, John Stewart, Elvin Bishop, Freddy Fender and Doug Sahm often brought San Antonio conjunto maestro Flaco Jimanez for an ensemble that later formed into the Texas Tornados. Also the bands I never heard of before or after were sometimes the greatest players in the world. There was never a shortage of heavyweight champion country-folk-rock music, what is now called "alt.country." The Flying Burrito Bros. were a regular (but I never saw them with legend Gram Parsons). The details of events leading up to Elvis Costello's shows there are for another story that could be a book. Probably Jerry Lee Lewis put on the most stunning experience. When the Killer was hot, a wild man in total control of his music and singing, he put on the best shows I've ever seen. Even when he'd had too much of something, he'd put on great shows on autopilot. Emmylou Harris has to be my personal favorite because I got to see and hear her career really began and take off with her early Palomino shows. One afternoon, while sitting at the bar, my girlfriend and I were amused by the shy long-haired young guy who introduced himself as "Johnny Cash's son-in-law" and asked the bartender who he needed to see for an audition. That led to Rodney Crowell joining Emmy Lou's "Hot Band." Later I was surprised to learn that the guitarist for the Palomino's house band was Telecaster-master legend Albert Lee. Soon Albert was also recruited. The Hot band also featured members of Elvis's old TCB Band and simply the greatest musicians around. By the '80s, Billy had passed away, and the Palomino building and operations expanded with a new generation of "cow punk" bands coming in. While staying very busy and attracting high quality talent, the excitement and the changing music industry of the '80s began to take a toll on the Palomino's magic, but there were still many great moments through that decade. Dwight Yoakum was a frequent opening act who caught a lot of people's attention. Lone Justice already had a reputation from the Hollywood club scene but their stunning performances, featuring Maria McKee were never captured on record. Many big name acts continued to play there during the '80s. Emmy Lou Harris continued to play there long after she could fill much larger houses. The rosters of acts began to include hard rock and Tejano bands. You just had to be there.

--Memories from the Ghost.

Guns of El Chupacabra Study Guide

--Donald G. Jackson

GUNS OF EL CHUPACBARA has truly earned the title of, "The Last B-Movie." We finished our work in April 1997 but realized the movie was way too ahead of its time. There was still a lot of crap hitting the video stores by a new wave of young armature digital wannabes taking themselves and their movies far too serious. I think it's finally over. People realized they can't do low budget versions of big movies anymore. You're either THE MATRIX or you're not. Who wants to see pale imitations when the ticket and rental price is the same? Now is the time to release something unique and original.

GUNS OF EL CHUPACBARA is a tribute and homage to the Roger Corman drive-in sci-fi monster movies and the Sergio Leone spaghetti westerns, along with DONALD G. JACKSON'S biggest influence the far out Ann Arbor underground — experimental movies of the 60s. Mockumentaries, a movie within a movie within a movie, space westerns, rock operas — the works. The sum total of everything JACKSON knows about independent filmmaking. Plus an opportunity to showcase some great new music. Even though we are now telling them what to expect it will still make people want to watch the movie for themselves.

Hopefully audiences will have fun and be entertained. The goal was to make GUNS OF EL CHUPACBARA "The Last B-Movie." And the ultimate independent film. Viewers who crave something fun and completely different will enjoy this multi-dimensional romp into the old west of the future that is a movie within a movie. And it's a lesson in breaking all the rules of filmmaking. It turns the B-Movie upside down and inside out! When enough people see this movie then the Higher Court of Cinema needs to put JACKSON and SCOTT SHAW on the witness stand for a long interrogation. And the rock operaness of the film — incredible new music by groups with some interesting names. SUN CITY GIRLS, COWBOY BUDDHA, SIN CITY BOYS, BURNT TATERS, and TOLEDO RAMBLERS. A great soundtrack that stands alone.

Viewers will enjoy repeated viewings with constant new discoveries. Like the mysterious pyramid, GUNS OF EL CHUPACBARA is encoded with traps and clever inventions that will leave the viewer both dazed and raptured.

Originally the filmmakers chose not to justify, explain, rationalize, or defend their work — but to let the film stand alone as a celebration of the cinema. Now JACKSON and SHAW are talking and remembering some of the more bizarre experiences creating the film. Recently JACKSON had this to say — "When I look back this is a film that should not exist. It was zen magic cosmic forces led us to some of those key locations and the spirit of spontaneous creation often took over. We'd have news crews watching us to see how we made movies without a script. JULIE STRAIN and KEVIN EASTMAND sat there under hot lights in full metal armor — when suddenly I was feeding them dialogue. I look back and am still amazed to this day."

From the personal side: A few quotes and random thoughts from JOE JUMPCUTTER — (a B-Movie fan and critic) All the mavericks have had their day — AL ADAMSON, JACK HILL, RUSS MEYER, HERSHELL GORDON LEWIS, GEORGE ROMERO, ED WOOD — and now finally the most radical far out independent visionary of them all — DONALD G. JACKSON. Over-looked and under-rated. Never really properly promoted. You can learn a few things from JACKSON'S ZENDANCE.COM website. He's worked with JIM CAMERON and shot 9 days of un-credited cinematography on TERMINATOR. Photographed 2nd unit on CAMERON's only music video. Worked with ROGER CORMAN. Jumped from a five thousand dollar budget on ROLLER BLADE to $15 MILLION on HELL COMES TO FROGTOWN. His films are hard to find and some haven't been edited for release — ONE SHOT SAM, PAGING DR. RRAISEWATER — and long anticipated ROCK N' ROLL COPS — created and directed by SCOTT SHAW. JACKSON produced with a vengeance and photographed 35 hours of zen footage. And JOE JUMPCUTTER had done some research on DR. SCOTT SHAW. Why did a Ph.D. hook up with B-movie maker DONALD G. JACKSON? How can one see the official director's cut of ROLLER BLADE SEVEN? — a movie who's style influenced a string of classics. JACKSON and SHAW claim no credit for their work in a string of "zenfilms" — Although JACKSON has always shot without a script when given the opportunity or thrown the script away when the movie started shooting — it was the two artists "synergy" that resulted in ROLLER BLADE SEVEN and culminated in the ultimate art movie — GUNS OF E CHUPACABRA.

A quote from a recent phone interview with JACKSON: "We' hired an editor to cut ROLLER BLADE SEVEN that took a high school teacher approach. It was frustrating. One day a miracle took place. SCOTT SHAW had never edited a movie in his life and the ¾ editing decks weren't familiar to him. Suddenly we fired the editor and SCOTT took over. Not only was he lightening fast from the start, but he performed some of the most amazing cuts I've ever seen." You can read more about the films of JACKSON and SHAW at their respective websites.

       www.zendance.com

                             www.scottshaw.com

Please contact us for any reason:
Donald G. Jackson & Company
1-877-385-5196
12400 Ventura Blvd. Suite 311,
Studio City, CA 91604 USA

DONALD G. JACKSON
Filmography

EVE OF DESTRUCTION (65)
Regular 8mm
I DONALD SUPERSTAR
and
I DONALD SUPERSPY (66-67)
16mm
SPACE STATION: W.A.C.O. (68)
Super 8 Film-o-Sound
THE DEMON LOVER (75)
16-35mm Blow-Up
I LIKE TO HURT PEOPLE (77-80)
16mm
ROLLER BLADE (84-85)
16mm
HELL COMES TO FROGTOWN (87)
35mm
ROLLER BLADE WARRIORS (88)
35mm
KILL-KILL, OVERKILL (89)
35mm
RETURN TO FROGTOWN (90)
35mm
ROLLER BLADE SEVEN (91-92)
16mm
RETURN OF THE
ROLLER BLADE SEVEN (91-92)
16mm
IT'S SHOWTIME (92)
16mm

LAST IMPRESSION (93)
35mm
CARJACK (94)
'film-look' Hi-8
QUEEN OF LOST ISLAND (94)
'film-look' Hi-8
LITTLE LOST SEA SERPENT (94)
'film-look' Hi-8
BIG SISTER 2000 (95)
'film-look' Hi-8
BABY GHOST (95)
'film-look' Hi-8
RAW ENERGY (95)
'film-look' Hi-8
ROLLER GATOR (96)
'film-look' Hi-8
TOAD WARRIOR (97)
'film-look' Hi-8 & digital
GUNS OF EL CHUPACABRA
(98-2000)
16/35mm & digital
New Films in Release
ARMAGEDDON BOULEVARD
(98) Home Video
RIDE WITH THE DEVIL
(98) Home Video
BILLY FRANKENSTEIN
(99) HBO
New in post from
SPEED-FLICK
ROCK N' ROLL COPS
PAGING DOCTOR PRAISEWATER

ONE SHOT SAM
DIARY OF A (MAD)
MICHIGAN MIGRANT FILMWORKER
SAMURAI SISTERS
HELL DOGS
UFO: SECRET VIDEO (86)
Re-release Special Edition
STEEL BOOGIE
FRANKENBLADE
VAMPIRATES OF HOLLYWOOD
THE DEVIL AND JACK DANIEL
HOLY TOLEDO
New Films in Development
JUDEE STRANGE
REV. DOCTOR
SAINT FRANCIS BLADE
a.k.a.
I LEFT MY ART AT EL MIRAGE
ROBOFISH
RevDonaldo - Hired Shooter
GALAXY OF TERROR (81)
New World
TOMORROW IN SPACE (82-83)
Graphic Films (Omnimax)
FORD OMNINEWS (84)
Graphic Films
(Omnimax/Imax)
THE TERMINATOR (84)
(uncredited)
Nine days additional
photography with
Gale Ann Hurd

and
James Cameron
SEASONS (85)
Graphic Films
(Omnimax/Imax)
CYCLONE (86)
(Cinetel)
stunt photography
with Fred Olen Ray
GRUNT THE WRESTLING
MOVIE (86)
New World Video
Second Unit
COMMANDO SQUAD (86)
(TWE)
stunt photography with
Fred Olen Ray
ARMED RESPONSE (87)
additional photography
with Fred Olen Ray
MARTINI RANCH (87)
(Warner Bros)
Bill Paxton rock video
2nd Unit with
James Cameron
KILL OR BE KILLED (89)
(AIP)
director of photography
SHOCK 'EM DEAD (89)
2nd Unit d.p.
with Traci Lords
TWISTED JUSTICE (89)

2nd Unit d.p.
with David Heavener
CLASS OF NUKE 'EM HIGH (90)
(Troma)
2nd Unit d.p.
DIVINE ENFORCER (91)
(York Ent.)
2nd Unit d.p.
POCKET NINJAS (93)
(Simitar)
photographed and directed
certain scenes
BY THE NUMBERS (98)
(Penthouse)
directed certain scenes
JULIE STRAIN SHOCKUMENTARY
(97-99)
STRAIN SISTERS
TRUTH ABOUT DOGS
Behind The Scenes
VAMPIRIA
LINGERIE KICKBOXER
Behind The Scenes
Making of HEAVY METAL
Eric Kroll Fashion Shoot
BROADCAST TELEVISION
BIG TIME WRESTLING (77-80)
Wide World Sports
TELE-EVANGELISTS (77-80)
W.W.S.
(*Technical note: It took
a truck load full of

equipment to produce
these TV shows
shot on quad tape.
Today, everything would
fit into a few small
cases - and produce
higher quality at a
fraction of the cost.)

DGJ Newsgroup Postings

Donald G. Jackson used the screen names Revdonaldo, MaxSamurai and occasionally OneShotSam, and Zendance98 in newsgroup posting—oftentimes responding to his own posts.

DO-IT-YOURSELF CINEMA!
Zendance98
11/5/98

Wow! Finally some passion about independent filmmaking! We're working hard to bring the first ZENDANCE FILM FESTIVAL to Hollywood. It is fun to make movies. If you do it only to make money, then most of the fun is gone. Make films because you love to make films. ZENDANCE will be showing VHS video projection, but films can originate in any format such as 35mm 16mm, Hi-8, DV, etc. Let's all make movies!

MaxSamurai
11/5/98
Are the 'do it yourself' cinema people actually making films or just talking about it? I'm shooting a 35mm feature with 100' loads on a World War II EYEMO. You can't get any more 'independent' than that!

Straight-to-video
MaxSamurai
11/5/98

There are plenty of video co's out there that will distribute your film if they
feel it has some 'commercial potential'---the market if tough compared to a few
years ago. It can still be done, but expect to sell in the low numbers.
I know filmmakers that are thrilled to sell 500 copies of their 'shot on video'
feature. In all honesty, it doesn't matter. The market is so small, you can
save a lot of money by shooting on DV or Hi-8. Save the 16mm til you have a
real budget.
My company MaxSamurai Extreme Cinema is looking for interesting films. Let me
know what you have. One VHS screener tells the story! (I know someone who shot
a Hi-8 feature called BIG SISTER 2000 and it just came out in every video store
except Blockbuster!)

Revdonaldo
11/6/98
It's fun to make movies and fun to show them. A friend runs the HOLLYWOOD UNDERGROUND FILM FESTIVAL at the Vogue theater in Hollywood. I believe they are having screenings once a month. There is usually an ad in the LA WEEKLY. I agree it's time to have fun with the cinema. Too many people take this all too serious. 'Having fun is what it's all about!'- Rinaldi (ROLLER BLADE WARRIORS 1988)

FREE FIRST ISSUE OF INDEPENDENT FILMMMAKER PUBLCIATION
Revdonaldo
4/7/98
The LIGHTSOURCE ENTERTAINMENT JOURNAL features articles on independent filmmakers. Issue number one tells about the making of GUNS OF EL CHUPACABRA. E-mail address for free sample.

CONRAD BROOKS(PLAN 9...) IN NEW DISASTER MOVIE
MaxSamurai
1/18/99
CONRAD BROOKS just left Los Angeles where he was shooting a new movie ONE SHOT SAM. His latest release in video stores is ARMAGEDDON BOULVEARD where he plays gangleader Rinaldil. Check it out!

LIVING LEGEND - CONRAD BROOKS
MaxSamurai
1/18/99
CONRAD BROOKS can soon be reached thru www.zendance.com
His most recent film is ONE SHOT SAM where he plays a 40's style detective who
visits Los Angeles to investigate a mystery surrounding the Flying Burrito Brothers.

CULT MOVIE ARCHIVE
MaxSamurai
2/4/99

Please e-mail me direct and I'll send you tons of info on the cult films of
DONALD G. JACKSON including HELL COMES TO FROGTOWN, RETURN TO FROGTOWN, ROLLER
BLADE WARRIORS, ROLLER BLADE, ROLLER BLADE SEVEN, KILL, KILL, OVERKILL, BIG
SISTER 2000,
LINGERIE KICKBOXER, ARMAGEDDON BOULEVARD, RIDE WITH THE DEVIL, and new movies
BLADE SISTERS and DEADBOYZ. Check out out site
www.zendance.com

MaxSamurai 1999 AFM Report
MaxSamurai
3/4/99
Official Screening Report from the 1999 AMERICAN FILM MARKET in Santa Monica, CA - 25 February - 5 March
RAZOR BLADE SMILE The Film Company, London Director - Jake West Vampires with guns! Influences seem to be MAX HEADROOM and lots of comic books. Great film for a first time director. Shot in 16mm. 35mm blowup print is excellent. A fun time at the movies. Scheduled for a theatrical release.
RESURRECTION Interlight Director - Russell Mulcahy I prefer his first film - RAZORBACK that had much better visuals and wasn't so grim.
SAMURAI FICTION Pony Cinema Director - Hiroyuki Nakano MTV meets Samurai Rock N'

Roll. Black and white. Widescreen. Some fantastic samurai sword battles.

FROM DUSK TIL DAWN 2: TEXAS BLOOD MONEY Dimension/Miramax Director - Scott Spiegel Everything a movie should be! Lots of interesting camera angles. Plenty of action. The Vampire Wild Bunch!!! Part 3 is finished, but not yet screened.

THE CORRUPTER New Line Cinema Director - James Foley Chow-Yun Fat has made better movies. The director has not. This is 'pure cinema!' Widescreen 2.35 to 1 with incredible cinematography. 'cherry picked' long lens shots, abstract angles, and visually interesting ways to present each scene. MaxSamurai's pick for the best film shown at the 1999 American Film Market.

TOBE HOOPER'S EGGSHELLS
Revdonaldo
5/19/99
Anyone know of a copy of Tobe Hooper's movie EGGSHELLS. There was an article
on the film in a 1973 issue of American Cinematographer. Film was shot in techniscope and made before TCM. Is it on tape? Visit the Revdonaldo website:
http://www.zendance.com

PRODUCER SEEKS NEW PROJECT
Revdonaldo
5/25/99
Anyone out there want to make a movie? I'm looking to help put together
something new.

Visit the Revdonaldo website:
http://www.zendance.com

THE LAST BROADCAST
Revdonaldo
8/6/99
I saw THE LAST BROADCAST shown at the DGA in Hollywood last year with
digital projection. It was far more impressive in every area than BWP. What a
shame it didn't get picked up by a major distributor.
Visit the Revdonaldo website:
http://www.zendance.com

CULT MOVIE ARCHIVE
35mm ZOMBIE MOVIE
MaxSamurai
8/22/99
Just took a look at the new film with CONRAD BROOKS on an upright 35mm Moviola. It is called UNDERWATER ZOMBIES OF
MALIBU. Doesn't look low budget. Director Lightmaster D did the right thing to shoot in 35mm. Now the movie can be show in theaters! I predict audiences will love it.

DISTRIBUTION
Revdonaldo
8/23/99
I've made independent films for 25 years and I know for a fact if you've got a
'fun to watch movie' then you'll find a distribution deal. I really don't think

there will be a lot of BWP type movies. I made a 'mockumentary' in 1986 called
UFO; SECRET VIDEO and another film in 1989
KILL, KILL OVERKILL that is very
similiar to BWP. One has been on USA CABLE
TV and the other is now being
distributed. More of us should build our own distribution network and help
each other instead of giving our films away.
Visit the Revdonaldo website:
http://www.zendance.com

ZEN FILMMAKING
Revdonaldo
9/2/99
grow the fuck up dude!
I was angry over this, and sent him this response:
I do not think that is a proper response. If those are the only words you can think of to use against me, you have a serious problem. Some of us are actually getting outside and making movies, while people like you sit here and criticize other people. You are the one who needs to get a life.
Cody
He responded tonight with this:
cody, you are trly an idiot, if you want to know more about me, type my name into yahoo search engine and see you little moron, Robert Rundle, I make films unlike you and your play pals!!!
 Just goes to show you, some people are out in another world. Doing things their own way.
Thanks Cody Visit the Revdonaldo website:
http://www.zendance.com

WWW.ZENDANCE.COM
Revdonaldo
9/4/99
ZOMBIE SUPER MODELS starring JULIE STRAIN. New on home video! Preaching the Gospel of Zen Filmmaking.

HONG KONG STYLE CHUPACABRA
Revdonaldo
9/6/99
Look out - October brings the release of a Hong Kong style action film -
THE GUNS OF EL CHUPACABRA
Visit the Revdonaldo website:
http://www.zendance.com

CHUPACABRA TRILOGY
Revdonaldo
9/10/99
Oct. 1, 1999 issue of FEMME FATALES has a new article JULIE STRAIN in
GUNS OF EL CHUPACABRA!
Visit the Revdonaldo website:
http://www.zendance.com

ARMAGEDDON BLVD.
MaxSamurai
9/13/99
Re: ARMAGEDDON BOULEVARD - Weird, but Good! Difficult working with low budgets, but this film really delivers in terms of artistry and originality. Rumor has it this will be one of the films show in October at the First Annual Zendance

Film Festival in North Hollywood. Watch the news groups or e-mail for details.

Blair Witch Project
Revdonaldo
9/14/99
BWP would have never made it without a multi-million dollar campaign behind it.
I think everyone knows how to shoot on video and trans to film.
Visit the Revdonaldo website:
http://www.zendance.com

ROLLER BLADE WARRIORS
MaxSamurai
9/15/99
 ZENDANCE is getting set to release the director's cut of this 1988 movie that starred Kathleen Kinmont. This will be the first chance to see the complete un-edited movie that has many scenes not shown on USA movies up all night. Shot in an interesting style by director/cinematographer Donald G. Jackson. He alternates between only two lenses - 18mm wide angle and 300mm telephoto.

INSPIRATION FROM 'LOAN SHARK'
MaxSamurai
9/15/99
The most inspirational independent movie of the year for me has been LOAN
SHARK. I understand it will be shown at the First STUDIO CITY FILM FESTIVAL.
Anyone have details???

Revdonaldo 9/15/99
BWP must stand for 'Boring Worthless Production'---LOAN SHARK is just the
opposite! The most exciting new independent film since El Mariachi. Forgive
me for telling the truth. I know it's very rare these days with big companies
spending millions of dollars to force BWP on the innocent ticket buyers. But
LOAN SHARK is the real thing. If you know anything about GOOD MOVIES, then
LOAN SHARK is fantastic!
Visit the Revdonaldo website:
http://www.zendance.com

NO BWP~!
Revdonaldo
9/15/99
BWP must stand for 'Boring Worthless Production'---LOAN SHARK is just the
opposite! The most exciting new independent film since El Mariachi. Forgive
me for telling the truth. I know it's very rare these days with big companies
spending millions of dollars to force BWP on the innocent ticket buyers. But
LOAN SHARK is the real thing. If you know anything about GOOD MOVIES, then
LOAN SHARK is fantastic!
Visit the Revdonaldo website:
http://www.zendance.com

WWW.ZENDANCE.COM
MaxSamurai
9/18/99
ZENDANCE is going to make all of the Donald G. Jackson films available thru www.zendance.com including
ROLLER BLADE (with behind the scenes)
ROLLER BLADE WARRIORS
ROLLER BLADE SEVEN
RETURN OF THE ROLLER BLADE SEVEN
ROLLER GATOR
and the just completed BLADE SISTERS

SHOT ON VIDEO FOR THEATERS
Revdonaldo
9/18/99
Does anyone know the FIRST THEATRICAL RELASED FEATURE FILM THAT WAS 'SHOT ON
VIDEO'?
I'm thinking it was one of three -
2000 MOTELS
MR. MIKE'S MONDO VIDEO
THE RESURRECTION OF ZACHARY WHEELER
Visit the Revdonaldo website:
http://www.zendance.com

POSITIVE MESSAGE SCRIPTS WANTED
Revdonaldo
4/20/99
Production company seeks POSITIVE MESSAGE screenplays with a spiritual message
for possible funding. Contact Revdo...@aol.com

Visit the Revdonaldo website:
http://www.zendance.com

HBO, SHOWTIME, HIRE LOCAL DV FILMMAKERS
FILMMAKERS STEP FORWARD!
MaxSamurai
9/22/99
Attention filmmakers! Step forward. Who's in this news group that has
actually made movies with theatrical release, television play, or that can be
found in video stores? Announce yourself! No kids with camcorders shooting 2
minute movies for the internet, please!

FUTURE OF INDEPENDENT FILMS
MaxSamurai
9/22/99
"In my opinion, the quality of the work is what ultimately matters.
Independent film making is not synonymous with B class distribution".-I don't
think your quote applies to THE BLAIR WITCH PROJECT. Very low quality on the
technical end. Most B movies are LAWRENCE OF ARABIA by comparison.
I'm still hoping to get more and better response to my question. What can we
do to help each other instead of taking an 'everyman for himself' attitude.

In the 1960's and 70's, we had the drive-ins. A good place to get your

inde horror movie or action film played. The 80's brought home video that put
every kind of product on the shelf. The 90's became more selective.
Distributors paying less, but wanting bigger stars and higher budgets. NOW - where do we stand as INDEPENDENT FILMMAKERS? Is shooting on DIGITAL and
SELF-DISTRIBUTION on the INTERNET the way to go? Please discuss.

ZENDANCE FILM FESTIVAL
Revdonaldo
9/23/99
What would independent filmmakers like to see at film festivals? ZENDANCE is
getting ready to launch and we're open for suggestions.
Visit the Revdonaldo website:
http://www.zendance.com

ZEN FILMMAKING
Revdonaldo
9/23/99
 Read the ZEN FILMMAKING article by Dr. Scott Shaw in issue Number 2 of THE LIGHTSOURCE ENTERTAINMENT JOURNAL. Shot with the camera that made BREATHLESS - the Eclair 35mm CM3.

INDEPENDENT FILMMAKERS WANTED!
Revdonaldo
9/24/99

If you make independent feature films, we'd like to hear from you! The new
ZENDANCE FILM FESTIVAL takes place in October 1999!
Visit the Revdonaldo website:
http://www.zendance.com

INDEPENDENT FILMMAKING
MaxSamurai
9/28/99
Are there any true INDEPENDENT FILMMAKERS out there who are making movies with their own money who hope to achieve artistic satisfaction and financial success?

SHOOT ON 35MM FILM!!!
MaxSamurai
9/30/99
THE NIGHT BEFORE HALLOWEEN, filmmaker MaxSamurai takes his 35mm World War 2 Eyemo camera onto the streets of Hollywood to capture a raw chase scene that
completes the new movie -SAMURAI SISTERS.

DONALD G. JACKSON
Revdonaldo
10/1/99
See the famous DEMON LOVER DIARY on Sunday October 3, 1999.
LACE, 6522 Hollywood Blvd.(323) 526-2911
Funded by the American Film Institute in 1975 it is a 'behind the scenes'

mockumentary on the making of the cult horror
movie THE DEMON LOVER which was
shot on 16mm/blowup to 35mm and played theaters
all across the country!
Arrive early! The film starts @ 7:00p.m.
Visit the Revdonaldo website:
http://www.zendance.com

OneShotSam
10/1/99
Jackson's own Super 8 documentary will be
released shortly along with the
re-release of THE DEMON LOVER

MEET JOE ESTEVEZ IN PERSON!
Revdonaldo
10/2/99
Meet actor JOE ESTEVEZ and filmmaker
DONALD G. JACKSON in person! Make this
movie if you can. It's a documentary on the making
of my first movie!

See the famous DEMON LOVER DIARY on
Sunday October 3, 1999. LACE, 6522 Hollywood
Blvd. (323) 526-2911

Funded by the American Film Institute in 1975 it is
a 'behind the scenes' mockumentary on the making
of the cult horror movie THE DEMON LOVER
which was shot on 16mm/blowup to 35mm and
played theaters all across the country! Arrive
early! The film starts @ 7:00p.m

24TH ANNIVERSARY OF DEMON LOVER
Revdonaldo
10/3/99
Make this movie if you can. It's a documentary on the making of my first movie!
See the famous DEMON LOVER DIARY on Sunday October 3, 1999.
LACE, 6522 Hollywood Blvd.(323) 526-2911

Funded by the American Film Institute in 1975 it is a 'behind the scenes' mockumentary on the making of the cult horror movie THE DEMON LOVER which was shot on 16mm/blowup to 35mm and played theaters all across the country! Arrive early! The film starts @ 7:00p.m

OneShotSam
10/3/99
THE DEMON LOVER will be re-released on home video this year along with bonus footage and 'behind the scenes' materials.

MaxSamurai
10/3/99
THE DEMON LOVER is a wild parody of low budget horror moves inspired by CHILDREN SHOULDN'T PLAY WITH DEAD THINGS, SIMON - KING OF THE WITCHES, and THE DEVIL RIDES OUT.

DEMON LOVER DIARY is an AFI sponsored 'behind the scenes' documentary of the making of the movie.

Bob Skotak who made the Demon suit went on to win two Oscars for SPFX~!

DEMON LOVER SELLS OUT!
Revdonaldo
10/4/99
The Film Forum had a packed theater tonight in Hollywood for the presentation of
DEMON LOVER DIARY directed by Joel DeMott. Now looks like there is some real
interest in a re-issue of 1975 horror movie THE DEMON LOVER. The film will
contain 'behind the scenes' including the 'making of the making' of the movie.
Fun stuff for low budget filmmakers to enjoy.
Visit the Revdonaldo website:
http://www.zendance.com

ZEN FILM MAKING VS. DOGME 95
Revdonaldo
10/21/99
Filmmakers interested in DOGME 95 might also enjoy checking out THE LIGHTSOURCE ENTERTAINMENT JOURNAL issues Number 2 - The Art of Zen Filmmaking and issue
Number 3 - Digital Filmaking by Jon Jost.
Visit the Revdonaldo website:
http://www.zendance.com

The American Film Market Review
Revdonaldo
2/24/00

The American Film Market opened today in Santa, Monica. 20 years since the
event got started. I saw it grow, and then slowly die. Welcome the Birth of
the intenet and new ways to promote inde films. The AFM is is history!
Good thing I wore black! The Market is completely dead. Same old crap we've
seen before. A social club where people pretend to play the game. Not even
the big companies were getting any buyers. More people crying tears inside
than all
the rain outside. No good new movies or screenings to attend. Where has all
the TALENT gone?
Anyone else have observations about the my observations?

ZEN FILM WORLD PREMIERE
Revdonaldo
4/7/00
ZENDANCE. COM
Presents
The World Premiere of R A W   E N E R G Y
Wednesday, April 12, 2000 @ 7:30 p.m.
with director/producer Donald G. Jackson
along with star Amanda Rushing and other cast members to answer questions about Zen-Filmmaking.

The event is sponsored by Cine-Nites at the Century City Playhouse located on 10508 W. Pico Blvd. (between Beverly Glenn and Overland) in West Los Angeles, CA

R A W   E N E R G Y is about three serial killers caught in a virtual reality dream trip.
MAN BITES DOG meets NATURAL BORN KILLERS. A whacky action spoof hosted on screen by famous Hollywood badman - WILLIAM SMITH.
 (The screening is FREE!)

TIMECODE - I saw it!
MaxSamurai
4/29/00
 I attended the 5:00 p.m. showing of TIMECODE at the NuArt. Got tickets and was in line about 4:30. The screening was sold out. Mike Figgis introduced the show and answered questions afterwards for about 10 mins. The outside line for the 7:00 was also sold out. The film was a DIGITAL PROJECTION (not on film as you suspected, but the regular theatrical release will be on 35mm). The Digital projection looked great. Figgis did a custom mix that he was also doing different for the 7 and 9 show. One word can summarize his technical achievement - INCREDIBLE! 4 different screens showing a 93 min movie all shot w/o editing. He did the show with 4 cameras shooting and did it 15 times. Figgis claims only takes 14 and 15 actually worked. It is amazing how he moves the camera thru the building, into limos, on the street, and back to different rooms. There are scenes that synch up with two cameras on the same scene. Perfect timing.

I've wanted to do an entire feature in one continuous take since I got interested in filmmaking. A.C. ANDERSON made a 30 min 16mm movie called P.O.V. that I saw in Ann Arbor in the 70's that I thought that was incredible. TIMECODE is 100X more incredible. The previews for 4 new movies shown before TIMECODE were all shot on digital. Digital filmmaking is here to stay! Very exciting times to be living in. TIMECODE: see it! I want to watch the movie again and listen to all of the scenes. It should be a big hit on DVD. You can play each soundtrack. And I really think EVERYONE in the sold out audience was a filmmaker! Maybe their is such a big interest in filmmaking now that you can target movies for other filmmakers. Talk about a niche market.

I'm excited. Time to grab the digital camera and go to work.
-MaxSamurai

OVER-REACTING TO CRITICISM
Revdonaldo
5/5/00
I agree with Rick. This newsgroup should be for inde filmmakers. We need to
be supportive of our individual efforts. As an artist, I'm not trying to
please anyone but myself. If my films find an audience, great. Nothing wrong
with being a 'commercial filmmaker. No reason to get so damn defensive and
make a scene.
I would like to see more honesty and less hype.

Revdo...@aol.com
Visit the Revdonaldo website:
http://www.zendance.com

DONALD G. JACKSON
Revdonaldo
 5/8/00
DONALD G. JACKSON
Producer/Director/Cinematographer of 35mm features that have appeared on Cable TV such as HELL COMES TO FROGTOWN, RETURN TO FROGTOWN, KILL-KILL, OVERKILL and ROLLER BLADE WARRIORS. Worked in every film format including Regular 8mm, Super 8, 16, 35,and Imax/Omnimax. Video work includes regular VHS, Super VHS, Hi-8, Betacam, and Digital.

RAW ENERGY has officially premiered on IFILM! Please watch my film and send a review!

RAW ENERGY REVIEW
MaxSamurai
5/10/00
RAW ENERGY
reviewed by D. Walker
 Some people come to Hollywood to get in the movies. Others come simply to experience the weirdness. If you are of the latter, you will enjoy RAW ENERGY, a movie that seems made for internet consumption! The opening advises us to play this film loud. If you live in an apartment next to rather conservative folks (or politically correct

liberals for that matter), the loud soundtrack might cause them to become concerned. Very concerned. Best viewed while reading apocalyptic websites.

MAX SAMURAI SEZ
MaxSamurai
5/14/00
RAW ENERGY
Dr. Samurai:
This is a great art film. It takes Natural Born Killers to the next level. The cinematography is great. The music is pumping. A Must See.

Mr Prophet Toy:
This film is as entertaining as it is bizarre and erotic.....the final scene is worth the price of admission alone.....trashy and psychotic look into the future of prime time TV shows like "Real TV" and "ET"

RAW ENERGY
reviewed by D. Walker
Some people come to Hollywood to get in the movies. Others come simply to experience the weirdness. If you are of the latter, you will enjoy RAW ENERGY, a movie that seems made for internet consumption! The opening advises us to play this film loud. If you live in an apartment next to rather conservative folks (or politically correct liberals for that matter), the loud soundtrack might cause them to become concerned. Very concerned. Best viewed while reading apocalyptic websites.

DON JACKSON AND MAXsamurai Rick SHITLY
MaxSamurai
5/18/00
ODDBALL221 inhaled too many chemicals when he used to pour foam for a North Hollywood maskmaker. He is one bitter and dark soul. Oddball 221 is actually special effect's loser of the decade SANDY COLLORA. IMBD shows him having only one credit, as a Production Assistant on a 1996 sci-fi movie. He is currently unemployeed because of his bad attitude with other workers. I understand from a few people who worked with him that he is constantly whining and complaining about everyone, so Don Jackson need not feel too singled out.. RAW ENERGY is an art movie and there are talented filmmakers like Rick Shipley and others who appreciate it. SANDY COLLORA needs to get a life. Now that Hollywood has kicked him out as a miserable failure, he can spend his days on the computer showing his bitterness towards those who actually make films. Pouring foam, sweeping up as a P.A. on a big production, and complaining doesn't make you a real filmmaker. Get off this newsgroup and get a life SANDEEEE!!

REVENGE OF THE DEMON LOVER
MaxSamurai
7/21/00

I just heard that they're making a sequel to the twenty-five year old
independent horror movie THE DEMON LOVER and doing a re-release of the first
one on DVD with "behind the scenes" making of and World Premieres in Michigan
and New York. Negotiations are underway for GUNNAR HANSEN (the original
Leatherface in TEXAS CHAINSAW MASSACRE to reprise his role of Professor
Peckinpah) REVENGE OF THE DEMON LOVER opens with Laval Blessing being let out
of the Zendance Assylum for the Criminally Insane.
MaxSa...@aol.com.

ANDY WARHOL WOULD HAVE LOVED DV
MaxSamurai
9/22/00
ANDY WARHOL would have loved DV! He was great at finding interesting people.
Locking off the camera and letting them talk!
MaxSa...@aol.com

IFC DV THEATER - BAD MONDAY
MaxSamurai
11/29/00
Does anyone have a VHS copy of BAD MONDAY show a few weeks ago on IFC DV
THEATER? I need to a copy for my collection.
MaxSa...@aol.com

RECORD ON DVD
Revdonaldo

1/5/01

RECORD ON DVD

Philips Consumer Electronics (NYSE: PHG) today demonstrated its first DVD-Video Recorder, based on DVD+RW technology at the Consumer Electronics Show. The DVDR1000 will be introduced into the U.S. market in the second half of 2001. Compatible with both existing and future DVD-Video and DVD-ROM equipment, Philips DVD-Video Recorder allows consumers to create their own DVDs and play the bare disc back on past, present and future players. The DVDR1000 features an AC-3 decoder/encoder for superior sound quality and an index picture screen, which allows users to see what has been recorded as well as how much space is available on the disc. In addition, Philips DVD-Video Recorder includes a digital i.Link data transfer (IEEE1394) for transferring camcorder footage to DVD, preserving the recordings in perfect digital picture and sound quality. The recorder also has a convenient editing capability, which does not require any special software and allows users to do linear editing directly on the recorder using the television as a display. In addition to DVD+RW and DVD-Video discs, the DVDR1000 also is compatible with CD, CD-R, CD-RW, S-VCD and VCD discs. "Only DVD+RW technology offers consumers compatibility that the DVD recordings they make will play back on existing DVD-Video players," said Thorsten Koch, senior vice president and general manager, Video, Philips Consumer Electronics, North America. "Since we expect the installed base of DVD-Video and DVD-ROM players to exceed 160 million by the end of this year, we think that this feature will be highly appreciated by consumers. Philips DVDR1000 broadens the functionality of the DVD-Video player by allowing consumers to simply press a record button to create their own DVDs." The Philips DVD video recorder will allow consumers to create their own DVDs, recording up to two hours of content on a single 4.7 GB DVD+RW disc in DVD quality. It also is possible to record up to four hours of better than VHS quality footage. For consumers who want to record even more content on a single disc, it is possible to create a double-sided disc with a 9.4 GB capacity DVD, which allows a total of up to eight hours of recording on a single disc. DVD+RW media are interchangeable between the PC and TV platforms, which means that consumers can record something with their camcorder, copy it onto a DVD+RW disc with Philips DVDR1000 Video Recorder, edit it on a PC and play it back on existing DVD-Video players and DVD-ROM drives.

HELL COMES TO FROGTOWN - DVD
Revdonaldo
7/14/01
Anchor Bay has released HELL COMES TO FROGTOWN on DVD. Worth checking out to hear the commentary by director Donald G. Jackson and screenwriter Randy Frakes.

ZENDANCE . COM
MaxSamurai
2/4/02

ZENDANCE.COM Joshua Tree, CA Cosmic Film Festival will host the World Premiere of GUNS OF EL CHUPACABRA along with other movies and live alt. country and bluegrass folk music.

THE DEMON LOVER
MaxSamurai
3/19/02
PSYCHOTRONIC NUMBER 36 has the true story of THE DEMON LOVER, (of interest to camera people - shot with a CP 16 and blown up to 35mm) along with a good interview about ZEN FILMMAKING, HELL COMES TO FROGTOWN, etc.
On newstands now!

THE DEMON LOVER 6-22-2002
MaxSamurai
6/12/02
FREE DEMON LOVER 1-SHEET POSTER 6-22 DGA LOS ANGELES DEMON LOVER DAIRY Special Screening (USA, 1980, 90 min) Sat Jun 22, 7:00pm DGA Theatre Donald G. Jackson shot THE DEMON LOVER - a 90 min horror movie for three thousand dollars in cash and the picture played theaters and drive-in's all across the country. Now the DGA is showing a behind the scenes making of the movie called DEMON LOVER DIARY. Shades of the BLAIR WITCH PROJECT and AMERICAN MOVIE - but it was made in 1975! It's a hoot - show up and ask for a free 1-sheet movie poster painted by Val Mayerik - the original artist of HOWARD THE DUCK. TED

NUGENT promises he'll be in attendance to deal justice!

Demon Lover Diary USA, 1980, 90 Minutes
Factory workers Don and Jerry are fulfilling a lifetime dream: they're producing their own low-budget horror movie. Jeff and Joel, lovers and cinema-verité filmmakers, and a friend of theirs named Mark have come out to Michigan to help the dream come true: they're shooting The Demon Lover for Don and Jerry. Two weeks after production starts, Jeff and Joel and Mark are fleeing Michigan – bullets ricocheting off the car – with their lives and film in jeopardy. "Real-life horror far more unsettling than any found in fictional thrillers. This is America... a funny, frightening, exhilarating film." — David Ehrenstein, The Los Angeles Herald Examiner.

HIGHLY STYLIZED AND INSPIRATIONAL
MaxSamurai
7/17/02
Now that I've seen the movie, I'm reading the reviews and not one seems to pick up on the most obvious thing that impressed me about the movie. There is no coverage. No traditional inter-cutting. No rapid fire editing. Instead, we have the bare bones minimal very selective and stylized interpretation of the scenes. Less is more. Many things are not shown. ROAD TO PERDITION is the closest thing to an "art film" we're going to get from a major release. This director had complete creative control - c.c.c. RTP is probably one of the greatest movie experiences I've had, bar none! This

movie is a celebration of the cinema that has me inspired once again to make movies.

HAS DIGITAL VIDEO KILLED INDE FILMMAKING?
MaxSamurai
4/29/02
Seems like the good daze of independent filmmaking - mainly from the 70's thru
the mid 90's all ended with the digital camera and computer. Has digital
killed inde filmmaking? Distributors are reluctant to buy films shot on video.
 The studios seem to be making the so-called "B-Movies" with major stars and
big bucks. Is there anything for the inde except festivals. I guess the main
point is can the inde make money with digital films??? Looking for feedback.

Revdonaldo
4/30/02
I think the point is that digital video has turned independent filmmaking into
a hobby and student dream process instead of making movies on 35mm and 16mm
that could be sold. The FILM part seems to have now been taken over by big
companies who can afford names and better production values. Does anyone
really care about digital films unless they have stars and or big buck
theatrical promotion!

85

Revdonaldo
5/1/02
In the "good old daze" all of my friends and associates were shooting 16mm so
their films could be shown at the Ann Arbor Film Festival - a haven for
underground and experimental films. Most of these filmmakers - myself included
went on to make commercial films that incorporated all the Ann Arbor-style
techniques. At one time it cost real money to make a feature film - and buyers
and distributors knew this so didn't mind paying decent money for the product.
Now the market is flooded with digital and everyone knows what is going on.
Some of the big boyz are shooting digital just for fun - but their real meat
and potatoes is still 35mm Sag films. I doubt there will ever be an area in
Beverly Hills know as "digital stars" BUT there are plenty of MOVIE STARS.
Visit the Revdonaldo website:
http://www.zendance.com

MaxSamurai
5/2/02
Maybe someone should write a new book -
HOW TO MAKE DIGITAL FEATURES THAT SELL -
Chapters might include:
1. How to raise one million dollars for production, stars, and promotion.
2. Why you should shoot on film instead of digital.
3. Realistic expectations.

Revdonaldo
5/2/02
I guess the reality is that digital video has killed the opportunity for anyone
to make money as an independent filmmaker. I knew alot of people in the 80's
and 90's who earned a good living producing independent features - many made
with private financing. There was a need for new product in home video and the
foreign market. Now the so called "B" movies are made by the majors. Everyone
is shooting on digital because of the low costs. I'd compare it to everyone
writing books because they can afford a typewriter. Having a typewriter,
computer, or video camera doesn't make you an artist. And there is more to
making a movie than telling a story. How many songs "tell a story" - most of
my favorite films go way beyond simple story telling. Embrace digital
filmmaking because it's not going away, but don't expect to make a living as a
digital filmmaker. Since 1990, there has really only been about 10 people
breakthru into the big time. Anyone care to name them? Chances of the new kid
on the block with a digital camera becoming the next Kevin Smith are slim to
none.

Revdonaldo
5/5/02
Super 8mm film now cost as much or more than 16mm - so it is pointless to

consider shooting Super 8 for commercial release. Nobody is getting sales and making a living doing this. At least with DV -
there are some success stories. You must have a good product and have money to
market it.
End of story.

Revdonaldo
5/7/02
I'm the first one to say that shooting DV is one heck of a lot of fun and a
cheap way to make movies. Nothing wrong with LOW RES for certain purposes.
All I'm saying is that the GOOD OLD DAZE of making money with independent films
- has been killed by the advent of too many DV cameras and student filmmakers
who'll give their work away for almost free hoping to break into an industry
that doesn't want them.

Revdonaldo
5/12/02
Long ago in a Galaxy far away - Hollywood - there was an opportunity for people
from Michigan, Indiana, Ohio, Texas, Florida to move to L.A. and get a job in
the movie business. Nice way to make a living even if it was working for ROGER
CORMAN. I moved out here in 1981 to join many of my friends. There was so
much demand for product when the video boom hit that studios couldn't keep up -
so there was an opportunity for anyone with a 16mm Bolex to make a movie. One

movie - ROLLER BLADE shot with out-dated 16mm reversal stock for five thousand dollars actually made ONE MILLION DOLLARS for New World Video. The filmmaker even made a couple hundred thousand for himself and got other deals. The whole point of this discussion that I started a long time ago when I originated this thread was - can it still be done? Has digital video killed inde filmmaking? Is there still a need for inde product and is it possible to make a living as an inde filmmaker?
Visit the Revdonaldo website:
http://www.zendance.com

MaxSamurai
5/18/02
Hollywood Video seems to have plenty of new Shot on Digital Video movies on the shelf recently. Titles are from companies like Full Moon, Tempe, and Brain Damage.
Mostly extreme gore horror movies and Urban gangster pictures - but looks like maybe someone is making a few bucks shooting on digital. I'd be curious to know more about these microbudget productions and what kind of money is being made?
How does one get a independent film into Hollywood Video stores? What is the submission process?

MaxSamurai
5/21/02
I am just amazed at the number of new digital features carried by HOLLYWOOD
VIDEO. Anyone checked them out? Seem to be mostly horror and urban action
titles.

DEPENDENT FILMMAKING
Revdonaldo
11/25/02
Here's a possible subject for discussion. Shouldn't what's left of
"independent" filmmaking really be "dependent" filmmaking because we are in
need of a supportive audience at this time. Big studios control almost
everything. Try and get your home grown movie in video stores or find a
meaningful distribution deal.
What can we do to promote an alternative cinema? Anyone else want to answer
this call to arms! It just seems that digital filmmaking has killed the what
used to be a good way to earn a living making movies.

MaxSamurai
11/26/02
Yes, independent filmmaking should really be DEPENDENT FILMMAKING because w/o
an audience - what's the point? Back to the old arugment - if you make a film
and no one see's it, did a tree really fall in the forest?

Revdonaldo
11/26/02
INDE ROADSHOW sounds great! Just like the old daze. Set up a tent and show
movies out of the trunk of your car. This just might work if promoted
properly!

Full Frontal Is The Worst Movie I Have Ever Seen
Revdonaldo
8/4/02
From a filmmaker's pov - why shoot on digital video if you're going to degrade
the image to look horrible as possible. After over six months of media hype,
FULL FRONTAL is a slap in the face to inde filmmakers!

SUCCESSFUL INDEPENDENT FILMMAKERS
Revdonaldo
5/5/02
Here's a list of successful independent filmmakers out of all that have tried
in the past 10 years - Please add to this if you can.
Darren Aronofsky Quentin Tarantino Christopher Nolan Kevin Smith Robert Rodriguez Daniel Myrick Eduardo Sánchez

ZEN FILMMAKING IS DANGEROUS
Revdonaldo
3/24/02
PSYCHOTRONIC VIDEO Number 36 has a seven page article on
ZEN FILMMAKER - DONALD G. JACKSON, creator of ROLLER
BLADE, HELL COMES TO FROGTOWN, and GUNS OF EL
CHUPACABRA. Because of the overwhelming response and flood of e-mails sent to
ZENDANCE.COM - We've decided to make this special offer. Jackson's first film
was shot for $3000
(three thousand dollars) and made it to theaters and drive-ins all across the
country. Jackson was the subject of an AFI sponsored documentary made during
the shoot called DEMON LOVER DIARY that played and won film festivals since
1980.
Both films were shown on a double-bill at the NU ART THEATER in Los Angeles.
Special Effects Wizards on THE DEMON LOVER BOB and DENNIS SKOTAK went on to win 4 Academy Awards.
DONALD G. JACKSON worked with JAMES CAMERON on the final daze of TERMINATOR and
also shot 2nd Unit with BILL PAXTON on CAMERON's Spaghetti western music video
- REACH. In celebration of the soon-to-be published book
SOLDIER OF CINEMA - LESSONS IN ZEN FILMMAKING aka

HOW TO MAKE LOW BUDGET MOVIES AND WHY YOU SHOULDN'T - written by DONALD G. JACKSON - Here's a special offer:
BUY THE DEMON LOVER 1-SHEET AND RECEIVE ZENDANCE. COM FREE CLUB MEMBERSHIP.
(limited time offer)
Cult-classic THE DEMON LOVER Full color theater 1-sheet posters created by cartoonist Val Mayerik (original artist of Marvel comic's HOWARD THE DUCK) recently discovered in a storage locker in Ann Arbor, Michigan. Extremely rare. This micro-budget16mm feature was blown-up to 35mm and played theaters and drive-ins in the late 70's and early 80's. SAM RAIMI attended a midnight show in Detroit with his pal BRUCE CAMPBELL and was inspired to make THE EVIL DEAD. Producer/Director DONALD G. JACKSON offers for sale a limited number of these impossible to find 1-sheet posters that are a part of independent film history. A must have for fans of low budget horror movies. Send $10.00 plus 3.50 postage for priority mail.Coming soon - THE DEMON LOVER DVD with never-before-seen SUPER 8 "behind the scenes" making of including "lost star" TED NUGENT, plus Jackson's pre and post-production Adventures in New York and Hollywood. This DVD is only available to purchasers of THE DEMON LOVE 1-sheet poster who also receive a BONUS FREE MEMBERSHIP in ZENDANCE.COM Members will receive free passes to the ZENDANCE FILM FESTIVAL plus opportunities to attend special seminars on ZEN

FILMMAKING. Visit the Revdonaldo website: http://www.zendance.com

Seeking independent video store owners/managers
Revdonaldo
1/19/03
HOLLYWOOD VIDEO stocks many independent features and I know for a fact some of
the budgets were far less than Five Thousand Dollars. YORK HOME VIDEO just put
out a movie called ANKLE BITERS. It is a brilliant John Woo - style
action/comedy. YORK looks for it to be a major hit because of the huge sales
conducted overseas at Cannes. The director is a friend and his total budget
was Nine Hundred Dollars. Not bad for a totally entertaining shot on video
feature.
My point is that a good movie will always find distribution.

MaxSamurai
1/20/03
I've never met an independent video store owner/manager who'd buy direct from
an inde filmmaker unless it was MONDO VIDEO in Hollywood. Selling one copy
isn't going to make a difference. The inde needs to make product that is good
enough to be picked up by the sub-distributors who sell directly to the large
chains - BEST BUYS, BLOCKBUSTER, HOLLYWOOD VIDEO,

WALLMART, and all the others. The only other alternative is selling on your
website,
AMAZON (who takes 50%). Why set low expectations? Make a good film that can
be distributed by the established companies.

MaxSamurai
1/26/03

YORK HOME VIDEO President,
Satanya York knows filmmakers are desperate people who mainly want to satisfy
their needs of seeing their films on the shelf in BlockBuster and Hollywood
Video. They believe having credibility could get them bigger budgets on their
next project. As a result, they are more or less giving their films away for
free in order to obtain distribution.
It should be noted that 95% of YORK titles are shot on film 35mm and 16mm.
Only on rare exceptions will she take something like ANKLE BITERS that was a DV
feature. The original distributor of this film was Yvette Hoffman of SPECTRUM.
 She failed to make a payment to the filmmaker and was in violation of her
agreement, so she returned the master. YORK took the movie for world-wide
distribution, but gave the filmmaker no participation in home video. She also
charged him to make M&E tracks, poster art, and duplication.
Last I heard the poor filmmaker owes YORK $12,500 for the privilege of having

his film distributed. Check out your local video stores mid-Feb to see ANKLE BITERS. A good example of what happens to talented filmmakers and why they can't make a dime.

HBO
MaxSamurai
6/8/03
I heard from an inside source that all the major cable networks including HBO, SHOWTIME, etc. are going to hire local DV filmmakers and give them an opportunity to have a showcase for their creations. This will include featuring talent from all areas of the country. They'll be showing local interviews, news stories, short films, DV features, etc. Now DV filmmakers will have a place to show their work, get discovered on higher levels, and also get paid. Sounds like a great alternative to all the mainstream shows and endless re-runs.

Soldier of Cinema
The Gospel of Revdonaldo

Highlights from the personal achievements and cinematic journey and gospel of Revdonaldo.

Someone once said that I was Hollywood's best kept secret. There's a few people who know about me. I've show many filmmakers the way to the light. Some made it light years beyond anything I could accomplish and others got lost to their own destiny.

Born April 24, 1943 I remember looking at the Sunday color comic pages and listening to a radio show called 'PUCK THE COMIC WEEKLY' where FLASH GORDON, PRINCE VALIANT, BLONDIE, and others were acted out like a radio show complete with music and sound effects.

My parents always took me to the movies where I was influenced by Saturday afternoon matinees with LASH LARUE, REX ALLEN, GENE AUTRY, ROY ROGERS, ALLEN ROCKY LANE and the serials KING OF THE ROCKETMEN, DICK TRACY, THE SECRET CODE, ZORRO, and many more.

On the radio I'd listen to BOBBY BENSON AND HIS B BAR B RIDERS, STRAIGHT ARROW, THE LONE RANGER, TOM MIX, THE SHADOW, and many others. BIG LITTLE BOOKS, comics, and newspaper strips all influenced my early life as a child. As a teenager I started to draw my own comic book and comic strip creations. Through an art magazine I joined the LYNTOP CARTOONIST CLUB where I met three people who would change my life: RICHARD LYNN, ROBERT ANTONICK, and CHUCK PENN.

Rick lived on a farm in Indiana where he collected comic books, daily strips, and corresponded with famous cartoonists. He was a fairly good artist who'd taken a mail order course in 'How to draw Comics'. His Indiana child-hood friend Chuck Penn enjoyed the comics and drew amateur cartoons. The Dayton college art student who had the 'cool drawing' style and served as a kind of role model was Bob Antonick. He drove a sports car, wrote sci-fi novels, had a cool philosophy of life, and sent me lots of inspirational letters and drawings. The four of us would get together for what we called LYNTOP CARTOONIST DAYS. My first trip to this convention was on the train because I was only fifteen years old. I was met at the train station by Bob Antonick and RickLynn. Antonick was driving a 1953 Studebaker. It was all so cool.

Rick has a collection of comic strips and books I'd never seen before including titles like FAMOUS FUNNIES that contained newspapers reprints of DICKIE DARE and unusual art I'd not seen including many EC COMICS, and daily strips with BEN FRIDAY and art I'd somehow missed.

On my own in Michigan, I continued to collect comic books, and clip and save newspapers strips such as JEFF COBB, STEVE ROPERS, TERRY AND THE PIRATES, ON STAGE any many more.

By the 50's I started to be influenced by certain shows on television. The early ones included SPACE PATROL, TOM CORBETT, SPACE CADET, CAPTAIN VIDEO, THE HUNTER, and local shows like WILLIE DO IT, THE GREAT FOODINI, CAPTAIN FLINT, CAPTAIN Z-RO.

Later shows that made big impressions included STONEY BURKE, MAN WITH A

CAMERA, and PETER GUNN. It was PETER GUNN that I saw long before being aware of creator Blake Edward's influences that pushed me in the direction of wanting to make movies instead of just trying to draw panels with cool 'camera angles' that Bob Antonick has been so inspirational about.

When Blake Edwards made EXPERIMENT IN TERROR,a black and white movie with all the stylized cinematography he used in certain episodes of PETER GUNN (THE CHASE - an experimental mostly silent episode), I was hooked on wanting to be a filmmaker.

Now I was affected by the 1954 widescreen DRAGNET preview. It kicked in what Jack Webb has said in the trailers. The movie used a crab dolly, hand-held camera, and would show you angles and scenes never before shown on the motion picture screen. It didn't, but what he said was one of the more influential things I'd remember. I've searched for years wanting to see this DRAGNET trailer. I was ten or eleven when I was it in the theater. Cinemascope was the big thing. The world was becoming more visually aware.

During high school other influences took place including my remembrance of a first tragedy. THE KINGSTON TRIO had changed my world with TOM DOOLEY. ELVIS was still the king. ROCK AROUND THE CLOCK with Bill Haley and the Comets. BUDDY HOLLY was different and fun to listen to. THAT'll BE THE DAY, OH. BOY, PEGGY SUE. I saw him on DICK CLARK AMERICAN BANDSTAND, ED SULLIVAN, and one day on the early morning radio news February 3, 1959---BUDDY HOLLY was dead.

THE KINGSTON TRIO, PETER PAUL AND MARY, THE LIMELITERS, THE CHAD

MITCHELL TRIO, BOB DYLAN, GORDON LIGHTFOOT took over my music collection. The BEATLES hadn't shown up yet, so I was finding cool things in folk music. DAVE GUARD AND THE WHISKEY HILL SINGERS. It would take me till 1991 to meet the incredible female singer JUDY HENSKE.

Mercury released the two best bluegrass albums in history -THE KNOB LICK UPPER 10,000 'Introduction' and 'Workout'. These three albums are still three of the four most inspirational albums I've ever heard. The fourth is THE FLYING BURRITO BROTHERS 'Gilded Palace of Sin'--- Two more. Capitol records released two albums by THE HEARTS AND FLOWERS.

I'd meet and get to know DWAIN STORY - Knoblick Upper 10,000 met Dwain at the Chestnut coffee house in Detroit and again at the Ark in Ann Arbor. Later I'd keep in touch with correspondence and phone calls. Dwain is the best tenor voice, flat top guitar picker I've ever heard. I visited him in Chicago on a cold winter night. He gave me original reel to reel tapes of his songs. Later I drove through the snow to the Aragon Ballroom to see a concert by ELVIS COSTELLO. I'd meet him twice. Dayton, Ohio. L.A. at the tribute to ROY ORBISON.

Influences in radio, newspaper comics, comic books, radio, movie serials, motion pictures, television shows, and then THE ANN ARBOR EXPERIMENTAL FILM FESTIVAL. Long before MTV, place to be every winter was Ann Arbor, Michigan. The show would run the entire week in Architecture auditorium. 16mm films from creative people all around the country. The place to be. And the band associated with the festival - COMMANDER CODY AND HIS LOST PLANET

AIRMEN. One festival they appeared on stage with PAT OLESZKO, a UOF M performance artist. I have some of this show on Super 8.

ANN ARBOR FILM FESTIVAL George Manupelli, founder of the festival created the most influential film of all time. DR. CHICAGO This film might be lost far as I know. It was 16mm black and white and ran two hours. Long takes, pan, tilt, zoom. I had to make films!

LIBERATION OF THE MANNEQUIN, MECHANIQUE CHINESE FIREDRILL, RICKY AND ROCKY, THE TRAGIC DIARY OF ZERO, THE FOOL. It was through the Ann Arbor Film Festival and the first 8mm Film Festival that I met GARY CROWDUS (I'd start CINEASTE magazine with him) and BOB and DENNIS SKOTAK. I'd join the MIDWEST FILM SOCIETY and be introduced to the NEW WAVE CINEMA of TRUFFAUT, GODARD, and many others. I'd also discover the films of ORSON WELLS and be influenced by CITIZEN KANE and TOUCH OF EVIL.

GARY CROWDUS would leave Warren, Michigan to attend NYU. He'd send me letters, clippings, and reviews of movies that would further change my life. SIDNEY FURIE WIDESCREEN TRILOGY: THE IPCRESS FILE, THE APPALOOSA, and THE NAKED RUNNER. In between A HARD DAYS NIGHT and HELP.

1962 working for an industrial photographer shooting black and white with a 4x5 speed graphic camera. Learned how to shoot and develop film. Make 8x10 enlargements and work in a darkroom. One night I got a new assignment. This is called a Bolex 16mm camera. I learned how to load the camera. First assignment was to shoot a high school football game from the pressbox. I got bored. I was too far away. Took the camera and got out on the field. Hand-held. Running with the team. The players loved it, but I was fired. The coach needed a record of the game.

I found an 8mm Bolex camera and started to shoot. My first effort was a 'rock video' made in 1965 to the tune EVE OF DESTRUCTION.

The only actor in the movie beside myself, I talked into going into photography in the Navy so he could send me free 16mm film. I got plenty of shipments of color reversal and black and white. My first two epics I shot and starred in called I DONALD SUPERSTAR and the B&W I DONALD SUPERSPY.

More Ann Arbor film festivals. Met and got to know independent filmmakers BOB AND DENNIS SKOTAK. They'd shot lots of 8mm films including lip synch sound and widescreen. Their epic was TIME SPACE that they'd hoped for a blow-up to 35mm and drive-in release by Roger Corman.

I had to make films. I sold precious collectable comic books and records to raise money. I met a fellow collector by the name of JERRY YOUNKINS. For good or bad, it launched me on my way as an independent filmmakers. We tried to raise money. A Detroit lawyers put together a limited partnership. It took him over one year to have the documents ready. It was a good package, but no buyers. I had to get creative.

TEXAS CHAINSAW MASSACRE had now changed by life. A 16mm motion picture shot with reversal stock using an Eclair NPR. I managed to track down director TOBE HOOPER and do a telephone interview. He was staying at the famous Tropicana Motel on Santa Monica Blvd. I'd be there in three years trying to sleep while worried the

MPAA was going to not give me first feature the R RATING needed to be released.

TOBE HOOPER gave me encouragement with two telephone interviews. Plus he put me in touch with GUNNAR HANSEN. It didn't hurt having LEATHERFACE himself do a part in my first movie. Also managed to get in touch with GEORGE ROMERO and have him as a guest at a Detroit comic book convention. We also had Alan Ormsby who'd made a film CHILDREN SHOULDN'T PLAY WITH DEAD THINGS.

I borrowed money from a loan company: $1500 on my household furniture and $1500 on my new 1974 Gremlin. $3000 in the bank and I started shooting THE DEMON LOVER. 16MM PARODY of low budget horror films. VAL MAYERIK (the first artist to draw HOWARD THE DUCK) played the good guy and JERRY YOUNKINS was the evil wizard.

When the producer/cinematographer of DEATH CORP proved to be unaffordable, he did visit us with his Eclair ACL and shoot a free test.

DANIEL PEARL who shot TCM was willing to do the job if I could have raised 150-K with the Detroit lawyer's LP. But no luck. BILL DEAR who'd shot a 16mm to 35mm Michigan motorcycle movie called FREEDOM, RIP would help, but I didn't have the money for his salary and equipment.

JEFF KREINES - who'd shot the wide angle lens, hand-held, continuos takes Ann Arbor Film Festival winner RICKY AND ROCKY agreed to be my DP. He owned his own Auricon 16mm camera with a fixed 10mm wide angle lens. He would show up from MIT with his girlfriend shooting a documentary about the making of my film.

DEMON LOVER DIARY would win prizes in film festivals all around the world. I had to rent a 16mm CP 16 with an 8mm zeiss distagon lens. The entire DEMON LOVER Feature would be shot handheld with a wide angle lens. When it became too obvious that Kreines and his girlfriend JOEL DEMONT were more interested in providing production resistance rather than assistance---they were deliberately sabotaging my film in order to make it all fall apart so they'd have their AFI sponsored documentary. It was ironic. I'd later learn that the AFI had given them $10,000 to make a film about a guy in Michigan who didn't have enough money to make a film.

JEFF KREINES and JOEL DEMONT are fired. A wild car chase finds them trying to leave town with all of my exposed 16mm film plus the rest of the raw stock. It took some tough words to persuade them to turn over the film and leave fast.

RESTART: I had to learn the hard way that it was a lot easier to shoot the film myself than to argue with a cameraman. The angles and lighting were all natural instinct. It was fun and it was thrilling. Helping on the crew were BOB SKOTAK monster maker, art director, and editor. DENNIS SKOTAK 2ND unit cinematography with his Bolex, second editor, and BRYAN GREENBERG, camera assistant and assistant editor. We made the film. We edited the film.

JERRY YOUNKINS and I took the work print to New York. EUE/SCREEN GEMS did the blow up from 16mm to 35mm. We did the sound mix in New York. Took the film in hand to Los Angles for a personal review by the MPAA. It was too bloody for their taste, but they understood it was a parody. They gave it an 'R' rating on the condition we'd make certain cuts. The certificate came in the mail. It said the film was rated 'R' and nothing could be added. We changed nothing and how three World Premiers.

In Jackson, Michigan the twinplex had a feature on the other side that was the cinematic event of all time. STAR WARS. We got on the front page of local newspapers and appeared on a local Detroit TV show.

Starting with $3000 cash loaned to me from two finance companies, we were able to network with friends, relatives, and businessmen enough money to do a 16-35 blow-up and make a total of seven prints.

My home town of Adrian showed THE DEMON LOVER at a drive-in world premiere. The drive-in across town was showing FOOD OF THE GODS.

We had midnight shows in Detroit. One night a group of young filmmakers attended to ask me questions in the lobby. They were excited, as I'd been by TCM and DEATH CORP of shooting in 16mm and blowing up to 35mm to play in a theater. I answered their questions along with Bob Skotak and his brother Dennis. They wanted to make a horror movie. It would be released several years later. THE EVIL DEAD. I'd spoke in the lobby that evening with Sam Rami and Bruce Campbell.

BOB SKOTAK decided he had to make the trip to LOS ANGELES and look for real work in the movie business. Soon he helped start ROGER CORMAN's NEW WORL SPECIAL EFFECTS DEPT. I remained in Michigan. Back working in a factory once again, but on weekends with a Bolex me and BRYAN GREENBERG had started shooting the World's First Wrestling Horror Movie - RINGSIDE

IN HELL. When we'd have extra money, we'd rent an Eclair NPR and shoot sync sound. DENNIS SKOTAK would run the Nagra. BRYAN would shoot the NPR and I'd mostly direct and do the Bolex work.

Soon BOB would need DENNIS to join him in California. Bryan stayed for awhile to help do a rough cut on RINGSIDE IN HELL. We took the edited work print to L.A. Visited with the SKOTAKS. Showed the film to a producer who'd make the influential film THE HILLS HAVE EYES.

Back to Michigan. BILL DEAR was now set with Michael Nesmith and Pacific Arts. They were starting to do rock videos and had a show called POP CLIPS. A job was offered to BRYAN. He was off to Carmel.

THE DEMON LOVER had caused me so much grief and financial worry. A small distribution company called 21ST CENTURY was getting the film shown in grind houses and drive-ins. Forgot the 3rd world premiers was the LYRIC THEATER on 42nd street. This is where a scene was shot for TAXI DRIVER. THE DEMON LOVER out-grossed CARRIE playing across the street. With no ads, this one theater took in $14,000 in one week charging admission of $1.50. The distributor complained this was low, but helped convince other theaters to book the film.

I'd tried it myself with a company in Texas called GRIMES and they'd played drive-ins and Florida. FRED OLEN RAY saw the movie and called me for a telephone interview. Independent Filmmaking's were always interested in interviewing me because I'd done it. Took a 16mm camera, made a horror movie, and played theaters.

BRYAN GREENBERG was in California working with Bill Dear and Mike Nesmith. I stayed on trying to improve RINGSIDE IN HELL. We even managed to record an album of country-rock tunes to include. I had a wrestling/horror movie very inspired by Robert Altman's NASHVILLE.

Discouraged at being the only member of my group still alone in Michigan, I gave in to offers from Bob and Dennis Skotak to join them in Los Angeles with the hope of getting a job working with them at the Roger Corman special effects studio.

It was 13 below zero when I got on a bus in Detroit with Dennis Skotak. I documented the entire cross country to Los Angeles with a Canon Super 8 camera. Stepping off the bus, we were picked up by Bob Skotak and his wife Elaine. A newspaper has revealed ELVIS COSTELLO was playing the coliseum. They let me off with instructions on how to find their apt in west L.A.

No better welcome to L.A. than seeing ELVIS COSTELLO! After the show, I took my first solo trip on the bus and found out Wilshire Blvd went for miles. It took several wrong buses before I ended up a the corner of Santa Monica a and Bundy. ARLENES DONUT SHOP. Now long gone, but the place where delicious orange donuts the best in the world were served. I'd taken them home by the box load on the plane when I'd visit. Down the street, Dennis had raved about the NUWAY CHILI DOG PARLOG. He was right. Incredible chilidogs.

The apt on Bundy offered a note that Bob and Elaine has gone out of town for the weekend. I had instructions on how to feed the dogs.

During the next few days I'd actually get hired as a special effects camera assistant on a movie called GALAXY OF TERROR. I'd watch Bob and

Dennis influence cast decisions and be responsible for the hiring of ROBERT ENGLAND, ZALMAN KING, and SID HAIG.

I'd meet RANDY FRAKES who'd later work with me to write and produce HELL COMES TO FROGTOWN. I'd start working with Randy on special effects and go to restaurants with the second unit director and art director - JIM CAMERON. Jim would ask me questions about independent filmmaking and how to raise money.

I knew JIM CAMERON when he couldn't pay his phone bill and was being evicted from his Venice apartment. I was with him to shoot and direct the famous maggot scene from GALAXY OF TERROR. I walked in the parking lot with Jim to the trunk of his car where he proudly showed me penciled widescreen story boards from a movie he'd been hired to direct called PIRANHA II-THE SPAWNING.

The Fourth of July 1984, Jim would personally call me to help him shoot pick-ups on a movie that the production company refused to put anymore money into. Jim and Gale Ann Hurd paid me out of their own pocket for nine days of additional shooting on one of the most influential movies of all time.

JIM CAMERON told me I'd saved the movie with all of my inserts and additional shots. The Production Manager DONNA SMITH failed to give me an additional photography by DONALD G. JACKSON credit that Cameron had promised me. World is when Ernie Farino showed Cameron the end credits, Jim stood up and shouted- Where's Jackson's credit! Donna Smith was silent until forced to admit she didn't want to spend the extra $500 it would have cost to have added my name.

I continued to shoot my 16 Bolex feature. Shot with out-dated ECO REVERSAL stock, silent, and with no script. ROLLER BLADE was in the works.

Suddenly CYNDI LAUPER was going to wrestling matches and so were rock stars. The phrase ROCK 'N ROLL WRESTLING was coined.

New World knew I had an unreleased wrestling movie. They hated the title RINGSIDE IN HELL. I found out the country-rock score wasn't clear for me to use. I suggested we call the movie I LIKE TO HURT PEOPLE based on a song we'd recorded for the movie. But I didn't have clearance for the song. New World executives suggested a simple solution. Have someone re-record a different song with the same title.

Sam Mann who was playing the villain in ROLLER BLADE went into the studio and recorded a new version of I LIKE TO HURT PEOPLE in ½ hour. A new score and re-cut of the film ended with New World Home Video advancing $50,000 on a movie that would earn them one-half million dollars on video sales.

It wasn't hard to convince them that ROLLER BLADE was the next big thing for them on video. New World released it as their first made for video feature. They took out full page color ads in BILLBOARD and VIDEO MAGAZINES. NEW WORLD VIDEO now had two DONALD G. JACKSON pictures in their library.

I LIKE TO HURT PEOPLE and ROLLER BLADE were making them some money in the video market. ROLLER BLADE was shot with my visa card for a cash outlay of $5000. It made almost one million dollars! New World had paid me $50.000 on

I LIKE TO HURT PEOPLE and a cash advance of $70,000 on ROLLER BLADE.

The two pictures combined made them over one and a half million dollars off their $120,000 investment in me. Ten times their money back.

When asked what I wanted to do next, they loved the title I'd found written spray painted on a brick wall. FROGTOWN. HELL COMES TO FROGTOWN.

During the production, they tried to change the title to the ADVENTURES OF SAM HELL, but later decided I was right. HELL COMES TO FROGTOWN was all set to be released in 1000 theaters. NEW WORLD PICTURES filed bankruptcy.

The offer from New World Video based on the title was $150,000 for me to shoot on 16mm non-Sag. After reading the screenplay, it was moved up to theatrical where the final budget was 1.5 million. I'll never know what might have happened if I'd done the film as I wanted on 16mm with complete creative control.

New World made good money with I LIKE TO HURT PEOPLE and wanted to do something similar and along the lines of my picture meets SPINAL TAP. The result was GRUNT THE WRESTLING MOVIE. The producer would later have a company called MORGAN CREEK. His name is JAMES G. ROBINSON

I shot second unit on GRUNT THE WRESTLING MOVIE. It was blown up from 16mm and played a few theaters.

JIM CAMERON hated the fact New World had forced me to cut most of the action scenes from the script because they were too risky on our 1.5 mil budget. He had a few schemes on how we could save the film with some re-shoots but New World wasn't in the mood to cooperate.

My next film would be a 35mm Sag film spaghetti western version of ROLLER BLADE. ROLLER BLADE WARRIORS along with HELL COMES TO FROGTOWN would become cult favorites on USA CABLE.

JIM CAMERON needed a second-unit director and cinematographer on his spaghetti western rock video. MARTINI RANCH 'Reach' with Bill Paxton and many guest starts including Lance Hendrickson, Kathryn Bigelow, and many others. Matt Leonetti shot first unit with Cameron, but you can't tell where his work leaves off and mine comes on screen. It was a 12 minute rock video. Cameron directed some of my shots, but mostly I was on my own.

My next job would be shooting a movie starring DAVID HEAVENER called OLD SCORES. It was shot in 16mm. I discovered ZIAD DOUERI and trained him to be my camera assistant. He was put through the SOLDIERS OF CINEMA boot camp. I worked him long and hard. He complained, but gave me the best results I've ever had from a camera assistant. ZIAD has since gone on to be first assistant camera on pictures including NATURAL BORN KILLERS, FOUR ROOMS, DESPERADO, DUSK TILL DAWN, JACKIE BROWN, and others.

TWISTED FATE was re-titled KILL, KILL, OVERKILL! Shot entirely hand-held in a style used before popular TV SHOWS like NYPD BLUE, and HOMICIDE, this film is also a regular on USA CABLE.

Second Unit Cinematography on SHOCK 'EM DEAD led to getting to know TRACI LORDS.

She almost played the female lead in RETURN TO FROGTOWN and ROLLER BLADE SEVEN.

After three pictures for YORK (the founder of the company was the makeup artist on ROLLER BLADE WARRIORS). She introduced me to DAVID HEAVENER who hired me to shoot OLD SCORES and be 2nd unit DP on TWISTED JUSTICE. Tanya York gave me my own company. THE REBEL CORP.

I shot two 16mm features at the same time - ROLLER BLADE SEVEN and RETURN OF THE ROLLER BLADE SEVEN.

It was at this time along with the association of SCOTT SHAW (who played HAWK in both movies) we created the style of shooting we'd start to call 'ZEN FILMMAKING'. Movies without a script. Spontaneous creation. We'd gather a cast who looked good on camera and inspired us. We'd find a great location like the El Mirage dry lake bed. The actors would put on their costumes. I'd load the camera. CREATIVITY would strike. The results were like nothing that could be achieved with a screenplay.

IT'S SHOWTIME was a 16mm feature about dancers. SCOTT SHAW was off doing his own movies and developing as a filmmaker after his experience with the REBEL CORP. I'd intended to shoot without a script and the producers agreed.

At the last minute in order to attach a female 'star' a script was required. I recruited a screenwriter. The sought after start hated the script. I used it as a guide, but was able to get JEFF CONAWAY (famous for TAXI) to improvise his part and really understand appreciate ZEN FILMMAKING.

The producers tried to have me fired, but they were startled by the visuals in the screening room.

The film looked GOOD and that's all they cared about.

Next came a 35mm feature. It was to be an art film along the lines of MY DINNER WITH ANDRE. JEFF CONAWAY who'd I'd worked with in IT'S SHOWTIME agreed to be the star. GOOD DOCTOR PRODUCTIONS has to have a script. I called the screenwriter from IT'S SHOWTIME. The GOOD DOCTOR producer loved the script. We shot it as written.

The 35mm dailies were beautiful. Then he decided not to let me edit the movie. He brought in an editor who was also a director. He convinced the GOOD DOCTOR to shoot additional scenes and add animation. The results were a disaster.

The footage shot as written bares a striking resemblance to the structure of JACKIE BROWN.

What if you could shoot an entire movie in one long take without having to do any cuts. Shot in 'real time'. I conceived the idea of doing a shot on video feature. It would be given the 'film-look' in post-production and buyers wouldn't know it wasn't shot on film.

CARJACK ended up being shot over a period of eight days. It cost $7500.00 $1500.00 was spent on the actual film. $5,000 was for my knowledge. One thousand was spent on art work for the poster and video box. Tanya York made the down payment on a new house with the money she made!

MICRO-BUDGET VIDEO. Shot on hi-8 with 'film-look'. Who would know or care they weren't made on film. The writer of IT'S SHOWTIME, THE GOOD DOCTOR MOVIE (LAST IMPRESSION) provided the scripts. They were difficult to shoot, cost too much time and money. After producing and directing LITTLE

LOST SEA SERPENT, BABY GHOST, and BIG SISTER 2000, I was ready to return to the most comfortable and cost effective method created for ROLLER BLADE SEVEN.

'ZEN FILMMAKING' created RAW ENERGY. Many a viewer has remarked if only it had been shot on film it would have been a hit at the various film festivals where it could have been shown.

ROLLER GATOR was 25% ZEN FILMMAKING and the remainder written on the set before we'd shoot.

TOAD WARRIOR sent forth the call for the return of SCOTT SHAW. He'd play MAX HELL and be part of the creative process of making this new ZEN feature.

EL CHUPACABRA started with a screenplay. It didn't work. Another script was loosely outlined. Failure. Return of the ZEN-STYLE and SCOTT SHAW. The title was changed to GUNS OF EL CHUPACABRA.

The series is now a trilogy- with two other titles CRIMES OF EL CHUPACABRA and GHOST OF EL CHUPACABRA.

Towards the end of 1997, we started a new company. HOLLYWOOD INTERNATIONAL has produced two digital features to be converted to 35mm release prints. 1998 the company will release three examples of ZEN FILMMAKING the 16/35/digital feature GUNS OF EL CHUPACABRA and the digital to 35mm features ROCK 'N ROLL COPS and PAGING DOCTOR PRAISEWATER

Next DONALD G. JACKSON has vowed to only shoot films in the 35mm widescreen format.

Video will be used only for location scouting, auditions, and rehearsals. The new philosophy is "If it's worth doing, it's worth shooting on film."

I've been influenced by the main sources I've listed in this article. I've seen close friends win Academy Awards who worked with me on my first feature. Other friends pioneer what was to become MTV. Associates who've ridden with me in my 1962 Plymouth include IRVIN KIRSHNER, who directed THE EMPIRE STRIKES BACK and JAMES CAMERON famous for TERMINATOR, and all of his other block-busters.

Author's note:
The Gospel of Revdonaldo was reflected in one flash of light, and I plan to later make additions and corrections. My current work includes the publication of The LIGHTSOURCE ENTERTAINMENT JOURNAL that will features articles and reviews on lost films and hard-to-find music that I consider over-looked and under-rated plus information on current music and film inspirations along with news of my own creative activity.

PART II
THE FILMS AND THE FILMMAKING

Making The Roller Blade Seven

For some reason there has been an ongoing interest in the films *The Roller Blade Seven*, its sequel *Return of the Roller Blade Seven* and the recut, more widely distributed, version of the two films *Legend of the Roller Blade Seven,* sometimes titled *The Legend of the Rollerblade 7,* (which we, the filmmakers, in no way endorse). To this day, almost twenty years since RB7 was released, I still get e-mails and letters from people asking questions about the true meaning of this movie. In other cases, some people have been very critical of this film. But, perhaps that is what is to be expected when you intentionally create a *Pure Art Film.* Some people just won't get it. In any case, I thought I would write a few words here about the creation of *The Roller Blade Seven* and how it took on a life of its own. To tell the whole story would no doubt fill an entire book. I will try to keep it brief.

First, and perhaps most important*, The Roller Blade Seven* can never be compared to a traditional film. Additionally, it should never be judged by those who wish to compare it to traditional filmmaking, as there was never anything traditional about this movie!

Furthermore, when viewing RB7 and *Return of the Roller Blade Seven* is essential to note that nothing happened randomly—every location, every scene, every segment of dialogue, every visual image, every edit, was a conscious action on the part of Donald G. Jackson and myself.

For those of you who are old enough, or for those of you who have looked back in film history to some of the Avant-garde movies made in the 1960's, *The Roller Blade Seven* is much more on par with those films than the films of today. These films were referred to as, *"Acid Flicks."* This was in reference to the mind-altering drug, LSD. Meaning, they depicted a landscape void of reality. That is perhaps the best way to describe *The Roller Blade Seven.* To bring this comparison up to the modern era, RB7 is much more like an extended *Music Video* than a film.

As we created RB7, Donald G. Jackson and I very consciously went about making a movie that pushed the envelope of traditional filmmaking. Along the way, several people warned us that we were doing just that and told us that we should stop. Of course, we didn't listen.

Some people have also criticized the acting in *The Roller Blade Seven*. Again, they are really missing the point. Who cares about acting! The Roller Blade Seven is about the essence of life—which, in this case, is detailed in the realms of a film. It is not about acting! The only reason any words were spoken at all was to provide some semblance of a story to lure the uninitiated and the unenlightened into the deeper spiritual perspective this film delineates.

Moreover, if anyone looks at the wildness of the characters that make up this film, they will quickly understand that traditional acting has nothing to do with the development and composition of these roles. In fact, it was our intention to push the actors into new areas of expression—the wilder, the more bizarre the acting, the better.

What is a film critic? With very few exceptions, a film critic is someone who wishes they could make a film but does not possess the talent or the dedication to do so.

Pre-Production

Pre-Production for *The Roller Blade Seven* went up in the autumn of 1991. Our offices were located in the *Hollywood Center Building* on Hollywood Blvd., in Hollywood, California. Quentin Tarantino had just moved out after putting the finishing touches on his directorial debut, *Reservoir Dogs*. Don and I named our Production Company, *The Rebel Corp*.

Back then, things were very different in Hollywood. If you have seen the film, you will notice that some scenes have upwards of one hundred people on roller blades, sword fighting, etc. All of those people happily worked for free—seeking only a spot in a Hollywood feature film. And, we thank them all.

The First Zen Film

The Roller Blade Seven began shooting on a rainy Saturday morning in November 1991. By the end of the first weekend, Don and I realized that any concept of traditionalism was out the window. We tossed out any predetermined notion we had about the film and simply let spontaneous creativity be our only guide. This was to become the first *Zen Film*.

For the next several months we shot the film whenever the inspiration struck. We refined the cast as we went along, adding new people as needed.

The story... Don and I didn't care about the story. The stories have all been told!

The Cinematography

For anyone who has the eye to take notice, RB7 possess scope and photographic composition beyond belief. This is in no small part thanks to Don who was a Master Cinematographer.

RB7 was shot on 16mm. The cameras we used were the *Aaton S16,* the *Arri BL,* the *Bolex Rex 4* with a 24 fps motor, and the 24 fps *Canon Scoopic.*

The Roller-Cam

While filming RB7 we created a new style of photography. We named it, *"The Roller-Cam."*

We had a masterful skater named Steve Wright who would shoot with Don's *Bolex* and skate alongside and around the actors. This is what gives many of the scenes in RB7 an ethereal sense of movement. In some scenes, Steve would skate backwards faster than most people can run. The stories I could tell you about some of the amazing things he did while shooting certain segments of RB7...

When people see the footage he shot, they assume we used a camera truck. No, that was just Steve.

For the martial artists who are reading this, there was virtually no choreography. Every fight scene was either completely spontaneous or rehearsed and filmed only once. This occurred due to the fact that 16mm film is not cheap!

The Names

Our Executive Producer had high hopes of making a lot of money on the film. I'm sure she was very disappointed. But, to that end, a few months into production, she had us add several, *"Name,"* players to the film.

Back then, in 1991, if you added known *"Names"* to your film, you could be assured of sales—particularly to foreign markets. Though that is no longer the case, back then, we happily obliged.

Don Stroud

The first inductee was Don Stroud. Don has had an illustrious acting career, including co-starring with Clint Eastwood in *Cogan's Bluff* and *Joe Kidd*. He co-starred in the James Bond film, *License to Kill*. He also starred in the Motorcycle Cult Classic, *Angel Unchained*. From my adolescence forward, Don had been one of my favorite actors. So, I was very happy to bring him on board. I had worked with him previously and there is nothing but great things to say about the man. He has remained a close friend.

We drove out to the *El Mirage Dry Lake Bed* a couple of times with Don and he was nothing but great. You know, he is just one of those masterful actors who UNDERSTANDS. He didn't care that we didn't have a script. He was happy to create his own character.

In fact, in doing so, he became two distinct characters. One was a guardian of *The Wheelzone* and the second was a conga playing desert dweller. For his second incarnation, we brought along Jill Kelly, (who I will discuss more in a few moments). She and her friend wildly danced around Don as his congas played on.

William Smith

The next inductee was William Smith—also a Clint Eastwood co-star and the ultimate Hollywood Bad Guy.

Another great actor, Bill actually cried when Don and I went to a house in the Hollywood Hills where he was staying to offer him the role.

Back then, Bill liked to drink a lot. He kept his gallon of Vodka close at hand. But, the masterful actor he was, it never slowed him down. His improve was great.

"*Can I go home now, Daddy,*" was his constant mantra.

Karen Black

The next inductee was Golden Globe Winner and Academy Award Nominee, Karen Black. Karen is a sweetheart—a very nice person. Don and I picked her up early one morning at her home in Woodland Hills. She climbed into the back seat of Don's *1962 Plymouth Belvedere* and we drove to this Art Farm, which we named, *"The Mushroom Ranch,"* located in the California *high-desert*. We filmed several scenes with her in a tribute to her Acid Taking Graveyard scene in *Easy Rider*. These scenes became some of the most magical in RB7.

There are no words that could describe the *Zen* totally of the moments we felt with Karen while we filmed that day. When I later edited the scenes we shot that day, they came into their own perfection and I truly believe they are visually the high point of the RB7.

Dialogue

Whenever any member of the cast needed words to memorize, we gave them a copy of either *Essence* or *Time*. These are two books that I authored, made up of spiritual aphorisms. The words in these two books make up much of the dialogue of RB7. Karen loved the books and virtually all of her dialogue is based on my writing from those books.

Time was re-worked and re-released in 1999 with the title, Zen O'clock: Time To Be and Essence was re-released in 2007 with the title, Essence: The Zen of Everything.

Don and I bumped into Karen at the twenty-five year reunion screening for the film, *Nashville*. This was held in 2001 at *The Academy of Motion Picture Arts and Sciences* in Beverly Hills. After the event all of the cast and crew, including: Robert Altman, the director, (who I had worked with on his film *The Player),* Karen Black, Jeff Goldblum, Keith Carradine, Ronee Blakley, Shelley Duvall, Henry Gibson, Scott Glenn, Lily Tomlin, Cristina Raines, etc., etc., etc. went to one of my favorite restaurants, *Kate Mantilini's*. At the restaurant Karen told us how descendants from the kitten she had brought back from that Art Farm still live with her.

Rhonda Shear

Rhonda Shear was the next *"Name"* cast member to be added to RB7. Rhonda is a very sweet, flirtatious lady. At the time she was in RB7 she was hosting a late-night T.V. show called *Up All Night*. This show broadcast weird art-house moves on the *USA Network*. A couple of Don's films regularly showed on the program and I am sure the reason the Executive Producer wanted her in the film was so RB7 would also appear on the *USA Network*. Though the original *Roller Blade Seven* was never shown on *Up All Night, Legend of the Roller Blade Seven* was broadcast several times.

Frank Stallone

The next cast member added was Frank Stallone. The previous *"Name"* talents were all cool beyond belief. Frank, well that was a bit different story…

We had Frank meet us at the Granada Hills home of one of the film's A.C.'s (Camera Assistants). We then loaded him into Don's car and headed for the location.

"Are the crew waiting for us at the location," Frank asked. Don and I laughed because he and I were the crew.

The Crew

During the filming of RB7 Don operated the camera; I did the sound. So, the process was, I would get the DAT up and running, Don would roll the camera, then I would go into frame with the slate, call the scene, slap the slate, walk out, then walk back in and act.

Needless to say, through Frank acted out his part and behaved like a true professional, he did not see the ART in that process.

De Soto Jungle

We took Frank to this location we had dubbed, *"De Soto Jungle."* There we shot the encounter between his character and mine where we battle with Samurai Swords.

It is hard to forget the look on Frank's face when Don handed him the rubber Black Knight suit we had picked up for him. His embarrassment radiated and I am sure he was wondering was the $6,000.00 we were paying him for one day of work worth it. *None-the-less,* he put on the suit and we shot the scenes.

It is important to note that on film we knew the suit would look fine. In the *up-close-and-personal*, however, it did look kind of fake.

A funny story involving Frank occurred after we filmed our first scenes with him and had returned to our AC's house. Don looked at me with fear in his eyes and said, *"What are we going to have Frank say?"* I suggested we go for a ride, which we did. We ended up at *Tommy Burgers* in the North Valley. We had a couple of burgers and etched out the basis of what Frank would say.

We returned to the garage of our AC, where Mark Richardson had constructed our sets. Filming continued...

Joe Estevez

The final *"Name"* talent to be added was Joe Estevez. Joe, perhaps best known for being the brother of Martin Sheen, is a great guy and has remained a close friend—who I have worked with several times.

Don and I had not met Joe prior to shooting with him that first night. But, we had seen him in the film *Soultaker*. This is the film that led Joe to indie film stardom.

The shoot was planned for stages had set up at our Hollywood office building. We also had a dressing room set aside for Joe. When he arrived, we lead him to it. But, Joe being Joe would have nothing to do with it. He just wanted to hang out.

Joe's a great actor. Like Karen Black, much of his dialogue in RB7 came from my two books, *Essence* and *Time*.

David Carradine and Erik Estrada

Don and I courted both David Carradine and Erik Estrada to be in RB7. I had worked with David in another film and, if nothing else, he is an interesting guy. To this day, his original *Kung Fu* T.V. Series remains one of the most important events in television history.

Don and I had both previously worked with Eric. So, we went to his house and discussed the role he would play. We had a pink Harley Davidson lined up for his character—playing off of his role on television series *CHIP's*.

Both David and Eric were up for doing the movie. But, due to contractual difficulties, brought about by the Executive Producer, neither of them appeared in the film.

Jill Kelly

Some people have noticed that we used a few Adult Film Stars in RB7. This is true. Jade East was in the film and Jill Kelly's first role on film was in this movie. To name just a few...

We had meet Jill, then known by her given name Adrianne Moore, through a friend of Don's who was a dancer in a strip club in Bakersfield, California—where Adrianne also worked. The four of us went out and had a great time getting drunk on margaritas in a Burbank, California hot spot.

For those of you in other parts of the country and the world, Burbank is the home of many of the major film and T.V. studios. So, a lot of industry people hang out around the city.

We hit it off right away and we asked Jill to be in the film. From the time we first meet her forward, I have nothing but nice things to say about Jill. She is super-professional and a very nice person.

After her appearance in RB7 she went on to become one of the top players in the Adult Film Industry. Don and I have worked with her a few times since RB7. And, she has remained a very nice person.

Traci Lords

Perhaps the saddest thing about the *"Name"* talent that was to be associated with RB7 was the loss of Traci Lords.

We heard Traci was looking for a new project. I had not worked with Traci before but Don had worked with her on the film *Shock 'em Dead.* So, she was offered the role of the female lead.

Traci, particular about the films she worked on, came by to look at some footage from RB7 with her agent. We met at *EZTV,* when it was located on Santa Monica Blvd. in West Hollywood. She liked what she saw—all the flamboyance and radical cinematography. She *"Got on the Bus,"* as we used to say.

Traci came by our offices the next day and wanted to know about her character. I silently laughed as Don attempted to explain that this was *Zen Filmmaking* and we simply allowed spontaneous creation to be our only guide. *"What, no script!"* Don handed her copies of my two aforementioned books and told her she could use any passage she wanted from them. Though not completely satisfied, she agreed.

One of the things that really impressed me about Traci was the fact that she understood her character was going to wield a Samurai Sword in the film. She wanted to look professional. So, each afternoon she would come by, we would go onto our back stages, and I would teacher her proper Samurai techniques. We gave her a Samurai Sword to practice with at home and each day she would come back having mastered the previous day's techniques. Few actors or actresses, take their roles this seriously—especially for an independent production.

Traci even re-dyed her hair blonde for the film—as per Don's request. This, just after she had taken it to a strawberry blonde. So, she was really up for the project.

The day came to sign the contract. Our Executive Producer, looking to her own future, had devised a contract that stated she could use any footage filmed for RB7 in any additional movie she desired—from here to eternity... Traci, obviously a savvy businesswoman, was not going to become *Stock Footage* and would not sign the contract. All she wanted was that wording be taken out. The Executive Producer would not budge.

Perhaps the most unfortunate thing about this situation was that I was the one elected to give Traci her contract. So, she blamed me. I received an understandably very angry phone call from her the night all this took place, stating, *"You're the Producer of this project—do something!"* But, I was not the one providing the financing. So, there was nothing I could do. Sadly, we lost Traci Lords.

But, back to the story line....

Return Of The Roller Blade Seven

During the filming of *The Roller Blade Seven* we realized that one film was just not enough to cover the entire subject matter of *Artistic Filmmaking* and *Cinematic Enlightenment* that we wanted to present. Don and I were sitting down, having a burger, at *Jay Burgers* over on Virgil and Santa Monica in East Hollywood and we had a revelation—we needed to make two films. As Don had a contract for two films with our Executive Producer, we decided that the best thing to do was to create a second feature in association with RB7. Thus was born *Return of the Roller Blade Seven*. With this film we decided to present an even more artistic landscape and provide clues and answers to some of the *Cinematic Zen Koans* presented in the first film. For this reason, if anyone wishes to truly understand what we were trying to do with RB7, the second film must also be studied.

More Gold

Upon the completion of filming each day we took our film to the lab to be developed. After we picked it up, we would head over to a *Telecine* house in Burbank, where a great Colorist named, Wilks Butler, did our color correction for us.

"MG," was the word, *"More Gold."* Don and I were both in love with the look of *The Golden Hour,* (the hour just before sunrise and just after sunset), and we attempted to make RB7 look as gold as possible.

Some of my fondest memories of RB7 are the hours, leading to days; we spent in *Telecine* on RB7. Wilks would have his runner Alex go and get us Chili from *Chili John's* in Burbank and we would eat while we watched RB7.

Magical Things

Many magical events occurred during the creation of RB7. One of the most striking was the fact that Don and I decided to go and have some *Production Stills* developed at this shop in Burbank. Inside, the walls were lined with photos of this one very beautiful girl. We asked about her. The story was, the shop had a photo day and she was the model. Looking at this girl's photos, I could not help but think, *"I would really like to meet her."* About an hour later, Don and I stopped at a *711*. Inside, a girl walked up to me and said, *"You look like a rock star."* Low-and-behold, it was the same girl.

Hard to believe, but very true. We gave her the role of Sister Sparrow in the film and she became one of the female leads.

Editing

Editing is where RB7 took shape. We began in a traditional manner—hiring the editor who had edited Don's film, *Roller Blade* to work while Don and I supervised. The editor made two big mistakes:

1. He just did not understand Art.
2. He taught me how to use the equipment.

I edited, while he would sit there and try to make sense out of the movie.

A Funny Story

One of the interesting things that occurred, that perhaps heralded our leaving the realms of traditional editing, was that while we were attempting to get the original editor to understand our style of *Zen Filmmaking*—one morning, upon arriving at the Sunset Boulevard building where the editing studio was located, Don went to the bathroom. With him he carried all of our DAT tapes.

We had recorded the sound for RB7 on the, (then), newly developed DAT (Digital Audio Technology) format.

Don left the bathroom with the tapes sitting on the sink. Once in the editing studio he soon realized what he had done and we quickly returned to get them. But, they were gone. We had hoped someone had just picked them up for safekeeping. So, we went and asked, suite-to-suite. But, to no avail. We put up a notice in the bathroom, but no one ever responded.

That's Hollywood for you. Had it not been for the fact that we had transferred all of our Beta Master Sources Tapes to 3/4 inch for editing, during *Telecine,* we would have had no audio for the films. It was as if some guardian angel was looking out for us…

The Editing Moves

Don and I quickly realized that the original editor was not the man for the job. We rented an editing suite at *Midtown Video,* across the street for *the Beverly Center,* and I went to work.

Never to live the life of traditionalism— while I edited RB7, we also cast upcoming features. There were times in that editing suite when we had upwards of twenty beautiful would-be Hollywood starlets hanging out and hanging on; willing to do whatever it takes to get a role in a film.

A friend of Don's came by one particular evening. In disbelief, he asked, *"Does stuff like this really happen?"* Yes, it does.

One More Time

People often comment about the multiple takes we repeatedly show in RB7. The reason for this is based in two unique perspectives. The first is, I decided to take the multiple angle cuts, which were being used in the martial art films of the late 1980's and early 1990's, to the next level. Let's give the audience, *"In Your Face ART."* I could go on and on about why. But, it is as simple as that… *Art for art sake.*

The second, more metaphysical, reasoning is that I was referencing that altered state of reality which occurs when you take hallucinogenic drugs—sometimes your mind flashes back over the same image several times. Though, in reality, it is the same. It, *none-the-less,* appears to be quite different and quite unique each time it is studied.

During the editing I would often look over at Don while I edited and ask, *"What do you think?"* after having laid in one, two, or three flash cuts. He would smirk, shake his head, *"Yes,"* and say, *"One, two, maybe three more."*

Though *The Roller Blade Seven* was the first film I ever edited, when I look at it today I believe it is some of my best work. Don Jackson never stopped talking about how much he loved the edit on RB7.

There was no precise technique that I used while editing the film. As is always the case with *Zen Filmmaking,* I simply allowed the moment to guide me and what came out was *Art.*

People often ask me why I have never edited another film in the style of RB7. You have to understand, when I edited RB7, this was before all of the effects, multiple screens, and color variations that came *hand-in-hand* with the digital revolution. All I had to work with was the film. I feel what I did with RB7 made the statement I wanted to make at that point in history. With all of the technology that has occurred since that point in time, what I did back then has since become very easy—it has become commonplace. You can see it on all the trendy T.V. shows.

Me, I have moved on. Though I will occasionally reference a moment of RB7 editing in my later films, all the flash cuts, and mismatched frame edits of RB7 have become so common, so expected, that now I am working from a different space of consciousness.

All the Rage

Don, who possessed a volatile temper, occasionally would go into a rage about various things while we edited. At one point, he got so mad he smashed his fist into the wall of our editing suite, breaking his hand. He went to the doctor. I continued to edit.

Dark Days

By the time Don and I took RB7 and *Return of the Roller Blade Seven* to *Rick Spalla Productions* in Hollywood to create the final master copies of the films, we had hit dark days. Don, being one of the greatest squanders of money I have ever known, (and I say that as a compliment), had spent our Production Budget and our Executive Producer had cut off any further funding. So, we were flat broke. This situation was amplified by the fact that my *1964 Porsche 356 SC* had blown its transmission and fixing it was not going to be cheap. So, I was delegated to riding my Harley Davidson to the Post-Production sessions—many times in the pouring rain. Finances got so bad I had to sell my *1930's D'Angelico New Yorker* guitar, simply to survive. For any of you who understand the value and rarity of these instruments, (basically, they are the *Stradivarius* of guitars), you can understand our plight. But, like the spiritual transformation presented in RB7—good overpowering evil, we continued to fight the good fight.

Though it was unplanned, I ended up doing the soundtrack for the two films, as well. This was mostly motivated by budgetary considerations.

I had spent my entire life as a musician. So, this was really no problem. The only downside, I only had one weekend, (two days), to compose and perform it all. And, this was prior to computer integration into music.

Plus, we planned to have music in every-single scene. So, it was not going to be easy...

I wanted the soundtrack for the two films to possess a very rhythmic-tribal vibe. The only problem was, my drum machine died just prior to my beginning the soundtracks. The situation was saved by a sweet, beautiful Chinese girl, via Hawaii, who had befriended me just prior to the beginning of RB7's production. She went to Guitar Center in Hollywood and bought me a new drum machine—which saved the soundtrack. I think I still owe her the money for it. *"Thank you Laurie!"*

Though it was not an easy accomplishment, with a little help from Mike Spalla, our On-Line Engineer, we finished the soundtracks and the films. When the two films were completed, we knew we had created works of *Pure Art*. Not commercial filmmaking. But, *ART!*

The Release of Roller Blade Seven

RB7 and *Return of the Roller Blade Seven* were released at the 1992 *American Film Market* (AFM). European countries were the first to purchase the rights. Don and I never saw a dime.

Little fanfare occurred upon the release of these films. This was in no small part due to marketing decisions made by the Executive Producer—which Don and I had nothing to do with. So, I began to send copies of RB7 out to the various industry magazines and to some industry professionals. If nothing else, it did get noticed.

If I may reiterate, it is important to note that to truly understand the message of spiritual evolution presented in *The Roller Blade Seven*, one must also view *Return of the Roller Blade Seven*. We made these movies *hand-in-hand*. And, though they each possess a unique and specific spiritual message, to understand the complete process of *Zen Cinematic Enlightenment,* one must view them both. This, however, immediately became nearly impossible once the Executive Producer took possession of them.

Stabbed in the Back

Soon after the 1992 AFM, as is so often the case in Hollywood, we the filmmakers: Donald G. Jackson and I got backstabbed. The Executive Producer decided the two features would market better as a single film. So, without telling us, she broke all our contracts and had the films reedited, titling it *Legend of the Roller Blade Seven.*

When one views *Legend of the Roller Blade Seven,* in comparison to *The Roller Blade Seven* and *Return of the Roller Blade Seven,* one can truly see the ineptitude of the Re-Editors. They simply took scenes I had edited from the original features and combined them into one film. Oftentimes, they misaligned the music hits which we had added to the original films. So, several visual situations occur and the hit goes off either too soon or too late. They also added some bad narration. The Executive Producer also deleted many of our cast and crew credits—most notably my Producer credit. Basically, our vision was destroyed. As such, in no way do we endorse the version of the film *Legend of the Roller Blade Seven,* sometimes titled *Legend of the Rollerblade 7—*

though this is the version which was released in the U.S. and is much easier to find.

But, it wasn't just Don and myself. While we were still casting the film, prior to shooting, a very nice girl came in, Allison Chase. She became, Stella Speed, the female lead of the two films. And, she can be seen featured in many of the film's photos. She was a real trooper, hanging out throughout the long production. Don and I gave her the *"Introducing"* credit in RB7, as this was her first film role, and second billing in *Return of the Roller Blade Seven*. But, her name was virtually wiped from the history of *Roller Blade* by the Executive Producer. It was very sad to see Allison's reaction to being excommunicated from RB7. But, there was nothing Don or I could do about it. The good news is Allison has gone on to win a *Grammy Award* for her work as a producer on a reality based T.V. show.

This is an important lesson to all actors, actresses, and filmmakers—be careful whom you work with in Hollywood, because the money has the power, and the power can do anything that it wants.

The Roller Blade Seven Trilogy

Initially, Don Jackson and I planned to make a series of three feature films in association with *The Roller Blade Seven*. This was to be known as *The Roller Blade Seven Trilogy*. This intended trilogy was in direct reference to the holy trinity of the Christian and Hindu religions.

We completed the first two of the trilogy…

Some people have mistakenly assumed that *Legend of the Roller Blade Seven* was the third installment of *The Roller Blade Seven Trilogy*. This is incorrect. The third film was to be titled *Wheelzone Rangers*. Though we intended to make this film, and a few times actually attempted to bring it up. But, this never came to be, prior to the passing of Don Jackson (RIP).

This is a film I still plan to make, however. At the appropriate time, when the necessary inspiration, financing, and cast are in place, Hawk Goodman, (my character), will reappear in *The Wheelzone*.

Moving On

Virtually immediately after the 1992 AFM, I began filming *Samurai Vampire Bikers from Hell*. The Executive Producer of RB7, true to her nature, had my cast and crew thrown out of our Hollywood office building and stages on the first day of shooting. This was obviously very uncool, especially after the months of undaunted effort I had put into RB7. Her actions were amplified by the fact that a large part of the time I worked on RB7, I did so without pay. But, in the long run, it was the best thing that could have happened to my production and to me.

My friends Ken Kim, Vince Spezze and I packed up the equipment. Vince and I then went to a strip club and got drunk. As if a veil of negativity had been lifted, I was free from all of the darkness that had haunted the production of RB7. I never returned to the *Hollywood Center Building*. I brought *Samurai Vampire Bikers from Hell* back up and finished it a short time later.

Don and I had begun playing around with the newly released Hi-8 format near the end of RB7's production. I loved the ease of the format. An actress, Susan Jay, who I had meet while we were doing some final casting for RB7, purchased a *Sony CCD*

V5000 camera for me—which became my main production tool for my next two films.

Don, inspired by my immersion into the Hi-8 format, went on to do his own video features. We did not work together again until 1996.

To some people, RB7 and *Return of the Roller Blade Seven* are weird or strange. To us, that is good. These films were created with Spirituality and Art as their central focus. And, true Spirituality and Art are never normal, known, or truly understood.

Like I always say, *"You may not like the ART of Picasso but you cannot say it is not ART!"* This is how I feel about RB7.

For myself, even to this day, I laugh whenever I watch these two films. The same was true of Don before his passing.

Sure, there is a lot of inside humor in *The Roller Blade Seven* and *Return of the Roller Blade Seven.* Sure, they are cinematically self-indulgent. Sure, they project an artistic landscape only truly understood by we, the filmmakers. But, it is essential to understand; *"Fun is what they are both all about."*

As it is taught in Zen, if you can remove yourself from the constrains of reality, enlightenment is found. These two films are designed to be like the *Zen Koan,* a subtle way to step beyond the realms of reality and embrace *Nirvana*.

The Roller Blade Seven
The Story of the Production

Fade In:

Ever since I wrote *The Stories of the Production* for *Max Hell Frog Warrior* and *Guns of El Chupacabra,* I have been deluged with requests to write one about *The Roller Blade Seven*. To begin with, there is a chapter in my book, *Zen Filmmaking* on the creation of *The Roller Blade Seven* that I believe provides a lot of insight into what went on behind the scenes and has a bit of a different focus than this discourse. I wrote that when Donald G. Jackson was still alive, and he really liked it. It was up on this website for a while—way back in the way back when. I recommend you read it if you really want some additional insight into the making of this film.

To be truthful, I have long thought to go back into my production notes and write a detailed book about *The Roller Blade Seven* as it was such a long, mind-bending experience. In fact, it was complete fucking chaos! And, I may still do that at some point in time. …In the meantime, for all of those of you who have wondered, I will tell you what I can tell you… I imagine that even this piece will end up being fairly lengthy. If you can get through it, I believe you will have a deeper understanding of what this film and this film's filmmaking process was all about and you will probably see why it would take an entire book to actual detail all of the finite goings-on.

There are a few prerequisites to the telling of this story that you readers should know about at the outset. As all movies are, this film was created based upon a conglomeration of personalities. Some of these personalities were good; some were not. So, I am going to tell this story as truthfully as possible. But, there are a lot of secrets. For those of you out there who are worried about what I might say; don't be. Though I am going to tell a truthful story here, your secrets are safe with me. And, I imagine as the story of the creation of RB7 is so vast, I will probably be coming back and doing tune-ups on this essay as new remembrances come to mind—which is something that is not uncommon among my web-based articles. Mostly, this piece is a study in psychology more than simply a fact-based dissertation on filmmaking.

To begin, there needs to be a little bit of a backstory about me.

…I truly do not know what caused me to decide to enter the film industry, as an actor, when I was in my early thirties. Having grown up in Hollywood, I had truthfully seen the downside of it all. Throughout the 80s, I had run a martial art studio, went to grad school, played music, painted, wrote poetry and novels, traveled the world, spend many a late night at underground Hollywood nightclubs, and was in relationships with a lot of various psycho bitches of one flavor or another. As the 80s were coming to a close, I had met a nice young lady, who I am still with to this day, and my life's focus began to change. Again, I cannot give you an absolute reason why.

By the early 1990s, I had thrown my hat into the acting ring. Though my early onscreen appearances were mostly small, they were in the A-Market, I had my SAG Card, and was frequently being hired as a Featured Day Player. Thus, I would be given my own trailer, treated very well, and was paid at that time a base-rate of $455.00 for eight for

TV and film and $1,200.00 for commercials. I was what may be called, *"A working actor."* Things were moving along in my career... I had been active for less than a year and I was doing pretty well. Out of nowhere one day, I was called on my voice mail, (we all carried pagers back then), by Donald G. Jackson. He had received my headshot and he was about to do a movie.

I have told this story before, but we never figured out who sent him that headshot. It was a color 8X10 of me holding two swords. Color headshots, being very expensive back then, were usually not sent out. I had a manager and an agent but they both said that they had not sent it to him. So, I guess our meeting was some weird destiny thing that may never be explained.

In any case, I called him back and he inquired if I could actually use the samurai swords. I, of course, could. So, he asked me to meet him at Gower Gulch in Hollywood the next day. As I was an inexperienced actor, making many of the mistakes that an inexperienced actor does, I agreed to meet him.

The next day, I arrive at Gower Gulch; which is basically just a strip mall on Sunset Blvd. and Gower. I was on time, as I always am. I began to stand there and wait. Sometime later, an African-American man with a jheri curl mullet began standing around, as well. I eventually inquired if he was there to meet Donald G. Jackson. He was. He was a strange little guy who I was told was into Wing Chun.

Normally, I only wait for a person for fifteen minutes. If they are not there by then, I'm gone. But, as I was an aspiring actor and all, I waited... Forty-five minutes late, here comes Don: a balding, portly, middle-aged man, dressed in camouflaged clothing. Every bone in my body told me to walk away. But, I did not.

Don had arrived with two young ladies in tow in a car driven by another man, who I will get to in a moment. He came up to me and the other guy that he knew. His first question to me was, *"Where's your car?"* When I pointed out my 1964 Porsche 356 SC his eyes popped out of his head. Don loved vintage cars. Instead of going with the man he came with, he asked me to drive, stuffed the two girls into my very small backseat, climbed in the front, and we were off. We headed to various Hollywood film equipment locations for him to check out some stuff he needed for the upcoming production.

Weird! I could not believe I was doing that...

A bit later that afternoon, we arrived at the aforementioned guy's apartment. He was a recent film school grad and had hooked up with Don somehow??? He had written a script for Don called *Roller Blade 3* and he was associate producing it with Don directing. The premise of the script was moving forward from Don's *Roller Blade* and *Roller Blade Warrior* films. We went into the rear small patio area of his apartment where I was asked to demonstrate samurai sword usage. The man with the jheri curl was to be my judge and jury. This both amused me and pissed me off. Again, I thought to leave...

The man impressed... I mean, why wouldn't he be? From there, within a few minutes, other members of the cast arrived, and I was training them how to do combat sword techniques. I had been hired. I was to be the male lead of the film as well as the sword choreographer.

I do not want to get too sidetracked into what went on with that film. I recently did a documentary about it called, *Roller Blade 3: The Movie That Never Was*. I recommend you check it out as it does provide deep insight into the life and mind of Donald G. Jackson. I will say that it too was complete cluster fuck. The film student seeing this, high-jacked the production, stole Don's investor, but the movie was never finished. I have written about it in a few essays.

After that, Don continued forward attempting to find financing for his next film. I continued following the path of an actor and did a few roles, which additionally laid the foundation for my evolving career. Don and I communicated over the next year, mostly via voice mail, and we met once or twice. Then, upon the completion of *Frogtown 2*, Don called me, invited me to his office, and said he really wanted to work with me and I should be in his next film, *Roller Blade Seven*. My course of destiny was set into motion.

Before I go any farther, I need to say that the moment Don got into my 356, as I was driving him to the hospitable for the final stage of his life in 2003, he said, *"I really want to apologize for what happen to you on Roller Blade Seven."* I will get to his reason for saying that near the end of this piece. But, keep that essential statement in mind as it is very relevant to my involvement in RB7. I will continue…

There was not a lot of money backing *Roller Blade Seven*. It was to be financed by Tanya York who had tapped into financing from an aging Hollywood insider. The first film she Executive Produced was *Divine Enforcer,* which she asked me to appear in, then *Frogtown 2,* (which I turned down), and now RB7. Don wanted me to be the lead, do the martial art choreography, write, and produce it with him. The only probably was, as we only had a $30,000.00 dollar budget and the film was to be shot on 16mm film, there was not enough money for me to be paid. He would be paid but I would not... (Though I was promised big money on the back-end.) Initially, that seemed okay, as it would be a good opportunity for me. Don was a known filmmaker. He was a friend of Jim Cameron, which I had confirmed when I had a small role in *Terminator 2*. His film, *Hell Comes to Frogtown* was frequently on late night TV, and I thought it would be a good progression for my career. As we were only scheduled for a one-month preproduction and production window, I thought I could easily make it through that timeframe without getting paid.

Again, I need to go into a bit into the backstory here... When I signed up to do *Roller Blade Seven,* I had never seen any of Don's films. I was not into that style of movie. As a dude, I enjoyed the action-flicks of Seagal and VanDamme, which were big at the Box Office during that moment of time, and the movies that came out of Hong Kong. B-Movies, Cult Movies, and the kind of films Don made, I had no idea about... I was into Film Noir. My mistake, I should have researched what I was getting into.

Anyway... On the very first day we began preproduction, I arrive at what would become our production office and I was ready to go. Niceties were exchanged, we talked about a few things, began to set up casting sessions, discussed ideas for the film, and the like... Around lunchtime, Don doesn't say anything, gets up, and walks out the door of the office. Initially, I didn't think anything about it as I thought he might be going to the bathroom or something. Time ticks on... He doesn't come back. I sat there for over an hour, starring off into space, when Tanya comes by—as our office was in her suite of offices, she inquired as to where was Don. I told her I didn't know. I told her he got up and just left without saying a word. I could see the anger rising her eyes, *"You two are working together! Tell him to stop behaving like that!"* Tanya who had a long relationship with Don, knew of his shenanigans, and I guess was trying to warn me.

Here's the thing… And, something I did not know at the time, Don loved to test people. He would always fuck with people's minds, just to see the reaction he got out of them. But me, I'm not easily pushed, nor am I easily tested. Though my first thought was to say, *"Fuck this,"* and leave the production all together, instead, I walked across Hollywood Blvd. and went to Bushido McDonalds, as Don liked to call it, and got a Big Mac combo. Awhile later, Don reemerged in the office after I heard Tanya going off on him from another office. With her as the money, he did not treat me like that again.

The rest of preproduction went as preproduction does. We would meet at the office each day, do casting sessions, and the like. We would go scout locations, check out equipment, and we became closer as friends. But, underlying all of this was this innate tension that Don emanated throughout his career. He was constantly testing and pushing people. He really treated most people like shit. This really worked against my mindset as that is not the kind of person that I am. He would even subtly fuck with me on various levels, during those early days, by bringing in other people and offing them prominent positions in the production or in the cast and so on.

This was one of the major faults of Donald G. Jackson throughout the years that I knew him and something that got him into a lot of trouble with a lot of people. For example, if a person said that they were a screenwriter, Don would tell them to write a script and promise that he would produce it. If they were an actor, he promised them a starring role. As Hollywood is all about dreams and the promise thereof, he made a lot of enemies via this practice.

For me, within a few days of preproduction, I was ready to walk. It was just a mind fuck mess! There was so much unnecessary tension... There are so many stories I could tell and maybe someday I will... But, not today.

The problem with my mindset and who I am is that I am not a quitter. If I say I am going to do something, I am going to finish it. I believe that this (my mindset) was the entire reason that Don and I remained co-filmmakers for all of those years; I got things done, when he could not.

There are a few preproduction stories I can relate to you that may add to your overall spectrum of understanding.

As the movie was based upon Don's concept of, *"Roller Blade."* ...It is essential to note that he came up with the title before the Rollerblade skates were even invented... Anyway, we were looking for a cast of people who could skate very well. (Obviously, I could not.) One afternoon, we were out in the back of the building that held our production offices, in the parking lot, testing the skating ability of a few potential cast members. Afterwards, we went back up into the office. Tanya called us into her office, which overlooked the parking lot. Very rudely, she tells us that we are not allowed to do that in the parking lot. I mean, she really went off...

A side not here, I am not dissing her when I say this as in her own book she states she was always a very bossy person. But me, I do not take well to authority. Be nice, and I'm all-good. Be rude and I react. I mean, I was already an accomplished person by that point in my life; okay. She was twenty-one years old. Treat me with the respect I am due!

Again, that is another one of those moments where I almost said, *"Fuck it,"* and walked out the door. I didn't need it! But, before the words could even finish coming out of her mouth, Don began to apologize. He went into a whole discourse about how when he worked at an auto factory in Michigan, he had a manager and he did what the manager said and so on… The way Don reacted provided me with deep insight into his hidden personality.

Another thing that was going on was that I had developed a number of actor friends in the year or so I had been involved in the industry. As this was my first big-film producer position, I wanted to bring as many of them into the production as possible. I invited them to the office and we would have talks. Some of them decided not to do the film due to their union status. A SAG union actor cannot be in a non-union film. I could skirt that fact because I was a producer, and the union cannot keep someone from producing their own movies. Others wanted to get paid but as we had a low budget; payment wasn't an option. I even contacted my agent, and she sent a few people over; one of which we cast. Mostly, what occurred was that through this process, I lost a lot of friends due to Don's behavior. He just loved to fuck with people, and he found a way to fuck with me by messing with the heads of my friends. But, one or two of my peeps did get on board.

Regarding the screen story and its development… It is true that *Zen Filmmaking* is all about not using a script. But, in the early stages of

Roller Blade Seven, Zen Filmmaking was not yet in existence. Don told me that he had shot his then unreleased film, UFO Secret Video without a script and that *Roller Blade* was largely done without a script but Don truly relied upon a screenplay throughout his career. Plus, Tanya wanted to know what we would be doing. Thus, it was decided that I would be the one to write a script. So yes, *Roller Blade Seven* did initially have a script, though it was never used. I wrote it!

If you feel like it, you can read the treatment I wrote for *Roller Blade Seven* in my book, *The Screenplays.* You will see that what we planned to shoot and what we did shoot were very different.

Preproduction was scheduled to take about a week. By the time we finally got ready to go up, we were over a month into the process. All this time and I had not been paid. Again, I should have seen the writing on the wall and left.

One of the interesting things that occurred, a day or so before we were to go up, was that a young, beautiful actress came in to audition. Before we could get very far in our conversation, she reached her hand across my desk, took my hand, and said, *"I'll do anything to be in this film."* We all understand what that means... Me, being me, I was about to walk her into the closed off back section of our building, where we had production stages, and well... You know... Just at that moment, Claudia, the girl who played Kabuki, literally burst through the door, sees our hands intertwined, and blurts out, *"What the fuck is going on here!"*

Claudia was a very interesting person. From Germany; she was an outspoken stripper by trade, a smoker and a drinker. She loved the Crazy 8's, as we call them on the street; Old English 800. A nasty street beer almost universally only partaken of by African-Americans. But me, I was right there with her. I was the only one who would drink that swill with her. Whenever she came by the office, which she did quite a lot, she brought a forty once bottle or two and we would pass it back and forth.

What would have happened between that actress and I given the chance, I guess I will never know??? But, she is in the film. Guess who she is?

On the first day of production, in the early AM hours, I loaded up all my swords, my Rollerblades, and stuff into the back of my 356 and headed over to Mark's house in Downey. Mark was to be an actor in the film as well as our Art Director. Good guy! He had done a lot of work with Troma. Plus, he was a great rollerblader and had several friends who were also great rollerbladers that he brought onboard.

You have to understand, by the first day of the shoot, I had no idea what was going to happen next. Though I was the only other producer on the set, Don had created such an anxiety-ridden preproduction that I didn't know if I would quit, be the star of the production that I was promised to be, be replaced, or what was to take place next??? This, even though I had brought some of my friends on board—one in a principal role. But, me being who I am, (the non-quitter) I played along.

The fact is, this was one of the ways Don used to manipulate people—always keep them guessing. But, the truth was, (as I realized later), his mind was so chaotic that he too didn't know what was going to happen next and due to his very deep rooted insecurities, he was always afraid of being rejected, so he power-tripped to such a degree to keep anyone from having the ability to hurt him. But, that's life... Creative people are generally the most fucked up.

We had a lot of people there on the first day of production. Mark had a lot of costuming at his home. He handled getting the cast outfitted. Then, Don and I gave the final approval.

ark lived within very close access to the L.A. Riverbed basin; which is where we planned to shoot. This is why we staged from his home.

Before I go any farther, if you care about the *Roller Blade Seven* and its behind-the-scenes, you really need to see the documentary I did titled, *Roller Blade Seven: The Unseen Scenes*. There's a lot of very revealing stuff in that doc that begins at this point in the production.

Just as we are about to begin shooting, it began to rain. Rain is a great, free, special effect. It is not, however, great for roller-skating. In the aforementioned doc, you can see my character being the first to take a fall on the slick path that we were skating along. For me, who had only been on rollerblades once or twice, it was a scary and dangerous experience. Even our RollerCam guy, a GREAT skater, took a dive with the Bolex in his hand on that day. You can see that in the doc, as well.

The first shots of the day were the *Roller Blade Seven* skating as a team. Next, were the villains. We finished the day up by doing some of the martial art confrontation. Here is where a lot was revealed to me about Donald G. Jackson...

Obviously, I was a well-trained martial artist. My agent had sent me a well-trained female Kempo stylist that we cast for the film. Plus, I brought on a few other people who knew their stuff. Don suggested I go and set up the fights. I figured I had some time so I was first working with the girl and her opponent. Maybe ten minutes into the session Don walks up, *"Okay, let's shoot."* But...

Here's the thing, Don didn't even care that the people weren't ready. All he cared about was getting something/anything on film. So, all of those one-on-one fights you see in the film were choreographed on the spot. I told them do this or do that, and that was that.

Now, here was Don, a guy who loved the martial arts and samurai films. Though he never trained, he was constantly referencing all things bushido. But, there he was, making a martial arts film but he did not care about the most elemental component of the film we planned to make, the fight scenes. Plus, he had no idea about how to shoot angles so that the fighting techniques looked like they actually connected. Mostly, I think it was once again his insecurity and his fear of someone, (i.e. me), taking his power away.

There was a high point to all this that came later in my filmmaking career, however. From this experience, I realized that on the indie level of making a film that employs the martial arts, it is better to just choreograph one technique at a time; film it, then move on to the next. That way, no elaborate choreography is needed to be learned by the cast members.

The Saturday and Sunday shoot ended.

The following week, we took the film to Fotokem to be developed. We then had it telecined. Don hated what he saw. Being on the other side of the camera, I was a bit more forgiving; understanding that the actors had virtually no direction from Don, the director. Don was like that, he never really directed his actors. But, I too saw the flaws.

We were in the office, discussing the results of the pervious weeks endeavor. Don was fuming as he often did. Blaming others, as he almost always did. We decide that we needed to let go of all the structure and throw all of the plans that we had for the film out the window and just go out there and film. It was then and there that I came up with the title, *Zen Filmmaking*. *"Let's just be Zen. This is Zen. This is Zen Filmmaking."*

The next weekend, we reconvened at Mark's house. Again, we had a very large cast; though many of the people, especially the friends I had brought on board, had quit. As we weren't shooting any dialogue on that first weekend, they felt like they were just being used as an extra. And, Don refused to call all but three of the original *Roller Blade Seven* back; one was Kabuki, the other was this great rollerblader and friend of Marks who play several roles including the banjo player and Fukasai Ninja, and the other was one of my friends, a highly trained martial artist.

Once everyone was suited up, we went down into the river basin and Don called everyone around him. There and then, he blew up. He began screaming at everyone. Telling them what horrible actors they were, how they had cost him and I thousands of dollars, and that they were total pieces of shit. I was in disbelief. I had never seen a director treat people like that. He went on-and-on insisting that they were all ruining his and my movie. Wow!!!

He went up to one guy, who had been using nunchucks the first weekend, grabbed them away from him, threw them on the ground, and told him he was an fucking idiot and didn't know how to use them. Now, this guy was a trained martial artist and I expected him to react. I mean if someone had come at me like that the least I would have done is told him,

"Fuck you," and walked away. At the worst, I would have kicked his ass. But, this guy took it. Did nothing but stand there. I could not believe it. The whole scenario I could not believe!

Eventually, Don was finished and we began to film. We shot the first words of dialogue recorded in the film—my character laying on the ground saying, *"I can't believe she made me wear these skates."*

We filmed all day. We did the big skate oncoming, leading to the big fight scene. We also did a little trick that Don suggested—individually killing off all of the main characters so if we saw their face in the final cut, we could show their character dying and thereby keep the story sound.

As the day was coming to a close, there they came, the police officers. Someone had reported us. As we obviously didn't have a filming permit, this presented a problem, as what often occurred back then is that the police would confiscate your film. Don had actually been arrested once. But, that was because he was filming a naked girl handcuffed to a fence.

What we did was to give all of our exposed film to our RollerCam guy and have him skate off into the distance. Don, Sergio (our AC), and I got the cameras and walked off into the sunset. As the cast was just the cast, we left them there to deal with the repercussions of which there were none. What could they be held responsible for?

That was the last weekend of big production on the *Roller Blade Seven*. After that, all things were kept smaller and more controlled. Though we did have a fairly large number of cast and crew members on several of the shoot days, there was never the massive amount of cast and crew as on those first two weekends.

As we moved farther into the production, we needed dialogue for the cast to speak. Don loved my books: *Essence: The Zen of Everything* and *Time,* which was later published by one of the Bigs as *Zen O'clock: Time to Be.* There it was, our script. People like Joe and Karen took to it immediately. They could just choose their aphorism and that was that. We were set to go...

In the past, I've spoken a lot about cast members like Karen, Joe, Bill, and Frank and their involvement in RB7 in interviews, articles, and the like. For Joe, Chris Watson asked me to write the introduction for his book on Joe, *Wiping off the Sheen.* There, I pretty much spell out our meeting with Joe and his involvement in RB7. The one cast member I have not spoken that much about is Don Stroud. So, I will do it here...

I first met Don Stroud on the set of *Divine Enforcer.* I could not understand why an actor of his caliber would be doing a movie like that. I mean he had a GREAT career from the 1960s forward. In fact, ever since I saw his film, Angel Unchained, in my early teens, he was my idol. I forever watched his career evolve. So, to get him in RB7 and to get to work with him was a dream come true.

For those of you who have seen RB7 and *Return of the RB7* you will know that Don plays the congas in those films. That was all his idea to bring his congas along. And, a great idea it was as that really added a lot to the films and gave us something to really build around. For those of you who have seen the 1978 movie, *The Buddy Holly Story,* you will know that Don did a great job of playing the drums and bongos in that film.

Though Don did play the congas live in the film I actually had to loop his playing when we were in post. Thus, that is me you are hearing not Don. I will explain the reason for this in a moment.

A funny note, Don is a great and humble person. When I first met him he was living in Brentwood but he later relocated to Manhattan Beach when I was living in nearby Redondo Beach. Every now and then I would bump into him and he would be all excited to see me and say, *"Hey Scott! It's Don... Don Stroud."* Like I didn't know. In fact, sometimes he would call me up and invite me over to his place or to go out to lunch with him or something. But, I just couldn't do it. I could not hang out with my idol. It was just too weird for me. Though every time I ran into him, I was very happy to see him.

That's the story, in brief, about my feelings about and interaction with Don Stroud... Great guy!

Anyway, with my two books as a basis for dialogue, the movies got made. There are a million stories I could tell you. But, that would take a book...

It is essential that before I get any farther, I detail a known fact about Don Jackson... At least, known to those of us who knew him. Don was a very dark individual. Though he referred to himself as, *"The Master of Light,"* and he could quote you biblical passages left and right, he truly embraced a negative energy. An energy that spread to all of those around him if you were not very careful. Basically, he was one of those spoiled children who never really grew up. He was probably allowed to throw temper tantrums as a child with no discipline as that is how he behaved as an adult. If he wasn't getting his own way, he went off. While we were doing RB7, I allowed his negativity to enter my life and I was doing things completely against my nature, behaving badly, and just not caring about people and life. Being involved with this movie truly took me to a really dark place. But, I ended up paying the price. Read on…

Anyway, we went into postproduction. But, not without a terrible toll having been taken on both Don and I. Due to all the chaos he invoked in our lives by the time we got to that stage we were both eating Xanax like baby aspirin—stressing massively. Me, who has had chronic anxiety problems from my adolescences forward, due to living through one of those childhoods that you never quite get over, was particularly susceptible. So, it was bad…

Plus, I went to the doctor somewhere around this time period. I had gone into the production weighting my standard weight of one hundred and fifty-five pounds. When I got on the scale and the doctor told me I was one and eighty-five pounds I could not believe it! …The thing was, Don ate all the time. We were constantly eating burgers, candy, chips and junk. With no time to work out, as RB7 was pretty much twenty-four-seven, I had put on the pound. Plus, Don had a hiatal hernia that he never had treated. Thus, he barfed all the time when he was eating: on the set, in his car, in restaurants, you name it. It was really gross. This just all added to the fucking mess that was this production.

As detailed, in my earlier writing on this subject, we went into the editing of RB7 expecting to have one of Don's previous editors do the job. Each day we would show up and try to guide him but he just wasn't onboard for what we were trying to achieve. We wanted something really crazy, artsy, psychedelic, and abstract. But, he was trying to take it mainstream. He just didn't understand our vision.

As stated in the past, he taught me how to use the editing equipment and I instantly took to it. Thus, we fired him, moved to a large editing suit, and I got down to business.

A side note here… Don made one of the cardinal mistakes of filmmaking while we were at the original editing facility. He arrived one morning. With him was all of our original audiotapes from the production where we had recorded our dialogue. We were recording our sound for the film on the then new DAT tape system. He went to the bathroom en route to the studio. There, he forgot the tapes. They were all in a paper bag. I was already guiding our editor when he arrived at the editing studio. He sat down for a time and then remembered he forgot the tapes. He went back to the bathroom to get them but they were gone. Someone had stolen them. He, of course, massively freaked out. We searched for them, asked people for them, put up notes, but nothing. They were gone. You have to admit, that is a pretty fucked up thing to do—to steal something that important from somebody. But, that was all just part and parcel to the RB7 experience.

The only thing that saved us was the fact that we had much of the dialogue recorded on our ¾ inch edit tapes. Without that, we would have been fucked beyond belief. The whole movie would have had to have been looped.

You can see, in the aforementioned doc, *Roller Blade Seven: The Unseen Scenes,* several of the scenes that did not make it into the final cut of the film due to the fact that we did not have the original audio recordings.

Big mistake on Don's part! In any case…

We moved to a new editing facility. It was a fun and interesting time at our editing suite. There were drugs, alcohol, and women in there all the time. It was a massive orgy. True hedonism.

Though we partied, I did do the edit.

One of the things that I realized doing the edit on RB7 was, though I have edited a lot of movies throughout the years, editing is not good for my brain. For after I would spend a whole day in the editing suite, looking at and cutting footage, I began to see life as an edit. It really messed with my psyche.

In terms of the footage used, we put all the best of the best into RB7 except for one very good fight scene. The rest of the footage we used for *Return of the RB7*.

Once we were done with the off-line edit, as it is called, we took it to an on-line editing facility. For those of you who may not know, making a movie on film is a complicated and expensive process. First, you have to buy the film, shoot it, develop it, telecine it, sync the dialogue, transfer it to time coded tape, do the edit, then take the footage to a facility where they can match the time code numbers to the original masters, and then create the final edit of the film. This final stage is called on-line editing. Though on-line has a very different meaning in today's mind.

We went to the on-line facility and did our final edit. By the time we had gotten there, we still had no soundtrack. I don't know what Don was thinking but he seemed like he had a plan. As was commonly the case, he did not. As we were closing in on the final construction of the movie, I was handed the task of creating the soundtrack as the budget had all been spent. I was given one weekend. That was it. I had two days to create an entire soundtrack for two feature films and Don wanted music to be laid over every element of the movies.

My girlfriend and I lived in a small flat right on the water in Redondo Beach. Though the location was beyond great, the place was fairly small. And, as it was an apartment, it was not like I could jam out with loud drums and guitars and stuff. And, this was long before the computer age of music when everything got easy. Thus, I came home on that Friday night bewildered; what would I do? The answer, I just did it. I sat down with what I had: guitars, a sitar, a sarod, tablas, a banjo, a drum machine, and synthesizers, and just got it done. I created and recorded the soundtrack on a Teac 4-Track Cassette Recorder that I had picked up in Tokyo. Monday morning, I arrived with the soundtrack and we laid it down.

One of the truly philosophic elements I learned while we watched the final playback of the final edit of RB7, in the on-line studio was, in filmmaking, sometimes you have to accept what you get. There is a scene in RB7 where Alison's characters skates up to Don Stroud, talks to him, and then skates away as Don laughs. When original laid down, we had Don's laugh loudly echoing as Alison skated away. It was really cool. In the final playback, the laugh was gone. The on-line editor had messed up. The on-line editor looks at us. Don looks at me. I look at him. To go back in and redo that track would not only mean a lot of time but a lot of money. Though I thought it was essential; Don just let it go. And, that is one of the sad facts of filmmaking—you may want something to be someway but sometimes you just have to let it go…

That was it. The films were done.

With the films done, it was time to shoot the poster…

As we progressed through the months, pretty much all of the original cast members had fallen away. As they weren't getting paid, they were all gone. I got it. Even by the end, Kabuki was gone and she took her leather jacket with her. Thus, we had to buy another one of the expensive jackets she wears in the film from a shop on Hollywood Blvd. so we could imitate her character in the final poster shoot—which was photographed at a high-end facility in Santa Monica.

One of the funny stories about that photo session is that if you look at the RB7 page on my site or in the Photo Book I create on *Roller Blade Seven, The Roller Blade Seven: A Photographic Exploration,* you will see that there is a poster shoot with Don (Jackson) in the shot. Tanya hated it. She made us go back and get shots were he and the guy who played Heavy Metal were not in the picture. Awh, the power of power…

By this point, we had been up on RB7 for months. I was dead broke. As I have detailed in the past, I had to sell my 1934 D'Angelico New Yorker and other vintage guitars I owned just to survive. In fact, I don't know that I have ever truly recovered from the financial loss I took on RB7 for after all of these years I still have not been able to replace that D'Angelico.

Though the movie was finally completed, the problem after all of this toil and turmoil was, I was about to have salt poured into my wounds. I found out that Don had been paying Alison, our female lead, throughout the entire production. (I wonder why?) Now, it is not that she didn't deserve it. But, there I was: the producer, the casting agent, the location scout, the still photographer, the choreographer, the screenwriter, the star, the soundman, the editor, the soundtracker, the..., getting paid zero.

The back-end money I was promised... I was paid zero. Plus, the movies were released without me signing a release for anything: not the words from my books, not the music I created, not my producing, not my acting; zero, nothing, nada... How illegal and immoral is that? The high point is, if you want to call it that, Tanya did not own any of the creative material in the films. Thus, any copyrights she filed in regard to these films were and are null and void.

As for the movies, then Tanya stepped in... She didn't like the fact that my name was all over the films. Thus, after she had made in the mid six figures, (that is in the mid hundred thousand dollar range for all of you people in other countries), in other words—a lot of money by releasing the original versions of the films internationally at the 1992 American Film Market, she then had a re-do edit done for U.S. release where virtually all of my screen credits were wiped from the films. She titled it, *Legend of the Roller Blade Seven,* a title I had actually come up with and suggested during filming. I got a lawyer involved. But, lawyers cost big money. Money, I didn't have back then. So, I was fucked. Fucked beyond belief. Thus, answering the question of why Don said on the way to his deathbed, *"I really want to apologize for what happen to you on Roller Blade Seven."*

Don and I fell away from each other after that for a time. I was obviously very pissed. Plus, he liked people he could control and I had already set about making my own films. But me, I was the one who got fucked. Not him. He continued to get financing from Tanya. ...In my life, my Porsche had blown its transmission while we were doing the on-line edit and that would cost big money to be fixed. I had none. And, that is just one elemental example of what was going on in my life. ...Don and Tanya, they were flush, thus they did not care. I was the source of not only their money but a film that has been in public discussion for decades and I was not paid a dime.

    I guess the final blow came when I was on my way to pick up this girl on my Harley to go and see Soundgarden at the Roxy. I had just found out that Tanya had me thrown out of our production offices and ban me from entering the building. This, after she had made all of that money off of my creative vision. Me, I was driving and a car hit me from behind. The guy didn't have any insurance, so my fully customized Harley Davidson was toast—gone forever; totaled. I was taken in an ambulance to the emergency room at Cedars Sinai. They wanted to check me in but I wasn't down for that. So, I checked myself out. This was obviously before the age of instant communication with everyone via the smartphones that exists today. Back then, if you didn't have the number memorized, you were out of luck. I called all the numbers I could remember to get picked up but nobody answered. I called my girlfriend, but she was at work and didn't feel it was right for her to leave—she's that kind of person: work before love. So me, my life in ruins, my body broken, bruised, and bleeding, I sat there on the steps of the emergency room of Cedars Sinai hospital for five hours waiting until I was finally picked up.

    Welcome to Hollywood.

    That's the story of *The Roller Blade Seven*.

FADE OUT.

THE ZEN

Max Hell Frog Warrior: The History and The Evolution

The film, *Max Hell Frog Warrior* has an interesting set of circumstance that set its creations into motion. Certainly, its evolution goes back to the cult film classic, *Hell Come to Frogtown.* From there, Donald G. Jackson and Scott Shaw set about creating an entirely new interpretation of its foundation.

Frogtown is a geographic region of Los Angeles, California that skirts the Los Angeles River. It first gained this name when it was overrun with frogs in the 1930s. A friend of Donald G. Jackson's, Sam Mann, lived in this area. As the story goes, one day the two men were driving around discussing movie ideas and Mann came up with the title, *Hell Comes to Frogtown.* As he had already starred in Jackson's films, Roller Blade and Roller Blade Warriors, he was the obvious choice to perform the roll of Sam Hell, the lead character of the film. There was a screenplay written for this film by Donald G. Jackson's friend and writing collaborator, Randal Franks. It was titled, *The Adventures of Sam Hell.*

Jackson initially planned to finance the movie with his credit cards as he had done with his film, *Roller Blade.* In the interim, however, he had become involved with *New World Pictures.* They liked the concept and they offered to finance it for him. The only problem was, he had to add a completely different cast than was his intention. His actor/friends were to be replaced by, *"Name Actors."* Sam Mann, the actual inspiration for Sam Hell, was to be replaced by the then very famous wrestler,

Rowdy Roddy Piper. Don asked Sam for his approval, which he gave.

Until his dying day, Donald G. Jackson regretted this decision. He was not only sorry that Mann had been replaced but the movie was eventually taken away from his creative control and it lost much of the visual landscaped he had hoped to create with it.

Approximately five years after *Hell Comes to Frogtown* was released; Don had formed a filmmaking alliance with Tanya York. She had a financier in place that was wiling to bankroll her first feature films as an executive producer. As she had a longstanding relationship with Jackson, the two moved forward and created *Frogtown II*. For Jackson, the only problem was, again, much of the creative control was taken away from him. Ultimately, he again, was left with a film that he did not like.

During this same period, just after the completion of *Frogtown II*, York wanted to finance another Jackson film. He offered up his Roller Blade series. The 1991/1992 outcome was the first and second Zen Films, *The Roller Blade Seven* and *Return of the Roller Blade Seven,* created by Donald G. Jackson and Scott Shaw.

After the completion of those two films, Shaw took the foundations for the *Zen Filmmaking* concept he had originated and went off on his own and immediately created, *Samurai Vampire Bikers From Hell* and several other films. Jackson also moved forward to create several script-based feature films.

In 1995, Shaw was in Thailand. Jackson contacted him to reconnect and make another feature film. When Shaw returned, the two set about creating the next Jackson/Shaw Zen Film.

Initially, the team toyed with the idea of creating a humorous filmed based on Jackson's, *Hell Comes to Frogtown* theme, titled, *Road Toad.* This film was to star Scott Shaw and co-star Julie Strain. The team eventually discarded this concept and then set about on the idea of, *Hell Comes to Hog Town.* This film was to be based on the artistic intent of the film, *Zachariah,* the First Electric Western, which starred a young Don Johnson. This film would have Shaw ridding in, (with an electric guitar strapped over his shoulder), on his 1966, bright yellow, Harley Davidson, Electra-Glide. He would then battle the forces of evil that were controlled by an evil warlord known as, The Hog, to be played by Joe Estevez. But, eventually this storyline was also put to rest.

What emerged from this period of creative interaction was Jackson's desire to do the story he had hoped to present with the original, *Hell Comes to Frogtown*—the story of a frog plague unleashed on the earth by an evil overseer who would eventually be destroyed by the antihero. Enter, *Toad Warrior.*

Toad Warrior AKA *Hell Comes to Frogtown III* went up in the winter of 1996 on a shoestring budget. In association with Jackson as the Producer/Director, Shaw was to perform the lead role as well as Co-Produce and Co-Direct the film. The team of Jackson and Shaw brought on their friend and frequent collaborator, Joe Estevez, to play the bad guy. They also brought on Jill Kelly, who had her first on-screen appearance in the *Roller Blade Seven,* and had since gone on to become a major force in the adult film industry. In addition, the team brought into the production: Selina Jayne and Roger

Ellis — both of whom had appeared in the *Roller Blade Seven* and had gone on to co-star in Shaw's, *Samurai Vampire Bikers from Hell* and *Samurai Johnny Frankenstein.*

Jackson and Shaw filmed, Toad Warrior in the high desert of California and various other locations throughout Hollywood, Los Angeles, and at their production offices in North Hollywood. Quickly, the production began to express and represent all the aspects of the bizarre *Zen Filmmaking* minds of the Jackson/Shaw team.

When production was complete on *Toad Warrior,* the team quickly moved forward onto other filmmaking projects. The next on the production schedule was *Shotgun Blvd.,* AKA, *Armageddon Blvd.,* immediately followed by *Ghost Taxi,* AKA, *Ride with Devil.*

As the 1997 American Film Market was quickly approaching, the production team of Jackson/Shaw knew that they had to compete several projects. Shaw took on the role of editor for *Armageddon Blvd.* and *Ride with the Devil,* while they turned *Toad Warrior* over to a long time friend of Jackson — the editor of a number of his films, Christopher Blade.

The 1997 American Film Market premiered several Jackson/Shaw films. They included the one's named above and a thirty minute, long-form trailer, of a film they had not yet completed, *Guns of El Chupacabra.*

Though the Jackson/Shaw team was happy to have *Toad Warrior* edited and available, it was never the film that they had hoped to make. Though the needed footage and scenes were all there, they were not constructed in a manner the filmmakers had hoped.

At the 1997 American Film Market buyers from Japan, Malaysia, and the Philippines purchased the rights to release *Toad Warrior* theatrically and show it in movie theaters. Shaw attended the Tokyo premiere of the film. Jackson and Shaw held back on U.S. sales, however, as they wanted to reedit the movie.

The following few years proved to be a very busy time for the filmmaking team of Jackson/Shaw. Though they had hoped to get back to the film *Toad Warrior* and re-edited it, this never came to pass. Shaw did, however, condense the originally edited footage of the film into what the team called, a Zen Speed Flick, and released it with the title, *Max Hell in Frogtown*.

By the early part of the twenty-first century, Jackson had become very ill from his battle with leukemia. He passed away in 2003. Soon after this, a distribution company somehow came upon a beta master of the film, *Toad Warrior,* and released it in a compilation DVD. Let alone the fact that Jackson/Shaw never wanted this version of the film released in the West, many of the titles and screen credits of this version were incorrect.

Due to copyright infringements, this DVD was eventually removed from the market. By this point in time, Shaw had already revamped the film and had released it as, *Max Hell Frog Warrior.*

As the unauthorized bootlegged version of the film had already been released, Shaw decided it was best to release an authorized version of *Toad Warrior* in order to help in countermanding any further unlawful distribution of the film's unauthorized version. He did this in 2007.

As of 2012, Shaw still plans to go back into the original footage of the film, reedit it, and create the film that Jackson and he had initially hoped for.

In recent years, there has been an ongoing interest in the film. Similar to the Jackson/Shaw creation of, the *Roller Blade Seven, Max Hell Frog Warrior* has continued to draw interest from critics and cult movie aficionados. So much so, that the writers of the HBO television series, Newsroom, mentioned Max Hell in an episode of their show broadcast in August of 2012.

Growing from the minds of Sam Mann, Donald G. Jackson, and Scott Shaw, the *Frogtown* series shows no signs of being forgotten in the near future.

Max Hell Frog Warrior
The Story of the Production

Fade In:

The Zen Film *Toad Warrior,* which became *Max Hell Frog Warrior,* was the third film that Donald G. Jackson and I completed as a filmmaking team. The first two were *Roller Blade Seven* and *Return of the Roller Blade Seven.* It is important to note that about a year ago a young journalism student contacted me and I did an extensive interview with him on the creation of *Max Hell Frog Warrior* titled, *Max Hell Frog Warrior: The Facts and The Fiction.* There is a lot of interesting information and insights into this film's creation in that article. But, as we have well passed the twenty-year mark of the inception of *Max Hell,* I thought I would take a few minutes and detail a bit more intimate information about this film's ideology and its production facts as there is a lot of ongoing interest in this film and there remains a lot of questions and incorrect speculation about what actually took place during its creation.

The Roller Blade Seven
To begin with, Don and I had parted ways upon the completion of *The Roller Blade Seven* under less than ideal circumstances. The money had run out on the production budget before we were finished. Don being Don had squandered much of the budget and Don, as he tended to be, was very self-involved. Thus, any remaining money he kept for himself and to spend on his girlfriends. …He kept the money even though I did much of the work on RB7: casting, producing, acting, editing, soundtracking, plus most of the words spoken in the film(s) either came from

or were influenced by two books I had authored: *Essence: The Zen of Everything* and *Zen O'clock: Time to Be*. But me, I walked away totally broke. In fact, I had to sell my 1930s D'Angelico New Yorker just to survive. That was a terrible loss that I have never been able to replace. (For the record that was one of the Masterpieces created by John D'Angelico himself and not one of the replicas that are on the market today). Plus, my '64 Porsche 356 SC had blown its transmission, and somebody had crashed into my Harley as I was driving it on La Brea in Hollywood; totaling it and injuring me. Thus, it was not a good time for me.

The fact is, I cannot discuss the creation of *Max Hell Frog Warrior* without referencing *Roller Blade Seven* as the two have a very close correlation. *Roller Blade Seven* was a chaotic production. It didn't have to be. But Don, being Don, made it so.

Have you ever had one of those life-experiences where someone is so based in a negative mindset that they bring out the worst in you? That happened to me, in association with Don, when we made RB7. This was amplified by the negative, petty actions of our Executive Producer. Though we made a great movie, that is still at the forefront of the Cult Film Hierarchy, it left my life a mess. The fact is, during production and post-production both Don and I were constantly carrying Xanax with us as there was so much perpetuated anxiety associated with the production of that film. As I have stated in several places, though I have written an extended chapter about the creation of RB7, which is presented in my book, *Zen Filmmaking,* I really want to write an entire book about the film as so much went on during production that understanding the process may truly help other independent filmmakers overcome obstacles and allow everyone to come to a better understanding about human consciousness.

One of the essential things to note is that when Don asked me to come on-board and make RB7 with him, the production was scheduled for one month. One month, I can handle that. So, when I showed up at our production offices at the Hollywood Center Building on Hollywood Boulevard on the first day of pre-production I had no idea the months-upon-months that it would take to complete that movie and its sequel. Now, think about taking months out of your life while making no money. As I am a dedicated, one-pointed person who doesn't give up, I did not leave the production. But, I did pay a very high price for my involvement with that film.

Moving On

By the end of *Roller Blade Seven,* I was ready to set out on my own and make my own films. As the video revolution had just hit and realizing I had the skillset to make it happen, I immediately went up on *Samurai Vampire Bikers from Hell* upon the completion of RB7. Don being Don, got jealous so he went off to work with Mark Williams who was both a part of the cast and the crew of RB7. Then, the Executive Producer of RB7, to play a petty little power trip, had me kicked out of our production offices and banned from the building. This, after she had already made thousands-upon-thousands of dollars on international sales of RB7 and *Return of the Roller Blade Seven.* Though Don and I occasionally communicated over the next few years, I did not have good feelings about him or the Executive Producer as they were both prospering off of my vision and my labor.

Then, in 1995, out of the blue Don contacted me via the Voice Mail system which was the main method of industry communication of the time. We all carried our pagers. He wanted to make another movie and he invited me to his production office in North Hollywood to talk about it. Though I had serious doubts about going, but as I had nothing else on my plate at the time, we set up a meet and I arrived.

To track backwards a bit... Don felt that Mark Williams, (a good guy), had gotten too dependent on the film financing Don had in place. Don hated people becoming dependent upon him. Though Mark was writing all of Don's scripts at the time; including: *Rollergator, Little Lost Sea Serpent, Baby Ghost, Pocket Ninjas,* etc., Don fired Mark in a rage. (Just a note: Don was prone to rages). But, Don was one of those people who couldn't work alone. So, he paid to have friends. As RB7 was already becoming a Cult Fan Favorite in Europe and as he remembered that we worked well together, he decided we should make another movie and, thus, he contacted me.

When I arrived at the production office, I was surprised to see how old Don had become in just the couple of years since I had last seen him. At the time, I didn't know that he had been diagnosed with leukemia—which was probably one of his main reasons for contacting me, as he knew I got things done and he wanted to cement his filmmaking legacy and needed someone like me to do that. We spoke for a while, hung out over the next few days, and I finally reluctantly agreed to make another movie with him. Keep in mind, I had a lot of trepidation about working with him again. But, we set up a weekly pay scale for me that was reasonable and we moved along.

Pre-Production

For the next few weeks, we would meet at the office every day about eleven, scout locations, do casting sessions, hang out with other filmmakers, get drunk at lunch, go to private movie screenings, go and see obscure alt country and bluegrass bands in the evening, hit the occasional strip club, (scouting for talent), and do what industry folk do…

In terms of the pending production, we toyed with a few ideas prior to settling on *Toad Warrior*. The reason we finally decided to make *Toad Warrior* was that Don's creative vision had been taken away from him on both *Hell Comes to Frogtown* and to a lesser degree on *Return to Frogtown*. He never really liked the finished films—though, at least at the time, *Hell Comes to Frogtown* was frequency playing on TV and that film had really cemented his career as a known filmmaker. But, as he was never content with the two previous features, he always wanted to make a more free-flowing version of a film with Frogtown as the backdrop. Thus, *Toad Warrior*.

Though Don was linked into a company that was financing his films, so money was free-flowing, we decided to keep the production small. And, as we both considered *Roller Blade Seven* to be a true Zen Film Masterpiece, we hoped to re-invoke the essence of that film in what we were next to create.

Another factor to keep in mind about the inception of *Toad Warrior* was that by this point in my career I had begun to see myself more as a Producer and Director than an Actor. Don, however, wanted me to star in the film as *Roller Blade Seven* was already gaining Cult Classic status, plus he wanted to capitalize on my martial art notoriety of the time as I was in a lot of magazines, had a very successful Hapkido Video Tape Series on the market, my books were being published, etc... Thus, he suggested that we Co-Produce and Co-Direct the movie, while I star in the film. I agreed and we moved forward with this as our basis.

As RB7 was already a legacy for us, we wanted to invoke that film's sensibilities. Thus, my character again wore a black suit, black shirt, and the elbow and knee pads from RB7—minus the skates, of course.

Production Begins

On the first day of actual production, which was a Saturday, we were scheduled to go up at about noon. We had the entire second floor of offices in a building on Lakershim Boulevard in North Hollywood, so we decided to dress the offices and use them as sets to establish the initial character interactions. As for our actors, the first to be cast was Joe Estevez. Also cast was a friend of Don's, (from the days when they both were working for Roger Corman), to play Humphrey Bullfrog, a couple of girls Don had previously worked with in films, (finished or not), a newly arrived couple from New Jersey who we had just met at a casting session via an ad we placed in Dramalogue the day before, and one or two other new faces.

The day of the shoot I got up, put on my black suit, and was preparing to go to my storage unit as that is where I kept all of my lighting equipment which I was going to bring to the set as Don only had a couple of cheap photofloods whereas I had a number of Fresnels, C-Stands, etc. As if a warning sign from the great beyond, the first thing that happened to me was I thought I had my keys in my pocket. I walked out of the door of my apartment, carrying some equipment down to my 356, but when I got to my car I realized it wasn't my keys at all. Thus, I was locked out. A bit nervous about time, I went to find the manager of my building who was always in the office but she was not there. With a bit of freak-out running through my veins, I went on a quest to find her and finally located her in her apartment. She got the pass key, let me in, I got my keys, loaded my stuff, and was on my way. I get to my storage unit but the moment I opened the door I realized somebody had broken in. Someone had rented the storage unit next to mine and had cut a hole through the wall. They stole all of my lighting equipment, all of my costuming, my first guitar, my power tools, and a lot of guitar and amp parts and accessories I kept in the unit. I was upset to say the least...

With the police report made, I sped to the set. Living in the South Bay area of Los Angeles, I was quite a distance from North Hollywood. As I was driving towards the freeway onramp, I see the train gates up ahead going down. Damn! It seemed like the very long train took forever to pass. Again, a sign?

In the interim of waiting for the train, I called Don on my large flip phone and used some of the very expensive cellular minutes of the day to leave him a message on his Voice Mail and tell him of the situation.

As I sat there waiting for the train to pass, me, I really felt like I had failed. Though the theft was obviously not my fault, it made me feel like a liar as I could not bring my lights. And, as a person who is always very punctual, being late made my adrenalin serge. It was starting all over again, the craziness of *Roller Blade Seven*... I thought to just call it quits and walk away... I still, to this day, wonder if that was the life-course I should have taken? But, I drove on...

On the Set

By the time I finally got to the offices, a lot had already been accomplished. Don had brought in a camera guy, Jonathan Quade, that he had previously worked with. Jonathan was actually a gaffer in the big budget industry but he did a great job of set design, lighting, and low budget camera work. (We went onto work with him on a number of films). He, in association with a Production Assistant, had already created the set where Joe Estevez's character is revealed with the parachute covering the walls. But, with my lights stolen, all we had to light the set with was Don's two photofloods.

Most of the cast was wandering around the offices as Jonathan, the PA, and I continued the staging. Don sat in his office, as he liked to do, talking on the phone, joking with the girls, and generally screwing around. Finally, Joe arrives and we get underway.

We took Joe to the set where he was to be seated upon his thrown. Don asks him what he wanted to use as a character name. Joe suggested Mickey O'Malley, as he saw the green, thought of frogs, and wanted to reference his Irish roots. Don immediately hated the name. But, Don being Don, he didn't say anything. Me, I also saw the problem... We had hoped Joe to be a very fierce and domineering character. But, with a name like that...

Taking a Turn for the Worst

There is a point in every film where if you are an observant filmmaker you can take note of where the film all falls into place or where it all goes awry. This was that moment in *Toad Warrior*... Joe deciding on his name and Don or I not wanting to force a change. Thus, the production took a wrong turn that it never recovered from. This, before the first scene was ever shot.

...That's the problem when you are working with someone you really like and who is a really good guy like Joe—you don't want to come off as harsh or condescending. You want to keep them happy.

In any case, the first scene(s) to be shot were Joe interacting with the character Cricket AKA Sandra Purpuro, (the newly arrived actress from New Jersey). We immediately realized that she was a very good actress. In fact, immediately after *Toad Warrior* she moved onto having a very successful acting career.

We also added a couple of adult film starlets to the scene to give it some depth.

The Hierarchy

I was a bit in question about how Don was going to react to my co-directing the scenes as this was the first time we worked together in that manner. Though I obviously had a lot to say during the filming of RB7, I never felt like I was the director and I never crossed Don's boundaries. But, he was totally cool. The thing to note about Don, as a director, is that he never really directed the talent. He just let them do whatever they wanted to do and say whatever they wanted to say—the way they wanted to say it. Me, on the other hand, I think natural inspiration is great but you need to give guidance to the actors, at certain points, so the storyline will stay on track. That's what I did...

We shot the scenes with Cricket and Joe. We then brought in his two minions: the boyfriend from New Jersey (Kent Dalian) and a Japanese actor, Tom Tom Typhoon. Don wanted the Japanese guy to communicate in English but as I speak Japanese, I directed him to speak in his native language as he spoke very poor English. When you see him totally going off at Joe, that was totally his idea. He really got the essence of *Zen Filmmaking* and took it to the next, necessary level. Joe's reactions to him are great. Those are probably some of the best scenes in the film.

We then went and did the Humphrey Bullfrog stuff which I just do not like. That character and those scenes were developed by Don and his friend. They are just stupid and they don't play well. Again, within the first few hours of filming, *Toad Warrior* was set on a wayward course.

As evening was coming on, we decided to go to this nearby park that is linked to an overpass above the 170 freeway. There, we filmed the park fight scenes and the various characters crossing the bridge. While we were filming, we left the Production Assistant to create additional sets in the offices.

Returning, we then filmed the scene where the two girls are in jail: Agent Banner (Camille Solari) and Dr. Trixi T. (Elizabeth Mehr). This set was actually just an enclosed deck outside of one of the office windows. I thought they did a great job constructing that whole dialogue driven scene. And, they did it with no guidance. They were both talented actresses.

After that, we filmed my character's interaction with Joe. We then brought in Selina Jayne, (the Spirit Guide from RB7), who I had remained friends with, to do a Fortune Teller thing with Joe. Though I love Selina and Joe, that scene just did not work. Then, Joe goes into the scene where he does the hokey-pokey with the one actress portraying Dr. Trixie T. Terrible! Terrible! Terrible! So bad, I could not even watch it being filmed. Though, for the record, it was totally improved.

We then filmed the scene with the girl singing in the club where my character gets a drink thrown in his face. That club scene was set up in the waiting room of our offices.

We finished that evening by doing the inner-office fight scenes where my character and the actress playing Agent Banner fights a couple of frogs.

Calculating the Consequences

If you look at the amount of scenes filmed in just one afternoon and evening, and if you know the film, you will understand that a good portion of *Toad Warrior* was actually created in that one day. Though we captured a lot of footage, the essence of what I hoped the film would become, was lost. It had become nothing more than a poorly acted, un-comedic (though it was trying hard to be a comedy), stupid storylined, production that was destined to just remain a mess. Yet, we continued…

Over the next couple of weeks, we filmed additional scenes. Next up was Conrad Brooks. I had never met Conrad prior to the day we first filmed him, but I did, of course, know of his previous work with Ed Wood. I immediately realized he was a really nice guy. I liked him a lot. And, I loved his style of acting.

We took Conrad to a location by the L.A. River where he and I interact with a couple of frogs. We then went back to the office and shot the scene in his tent. A tent that was constructed from the same parachute used to line the walls of Joe's lair.

For some reason, Don wanted to bring Conrad back as the character Swamp Farmer from another of Don's films, *Rollergator* and have the talking Baby Gator in the scene with him, as well. I like Conrad's performance, but Baby Gator just added additional, unnecessary, stupidity to the film. That is the thing when you are working as a team member with someone, you may not always like their choices but you have to allow them their creativity.

A day or so later we went to do an evening shoot at an old bridge that Don had titled, *"The Bridge of Broken Dreams."* There, we took an actress we had just cast that afternoon. As she was new to L.A. I warned her about doing what she did; i.e. getting in a car at night with men she did not know and was not even aware of where she was being taken. In any case, she is the character that my character continually tells to, *"Shuuu,"* every time she tries to speak. We also did the scene where my character kills a frog at night with the bridge in the background.

Referencing the anxiety that took place during the filming of RB7 and how this same style of emotion engulfs other people… Don had this Production Assistant who had been working with him for a year or so. He did the voice of Baby Gator during the filming of Conrad and myself in the tent. He was also the one wearing the frog mask that my character kills in the aforementioned scene on the bridge.

Don had begun to get increasingly annoyed by this man. I thought he was fine but, again, Don found him becoming too dependent on his money. I suppose this change of heart had a lot to do with my now being part of the team as I was a fully functioning filmmaker and there was a lot of things that I could do that this man could not. As he had begun to annoy Don, Don had become more and more short with him. At one point that evening he yelled at the guy to get something out of the car. Instead of taking the frog mask off, he ran all the way to the car and back with it on. Thus, equaling a massive anxiety attack. It was the next day that Don, in a rage, fired him. The man called me up that night wondering what had happened and if I could ask Don to let him come back to work. I told Don the story but Don was the source of the money for this project so there was nothing that I could do as Don did not want him back.

The Lies Actors Tell

Don and I continued forward hanging out every day and occasionally filming over the next few weeks. One of the interesting stories, that I have told elsewhere, happened when we cast this girl because she told us she was an avid motocross rider and owned her own dirt bike. We thought this would be a great addition to add to the film. We called her character, Road Toad. We meet her up on the dirt section of Mulholland Highway, where she promptly fell off of her bike and broke her clutch handle. Every time she got on, she fell off. Finally, to save any hope of making the entire situation equal anything, my character asks her if I can borrow her motorcycle.

From this, we film me riding it for a bit. Keep in mind, I was shifting with no clutch. After that, the girl rode off. (I hope she made it home safely). But, we never heard from her again.

Tough we periodically shot a scene here or there, we only did serious filming maybe three or four additional days to create *Toad Warrior*. …Compared to the days-upon-days-upon-days of full-on production we had previously done on RB7, *Toad Warrior* had very few actual days of production.

Expanding the Cast

I had brought on Roger Ellis who had played the roll of Stealth in RB7 and I had used in much bigger roles in *Samurai Vampire Bikers from Hell* and *Samurai Johnny Frankenstein*. He became Overload War Toad. Roger was a great actor and really added some good stuff to a very faltering film. We did all of Roger's interior scenes at the garage/stage of Jonathan Quade, the aforementioned cameraman, who worked with us throughout the entire production. This is where the infamous spank scene(s) take place, which was the idea of yours truly.

The girl in those scenes was a great up-and-comer named Robin Kimberly. She made her living as an exotic dancer. I remember her telling me she hailed from Alaska, and I really liked her as a person and an actress. But, she was one of those people that we never heard from again after her days on the set. She played the role of Agent Spangle. And yes, the female agents in the film were intentionally named: Agent Star, Agent Spangle, and Agent Banner. That was on Don. …A sign of his abstract patriotisms.

Next up was Adrianne Moore AKA Jill Kelly, a girl who did her first onscreen performance in RB7 before becoming a major force in the Adult Industry. In the opening scene we find her character being chased by frogs out at the El Mirage Dry Lake Bed. The work we did with her character really adds positive aspects to the overall film.

El Mirage is one of the places where the, *"Magic,"* that I often speak of in association *Zen Filmmaking,* took place. We went there with only a basic idea about what we would film. But, when we got there we noticed a couple with their pair of ultra-light aircraft. Don asked if we could use them. They said, *"Yes."* With this, we added the entire opening scene to the film, providing a lot of production value. …We had no idea this would take place, but we allowed the spontaneity of Zen to be our guide and, thus, True Cinematic Magic occurred.

Something to Scream About

Elizabeth, the girl who played Dr. Trixie T., was soon to be moving and she invited us over to her large house to film. Here, we created the lab set. Overall, she is a great girl and a good actress; I really liked her but many of her scene were too comedic and just added, in my opinion, to the overall failure of this film. This is the case with the lab scene that we filmed at her home. Her and another girl, (one of her friends that we never met before or after that moment in time), go into this whole fake British accent thing, talking about the development of the frog plague. Again, both very nice people, but the scene just did not work!

One of the now-funny occurrences that took place that night was Don had left the set as he had something else to do. We had been there for awhile and I asked if anybody wanted something to eat. Some did, so we sent out. One girl who I had cast earlier that week, a new arrival from Japan, initially said she wasn't hungry but then, all of a sudden, after we had recommenced filming, she completely started freaking about the fact that she was hungry and she wanted something to eat. I told her we were busy and reminded her that she said she didn't want anything but this did not stop her. I told her I would give her some money if she wanted to walk over to a local fast-food place but she would have none of it. She really was causing a scene. Finally, I took her outside and firmly explained to her in Japanese how unprofessional she was behaving. She calmed down, told me she was sorry, and she kind-of shut up. This is just a reminded to you filmmakers out there, sometime the people you cast can become a real problem to your production.

Going Nuclear

We also shot exteriors at this one location in the West San Fernando Valley that used to house nuclear silos. That is where you see Sargent Shiva and my character do the Kurosawa influenced, long lens, sword fighting scene(s). I know a lot of people have discussed this scene in their reviews, incorrectly claiming there was only one take that was reused. But, if you actually take the time to study the film you will see there were several takes. We also shot some of the other additional exterior scenes out there that day.

Though there were a few more days of filming small things, here or there, that's what it took to create *Toad Warrior*.

It is essential to note that the moment Don and I began working together again, we did not wholly focus on *Toad Warrior*. We, almost immediately began to formulate, come up with other projects, and begin filming them, as well. Most notable filmed around this same period of time were the films that became *Shotgun Blvd.* and *Ghost Taxi.* Though none of these first, *"Next Generation Zen Films,"* rose to the cult status of *Max Hell Frog Warrior,* at least in my opinion, they were all better films than *Toad Warrior.*

Post Production

Post Production on *Toad Warrior* did not happen right away. As stated, we began working on other films. Finally, as the 1996 American Film Market (AFM) was approaching, we set about editing the movies we had in the can. I did Shotgun Blvd. and *Ghost Taxi* and one of Don's friends began to work on *Toad Warrior.* But, he was using some weird editing system that did not output in a high enough quality format so Don went into one of his rages and fired the guy. He then gave the footage to one of his longtime friends, Chris—a true film editor and a man who had edited some of Don's previous features. Don and he sat down and they did what they did.

I don't know if it was the lack of technology at the time, laziness, or just the fact that the editor was more locked into a sense of Traditional Filmmaking than *Zen Filmmaking* but he and Don really missed the mark on the original edit of *Toad Warrior.* The fact is, though they probably grabbed the best of the footage there was, so much more great footage was left unused. More than simply not liking the finished product, the fact is, the film really bothered me. It bothered me that so much footage was left on the preverbal cutting room floor. Plus, the story construction was shoddy. And, Chris knew it. He didn't like the edit either. He asked me if I wanted to redo it. But, there wasn't time. To me, the edited film kind of felt like they were just filling in the required eighty-two minutes that it takes to make a movie viable for international sales.

AFM

As AFM was coming up fast, Don and I gave the edited *Toad Warrior* to a sound design company to finish up the soundscape. We both watched the final product and didn't like it. But, as the hotel rooms that they turn into AFM selling suits on the Santa Monica coastline are expensive, we had to have product. Thus, posters were created, a selling staff was hired, and Don and I hung out at AFM, did some interviews, and watched a lot of movies.

One of the funny experiences we had at the 1996 AFM is when Jill Kelly came by one evening. We walked around the expansive hotel, full of buyers from all over the world, and all eyes were on us. Well… They were actually on Jill. She was a beautiful sight with her long blonde hair, her big platform shoes, and the white, virtually see though clothing she was wearing.

Though we didn't like *Toad Warrior,* three countries did buy the limited theatrical rights we were offering to be shown only in theaters in their country. Japan, Malaysia, and the Philippines being the buyers. After AFM, Don being Don absconded with all of the money from the sales. Lesson: people never really change.

Post, Post Productions

Post the 1996 AFM Don and I buried the film. We planned to reedit it but we were busy and we never got around to it.

By the early 2000s, Don was in his late fifties, getting very sick, and wasn't really able to do too much. Me, I did take the original film and created a Zen Speed Flick Version of *Toad Warrior* titled, *Max Hell in Frogtown*.

For those of you who don't know, a Zen Speed Flick is a film cut down to its most essential elements. This re-edit really gave the film a new vision. Gone was all the bad implied humor, leaving only the best of the best. Don loved it and I liked it a lot better than the original version.

Max Hell Frog Warrior

In 2001, as computer editing had become a realistic possibility, I pulled the original edit of *Toad Warrior* into my MAC G4. I begin the process of a re-cut in an attempt to make it a better movie. I removed some of the scenes that really bothered me, tuned-up some of the others, and added a bit of unused footage. I did not, however, go into a full blown reedit. What emerged was *Max Hell Frog Warrior*. Better than *Toad Warrior?* I think so. As good as this movie can be? No.

The Next, Better Version

I have personally sat down, looked through the footage, and started to do a completely new, better edit of the film four times over the past fifteen years or so. I do this, because as stated, there is a lot of great, unused, never before seen footage that could reveal an entirely different and better movie. Each time I have sat down to do this, however, I get maybe a half hour or so into the storyline development and something stops me. ...I don't finish. Then, I dump the edit. Though I know I really should complete the process something has always stopped me from doing so. What, I don't know?

Perhaps at some point, I will compete this process as I know there is a better film hidden within the footage.

Though I suppose there is a million subtle stories I could tell about the creation of this film, in this piece I have provided you with an overview of the All and the Everything of *Toad Warrior* AKA *Max Hell in Frogtown* AKA *Max Hell Frog Warrior*. I hope this provides you with some factual insight into the actual goings-on. Any specific questions, you can always ask...

Be positive and smile.

FADE OUT.

THE ZEN

The Saga of Guns of El Chupacabra and the Art of Zen Filmmaking

Dateline, February 1997:

Donald G. Jackson and I were driving down the road in Baja, California, Mexico in Don's *1962 Plymouth Belvedere*. We were scouting locations for a new film. The sun had just set and the sky was a darkening azure blue. Up ahead of us, about one hundred yards, was a white sedan. Don and I were laughing when all of sudden we saw something large dart across the road in front of the white car. The car swerved to avoid it. The car hit the side of the road and flipped over. By the time we reached the car, the occupants were already climbing out through the windows. We helped them get to their feet as they told us that they had swerved to avoid hitting a Chupacabra. We instantly knew the subject for our next film.

The Chupacabra is the Latin equivalent to the Big Foot of North America, Yeti, the Abdominal Snowman of the Himalayas, or the Lockness Monster of Scotland—in other words, a mythical creature that wreaks havoc and basically kicks butt.

The word Chupacabra literally translated from Spanish means, *"Goat Sucker."* The legend of the Chupacabra first arose in Puerto Rico and then spread throughout the Latin American countries about this creature which would suck the blood from farm animals, leaving their rotting corpses in the fields.

Even the *X-Files* did an episode on the subject...

Pre-Production

Giving into the fact that the previous summer Don and I had gone through hell attempting to cast suitable talent for a few feature films we made, we decided not to go through all of that again and, instead, bring only film-family members into this project—people we could trust and rely on. From this, we would be allowed to keep all of our energy locked into this project and not let it get dispersed by all of the problems associated with the *wanta-be* actors and actresses of Hollywood who just do not have a clue: *"I can't be in a movie today because I have an acting class to go to." "I have to leave the set because I have an audition." "You'll have to talk to my agent." "I can't be in a movie that doesn't have a script."* Etc. and so on...

Our initial central cast was composed of Conrad Brooks, one of the last remaining actors to have appeared in the films of Ed Wood. Robert Z'Dar, who had appeared in such *A-Films* as *Tango & Cash, Mobsters, and Maniac Cop*. Julie Lunar Strom, a girl which our friend Eric Brummer introduced us to when we were filming *Ghost Taxi*. Jeff Hutchinson, who had starred in Don's *Roller Blade* and *Little Lost Sea Serpent*. Sam Mann, who appeared in Don's *Roller Blade Warriors*. And myself, as the lead character.

The concept for the film was to make a movie within a movie, within a movie. There is a documentary film crew out interviewing people and collecting news footage on the remains left by the Chupacabra, government agents hunting it down, and then there is my character, Jack B. Quick, Space Sheriff, who is fighting the various foes who released the Chupacabra. As the plot unfolds, it is detailed that the origin of the Chupacabra is unclear, it could be a mutated earthly creature, a genetic experiment gone bad, or even an alien. What it actually turns out to be… Well, you need to see the film.

Day One

The first shot of the movie was staged at *Vasquez Rocks*. We had Conrad looking for his lost dog, Whitney. Immediately, the Chupacabra kills him.

The great thing about allowing the spontaneous Zen energy to guide us to initially shooting at *Vasquez Rocks* that day was that there was a major film crew at the same location. Thus, the Park Rangers did not kick us out for not possessing a filming permit—assuming we were a second unit team for the big film crew. In addition, seeing our opportunity, we took some production stills by the lighting trucks and lines of anvil cases that we could use for publicity shots if necessary. Conrad, on the other hand, chose to go up and grab a bite to eat at the production's craft service table.

Lesson One of Zen Filmmaking

Make all unpredicted situations work to your advantage.

Location Two

We then drove to the *Mizrahi Movie Ranch,* which is in close proximity to *Vasquez Rocks*.

Bob Mizrahi lives in this great old house up in a canyon about an hour outside of L.A. This ranch house used to be inhabited by Hoyt Axton. On the property, for some unexplained reason, there are numerous old broken-down bulldozers, trailers, cars, and various other large metallic objects. A great set for filming.

Lesson Two of Zen Filmmaking

Don't waste time, money, and energy attempting to create your sets when you don't have to. Instead, travel to them and allow their natural aesthetics to become a part of your film.

On the ranch that day, we filmed Z-Man Lord Invader's (Z'Dar) discussion with his minions, the Texon Five. His capture of the news reporter (Strom) who had been documenting the Chupacabra attacks. We then filmed Jack B. Quick, Space Sheriff, my character's encounter with Z-Man; which ultimately leads to my being chased by the Texon Five—who my character eventually disposes of.

From the inception of this film, it was Don and my concept to make it a *shoot 'em* up movie; reminiscent of Sam Peckinpah's *The Wild Bunch*. It was planned that this film would also mirror the intent, though not the content, of the 1971 film *Zachariah*. That film was billed as, *"The First Electric Western,"* ours would be, *"The First Zen Space Western."* Thus, there was going to be a lot of gunplay.

One of the interesting paradoxes of the California film industry is; anyone who is twenty-one years old can go out and by bullets with no questions asked. But, you can only buy blanks if you have a permit. As our production team possessed no permits, we bought real bullets. Thus, all the semi-automatic pistols, AR 15's, AK 47's, and shotguns which are used in this film, are loaded with live rounds. *Hey, blanks mess up the barrel of gun anyway...*

Our filming continued forward and followed the path of spontaneous creation. *"Scripts are for sissies,"* was our motto. We continued filming up until the 1997 *American Film Market.*

For the 1997 *American Film Market* (AFM) we created a poster in direct reference to *El Mariachi* and edited a six-minute work-print trailer for the film—then titled *El Chupacabra.*

At AFM, two films Don and I had created the previous year: *Toad Warrior* AKA *Max Hell Frog Warrior* and *Shotgun Blvd.* sold very well. Virtually all of Asia, South America, and much of Europe purchased these films. This international interest was in direct contrast to the reviews many U.S. magazines gave these movies—not understanding that they were created as a visually moving *comic books* and should not be compared to much higher budget films.

From the moment the market open, *El Chupacabra* was such a hit that virtually every territory desired to buy it, based solely on the trailer alone. This made Don and I realize that we really had something special—that we should pull it back until we had completed the film and could take it theatrical—at least on a limited scale.

Shooting Continues

At the end of AFM we decided to have David Heavener of *Twisted Justice* and *Fugitive X* fame do a cameo in the film. He had done a cameo in Don's film *Kill Kill Overkill* AKA *The Fate Brothers,* and was a longtime friend. Though a lot of bad things have been spoken and printed about Heavener in the film industry, his previous over the top type of performances were perfect for this film. We plugged him in as a cohort of Jack B. Quick. In addition, we met and added a needed Latino actor named, Hervey

Estrada. He played the masked Mexican wrestler, The Santiago Kid.

Over the next few months we shot predominately on weekends to accommodate people's schedules—creating the storyline as we proceeded. We used the O.J. civil trial, with all of its news crews as a backdrop and we had fight scenes with actors in full monster make-up at Los Angles Union Station. We had them run up and down the long futuristic halls and escalators of the Metro Link where Arnold Schwarenegger's *Total Recall* was shot. We even did scenes in the highly secured lobby and elevators of *The Bonaventure Hotel* where Schwarenegger's *True Lies* was filmed. When, and if, the police ever showed up, we would simply tell them that we were filming a birthday video. We even had our reporter (Strom) abducted at the *Cinco de Mayo* festivities at *Olivera Street*.

Lesson Three of Zen Filmmaking

Just do it. Ninety-nine of the time you can get away with it.

If the police stop you, never tell them you are making a movie, because no matter how small your crew is, they will assume you have money and can fine you or confiscate your equipment.

September 1997

Guns of El Chupacabra was the new title. I edited the film. It was all we had expected with the continual gunplay, martial art fights, and comic book storyline. There was, however, something missing.

When we had begun the film we were going for the PG crowd, no nudity and only stylized violence. When the first edit was complete, we realized that this film had become much more than we had realized it would. It was so artistic we knew we had to take it to the next and final level. We decided to shoot some more footage.

Lesson Four of Zen Filmmaking

Never let your storyline dominate your artistic vision. Too many would be filmmakers attempt to write what they believe is a *"Good Script"* and then try to film it. Without an unlimited budget, it is virtually impossible to get what is on the page upon the stage.

Filming Recommences

Having again attempted to cast a few actresses through *Dramalogue* and again running up against the same resistance. …Having to justify to these people, who have never done anything except maybe be an *extra,* that we were, in fact, experienced filmmakers and our style of *Zen Filmmaking* did work. Finally, we said, *"Fuck it."* We went to two porno agencies and got a few of girls.

Using porno girls is one of the best things you can do when your production needs nudity. These girls are extremely reliable. They don't forget to make the call time or decide that any day now Spielberg will be calling them so why should they do a B-movie. They are professional and, most of all, they are more than willing to take their clothing off. Mostly, they are really happy that they do not have to have sex and that they can actually send this movie home to their parents in Ohio and show them that they really are actresses.

We shot a few days with the girls from these agencies. But, something was still missing…

Julie Strain

Out of the blue, Julie Strain called Don. She had done a few movies with him earlier in her career: *Queen of Lost Island* and *Big Sister 2000*. She was just phoning to say, *"Hi."* Don asked, *"Would you like to be in Guns of El Chupacabra?"* *"Sure, can my husband Kevin (Eastman) be in it too?"* *"Of course."*

In *Zen Filmmaking* friends are good, especially if their husband is the co-creator of *The Teenage Mutant Ninja Turtles*.

Julie and Kevin showed up at our castle/warehouse stage. With them came the nationally syndicated television show *Strange Universe,* who interviewed all of us for the film. Great publicity!

Julie played the role of Queen B. A name I came up with in direct reference to the film *Dolomite*—in association with her actually being a queen of the B-Movies. Kevin was King Allmedia.

Julie and Kevin are really great people. Kevin is the nicest multi-millionaire you will ever want to meet. He calmly sat in his full metal armor costume, under the hot lights, the whole time we did his scenes where Julie and he send my character on a mission to save the Earth from the Chupacabra. Then, at the end of the film, they knight me, *The Reverent Doctor Saint Francis Blade.* He even did his whole *Strange Universe* interview in his costume. I have only the best things to say about both of them.

Rocket Ranger Dan Danger

After filming with Julie and Kevin, I again edited the movie at our production offices in North Hollywood—adding their scenes. They looked great! But, in watching the movie, there was still something missing from the film. Don and I pondered this dilemma while we filmed a couple of other movies. Finally, Don came up with the idea, Rocket Ranger Dan Danger.

What we needed for the film was one of those narrators—similar to the ones that appeared on the television shows of the 1940s and 1950s. Someone who would help to usher the story along and announce plot changes. Of course, as per our cinematic style, this had to be a BIG character.

We call up our friend Joe Estevez. The night before his shoot, I studied the film to find out where plot twists needed to be revealed and when to shift the audience from the obvious story development that was being presented. I typed up a list of scenes for him and the next day we headed to Bronson Caves, where an untold number of television series and movies had been filmed. Perhaps most notably, it was used as the Bat Cave for the 1960s television series *Batman*.

Joe took to the role and was great as always. We had completed out film!

Lesson Five in Zen Filmmaking

Zen Filmmaking is a spontaneous process. Just as the Zen understanding of enlightenment teaches that though you may meditate for years, it is not until the moment when you step beyond your thinking mind and realize that you are already enlightened that you achieve *Satori*. Thus, if you acutely plan your productions with screenplays, storyboards, and locations, there is no room for the instantaneousness of filmmaking enlightenment to occur and you will always be lost between the way your mind desired the scene to be and the way it actually turns out.

Lesson Six in Zen Filmmaking

In *Zen Filmmaking* nothing is desired and, thus, all outcomes are perfect.

The Essence of Zen Filmmaking

Zen Filmmaking teaches the concept of the Anti-Story. The stories have all been told. As such, attempting to re-tell them is a waste of everyone's time. This is especially the case with independent filmmaking. Why try to re-tell a story and compete with a production that had a million times your budget? Create your own instantaneous art and it will be what it is. Fuck the story! Who cares?

If you believe that you are going to be the next Martin Scorsese or Quentin Tarantino and whatever project you are working on is going to launch you to that level, you will continually be disappointed. As the Buddha said, *"The cause of suffering is desire."* So, just allow your film to be what it is—pure and artistic in its own right.

Art is art and that is how you should view your filmmaking. If you imitate, you are compared. But, if you create original cinematic art, though some people may not like it, they will, *none-the-less,* have an emotion about it. And, that is the essence of art—emotional response.

In *Zen Filmmaking,* embracing the spontaneous storyline does not mean that you let your actors improvise their dialogue. If you do this they will talk about so many things that have nothing to do with anything, that any concept you have for the film will be lost in meaningless dribbling dialogue. The problem with most actors is that they believe acting is solely related to talking. It is not! To this end, you need to control the patterns of dialogue in your film. Thus, *Zen Filmmaking* teaches that you create and feed actors their lines just prior to shooting the scene. At this stage, if they understand the process, only then they may add their own twist to what is being said.

In *Zen Filmmaking* one action or situation will mystically lead you onto the next and the next. First, get all of your elements in place at the location where you will film. Study which cast members are there, what props you have, and the present energy of this situation. All of these factors will direct you into what type of scene you will shoot. Then, let spontaneous creativity flow!

Zen Filmmaking allows you to be you: *your vision, your understanding, and your creation.* This is where art is born and enlightenment given birth to.

Post Note:

Guns of El Chupacabra was completed in late 1997. Its first theatrical screening took place at the *Directors Guild of America* in January 1998. It was then screened at *Sony Studios* in that same month. The film was exhibited at the 1998 *American Film Market* and found wide success, particularly in the South American and Asian Markets.

In 1998, Donald G. Jackson and I created *Guns of El Chupacabra II: The Unseen.* Initially, this film was released solely to the South American market but in 2008 was released internationally.

Before his passing, Don and I planned to add a third film to the series, making it a cosmic trilogy. This is a film I still plan to make when the inspiration strikes.

As time has gone on, as was similar to what occurred with *The Roller Blade Seven,* more and more people have come to embrace *Guns of El*

Chupacabra. In recent years it has won awards a several international film festivals.

Guns of El Chupacabra: The Story of the Production

Fade In:

As we have recently passed the twenty-year mark of the beginning of the creation of the *Zen Film, Guns of El Chupacabra* and as I continue to receive a lot of questions about the process of filmmaking used in making that movie, I thought I would take a few minutes and write a little bit about this *Zen Film*. I should begin this piece by stating that there is a chapter devoted to the creation of *Guns of El Chupacabra* in my book, *Zen Filmmaking*. That chapter is a great source for a lot of the inside-inside and the philosophy about what went on during filming. But here, I thought I would spell out more of the A to Z about the film, to give all of you who have wondered a bit more insight into the film's actual creation.

To begin with, Donald G. Jackson and I were friends. That is the best way I can describe our relationship. Being friends, sometimes you are more forgiving of a person's behavior than you would be of someone with whom you are not friends. In brief, Don was a psychologically complicated guy who had a lot of inner-demons. I say this to illustration how and why he and I had a bit of an on-again/off-again turbulent relationship, even during the filming of *Guns of El Chupacabra*. ...We were two very different people. I guess that he had undiagnosed bipolar disorder as one minute he would be fine and the next moment he would be completely freaking out. For anyone who knew him they will instantaneously confirm this fact. With this stated, he always treated me with the utmost respect—at least to my face. From this relationship, even amidst

Don's chaotic mindset, we made a number of seminal films together, including what eventually became *Guns of El Chupacabra*. This film is one of the two films that we made together that Don and I both considered to be *Zen Filmmaking* masterpieces. The other being, *The Roller Blade Seven*. Though I would add *The Rock n' Roll Cops* to that list, as well, but Don never got to see the finalized version of that film.

    The reason I begin by discussing the mindset of Donald G. Jackson is to illustrate what it was like to work with Don. It was not easy. Moreover, it is also important to note that Don was a horrible confiscator of other people's creative ideas: i.e. my idea about doing a film about the Chupacabra or a similar creature which I had relayed to him a few months previous to the beginning of filming. We even started to do my film, Surf Samurai from Atlantis, which was to highlight a Sea Monster— artistically referencing films like *Creature from the Black Lagoon* and *Return of the Creature*. But, we got sidetracked and that film was never completed... In any case, I hadn't seen Don in a few months before we began filming. I had gone off to Southeast Asia and, as I tend to be, was very happy living in Thailand. But, I had gotten attacked by a few knife-wielding foes one night. Bangkok can be a very dangerous place. Though I overcame my five attackers fairly readily, I did have a serious cut down the center of my face which brought me back to L.A. in a rush to see a plastic surgeon. I had been home maybe a week or so and one day, out of the blue, nearing the end of 1996, Don called me up and tells me that talk of the Chupacabra is all over the internet and we should do a film about it. Okay, but didn't I already suggest that a few months ago... In any case, we got together and we started preproduction. The only missing fact was, he had already taken my idea and had started filming. I guess he had hoped to grab my idea and create a film about the Chupacabra without me. But, I didn't find this out until later.

The problem was, as was always the case with Don, he had great creative ideas but he couldn't get anything done. He always surrounded himself with a less than ideal cast and crew. So, in essence, due to his lack of precision crewing, everything he had previously filmed was basically uselessly. ...At least in terms of the technology that was available at the time. And, he had filmed it on 16mm so that process wasn't cheap. Enter, me... My acute focus and my ability to get things done is what made *Guns of El Chupacabra* move forward and finally get finished.

Initially, we called the movie, *El Chupacabra*. With that as our inspiration we went out and began to film.

A friend of Don's, Bob Mizrahi, was living at this great ranch north of L.A. I am told that it was originally owned by Hoyt Axton. The great thing about this ranch was that not only was it secluded but it had hills surrounding the property. From this, we could fire live ammo, (of which a lot was shot during filming), with no worry of stray bullets traveling onto other people's property. Moreover, there were several abandoned bulldozer and other heavy machinery that gave the place a great look. We filmed many scenes at this location over several visits.

Initially, I was not sure about who my character would be or how I wanted to guide that character's development. Originally, I had thought about doing a professor sort of thing. From this, on the first day of shooting, I brought along some old-school desert expedition sort of wardrobe. But, as I always wear a sport coat, slacks, and tennis shoes, I just kind of ended up in front of the camera wearing what I wear. It was shortly after that Don and I realized that we really needed to take the storyline to the next level and not make it simply Earth based but intergalactic. Thus, it was Don who came up with my character's name, Jack B. Quick, Space Sheriff.

As was the case whenever Don and I worked together, we would meet at the office everyday at about eleven, do preproduction, location scouting, casting, and other stuff during the week and film mostly at night or on the weekends. Those were always fun and fulfilling days. This was the same path we followed with *El Chupacabra*.

When we began filming the movie we didn't have a monster. We simply did character development. It was Don who contacted the Executive Producer of Roller Blade Seven, knowing that she was in possession of a monster costume. This suit was originally made for a movie that never was filmed. One Saturday morning we went over to her house and picked up the costume. *El Chupacabra* was born.

While we were there she made Don promise her that he would not damage the creature costume as she wanted to use it in an upcoming film. He, of course, promised her that he would keep it safe and sound. But, I will discuss what came next in a moment…

For anyone who has seen the movie I am sure you will agree that it is a really great monster costume. When it was created, it cost a lot of money. The problem was, it was made for a fairly small and thin person. So, none of the men we knew could fit into the suit. But, the girl who was playing the character Linda Marshall was willing to climb into that costume. Me, I would have been way too claustrophobic to have ever gotten into a monster suit like that, as there was no self-way in and no self-way out. It had to be put on and taken off by someone else. As such, on the first day we filmed with her in the costume, she brought along a friend of hers whom we dubbed, The Monster Wrangler.

The first day we used the suit was a few months into production. We took our skeleton crew, our monster, her Monster Wrangler, and we went to Bronson Cave—which is a great Hollywood landmark that has been used in an untold number of films and TV shows. We filmed the reveal of the monster and my character fighting the creature.

An important note to keep in mind is that in the traditional Monster Flick, the monster is never revealed in broad daylight. The monster is always kept somewhat hidden and allusive to the seeing eye. We totally broke that rule with *Guns of El Chupacabra,* however, and let the monster be right in the face of the audience.

Filming went along for several months. Don and I also did a few other films in the interim. I was also very active in writing books and article about the Martial Arts and Zen at that time, so those projects took up a lot of my time when I wasn't working on the film. I also completed another Master's Degree during this period so it was a busy and productive period of time for me.

Filming on *Guns of El Chupacabra* took us over a year. In fact, it took us close to two years to actually finish the film. I have one of those very prominent memories etched into my mind where Don and I were on the roof of *The Broadway*

Building on the corner of Hollywood and Vine, where we filmed many a scene, and Don looked at me, shook his head and said, *"We've been filming this for over a year..."* Yeah, we had... Pretty scary... Where did the time go?

Speaking of *The Broadway Building,* that is where my character encounters the crew of ninjas and martial artists. That team was brought on by a guy who Don had met several years the previous who wanted to make martial art movies. As Don told it, that guy simply walked into his office unannounced one day and said he had money from a guy in prison who could finance films. But, the money never came through but that guy, like so many people who inhabited the world of Donald G. Jackson, continued to pop up hoping to break into the game.

This is one of the things that needs to be said about Don—he promised everybody everything. He told people what they wanted to hear. If they were an actor, he promised them a starring role. If they were a writer, he promised them he would produce their script. But, he never did... Hollywood is a cutthroat place where everyone expects to be a star and when someone promises you this dream... Well, when they don't follow through, things can get sketchy. Don made a lot of enemies.

The martial art troupe that the aforementioned guy brought into the production were all great martial artists and very professional. I think they added a lot to the overall presentation of the film. They guy himself, however... Well, I guess he suffered from a Napoleon Complex as he was very short. The day we filmed those scenes he kept insinuating that he wanted to fight me. Oh please... Get a life...

I only saw him one time after that, a couple of years later, when Don had an office in Santa Monica. He showed up out of the blue, was friendly and kept saying, *"You're like Don's son. Look at you two. That's why you never wanted to work with me, Don. You have a son…"* Again, Oh please… I'm told that guy died soon after that. Though much younger, he died even before Don passed away. RIP.

If I sound all over the place in talking about this film, that is because that is how it was created; very randomly. If I looked at my notes, I could tell you exactly happened when but that is not at all how I remember the creation of *Guns of El Chupacabra.* It went in spurts. We worked on it and then we didn't.

At the 1997 *American Film Market* (AFM) Don showed up having created a twenty-minute trailer for the film. I had been in Hawaii with my lady for a time and returned the day before the '97 AFM was to begin. Don had the tendency of being jealous and vindictive. Thus, he created the trailer without my input and I, the star of the film, was barely in it. Though I suppose I should have been angry, knowing Don I found that very-very amusing.

Don was one of those people who like to subtlety mind-fuck people. He thought that was how he could get over on them. Me, I was at one of those points, that happened several times throughout our partnership, where I was just going to tell Don to, *"Fuck off."* But, he kept insisting that I needed to be at AFM as I was the star of several films and he was distributing a couple of my Zen Film… So, I showed up. Though we didn't offer *El Chupacabra* for sale, we test-screened it to several buyers and they were all very impressed and interested.

Sometime soon after the '97 AFM we went into our second segment of filming. We changed the name of the film to *Guns of El Chupacabra* and we had recruited a few new interesting cast members. This is where the Santiago Kid as well as Maria-Maria came into play. This is also where we recruited a few porn girls to take part in the movie. Which I guess is an interesting story in and of itself to tell…

Don and I wanted to add some nudity to the film. Like the creature, we wanted this nudity to be in your face with no explanation or reasoning. We tried casting actresses for these roles but it just did not work out. In one case, the cast, the crew, he and I arrived at the office early on Saturday morning, we packed up all the equipment, but the girl who was scheduled to do the nude role did not show up. We called and called but nothing… So, all that time and energy had been wasted.

It was at that point Don came up with the idea that we should go to the major adult film-casting agency here in L.A., where he was sure we would easily be able to get some female talent who were willing to work in the nude. As there was no on-screen sex involved, something that these girls did for a living, he was certain we could find the right actresses. We went there, paid the two-hundred dollar casting fee, looked through their books, chose some girls, and got their numbers. Over the next week, we had them come by our offices, take off their clothes, and see how well we would be able to work together. A few girls were decided upon.

As *Zen Filmmaking* is all about living in the moment, we rarely planned what we would do next. On the day we were scheduled to work with the first two (nude) girls, both high-end adult stars of the time, we had them meet us at our North Hollywood offices along with other cast members such as the Santiago Kid and Maria-Maria very early on a Saturday morning. We planned to go to Bronson Cave to shoot. With a few cars of cast and crew following us, we arrived. But, the *Power Rangers TV Series* was filming there. There was tons of star trailers and crew trucks. ...Couldn't film there...

Next stop, we thought to go out to *The Mizrahi Movie Ranch* as we called it. Don's friend's place. We drive all the way out there, cast and crew following us. We pull in and a new owner of the property had taken over. He had evicted Bob. He tells us, *"Get off my property!"* Wow... Okay, now what?

Finally, the Santiago Kid, who lived out in the Palmdale area, suggested the desert ranch of one of his friends. Having already paid for the talent, and with nowhere else to film, we had no choice but to check it out. Again, with several cars in tow, we made our way a hundred miles northeast out to the desert.

Arriving at that desert ranch, it was a visual very nice location. It reminded me of an old run down chicken farm, though I do not actually know what it once was. But, we were free to shoot there.

With no real storyline in mind, we looked around and noticed a few chicken wire cages. Don and I decided that would be a great place to put the girls, detailing that they had been capture by El Chupacabra to be eaten later. Then, my character would arrive to rescue them. Finally, filming was underway.

I can only imagine what the porn girls and their manager were thinking with all of the running around. *Zen Filmmaking* and all... But, they were getting paid their day rate so I guess they really didn't care. Overall, we became friends and used the team in a few other films.

Filming went well at that ranch. We shot there a couple of times. Like *The Mizrahi Movie Ranch,* it was isolated and cinematically very interesting. We did have a problem when we were firing some AKs out there one time, however. Not realizing how far a bullet will actually travel, I guess one of the distant neighbors had a few shells flying by his head and had to drive over and ask us to stop firing in that direction. Luckily, nobody got shot.

The third phase of filming *Guns of El Chupacabra* came about when Don enlisted Julie Strain and her then husband Kevin Eastman, co-creator of the Teenage Mutant Ninja Turtles, to get on the bus. They were and are both very nice, very talented people. And, at the time, Julie had a great PR team behind her. From her being a part of the production we got interviewed on a couple of TV shows and a few magazines wrote articles about the film due to her being a part of the cast.

The majority of the scenes involving Julie and Kevin were shot at a location close to the L.A. River not far from Downtown. This space was owned by an artist who did some great gothic paintings. You can see some of them in the background of their scenes.

All of Julie and Kevin's dialogue was created a few moments before filming by Don or myself. We would roll camera and Don or I would feed them their lines, one line at a time. Then, cut. They did a great job. This is also the place where Julie knights my character, the Revered Doctor Saint Francis Blade.

This is a character evolution that was developed by Don. He thought my character should have some reward upon the completion of his mission. And, that was it, being knighted. Don, who was very Christian and very religious in his later years, wanted to evoke the power of Christianity in all of our films whenever he could.

It would be impossible to discuss the making of *Guns of El Chupacabra* without mentioning Conrad Brooks. Though he did not end up having a large role in the film, he was elemental to several important moments.

First of all, Conrad is a great guy. He comes from that old-school of acting (or should I say overacting) and I simply love his performances.

Conrad is a very nice guy and perhaps that was his downfall—at least in terms of working with Donald G. Jackson. For if Don found someone he could vent his anger upon, look out. Conrad often served that purpose as Don would just scream and scream at him. For example, when we were filming at *The El Mirage Dry Lake Bed* and my character was driving up to meet Conrad and a female cohort, Conrad kept missing his mark as he walked into the scene. Don just let loose on him several times. But finally, Conrad explained that he had cataracts and, as such, the high light of the desert made everything just a blur. From this, he was unable to see where his mark actually was. In the next take, as Don filmed from the backseat and my character drove into the scene, Don said, *"I guess I shouldn't have been so hard on him."* But, he never apologized. That's just who he was.

I believe this abusive mindset was one of the key downfalls to the overall career of Donald G. Jackson. He would test people and if he would find them venerable, he would go after them nonstop. Conrad was often on the wrong side of this abuse.

Though Don was certainly one of the most instrumental figures in relaunching the career of Conrad Brooks, why Conrad put up with it, I do not know? But, he did. In fact, Conrad loved Don. I think back to a time when I was teaching a course on filmmaking at U.C.L.A. and one of my students needed an actor for a scene he was shooting for his class project so I suggested Conrad as his day rate was only $100.00 and, hey, he was in *Plan 9 from Outer Space*. The moment Conrad got on set he thanked Donald G. Jackson. This made me smile, *"Hey Conrad, it was me who got you the gig!"* But Conrad, like so many other people, simply assumed that Donald G. Jackson and myself were one inseparable team, but we were not.

I know I have told this story somewhere before but when Don and I were filming *The Rock n' Roll Cop,* just after *Chupacabra,* we had brought on this one guy who was the godson of actor William Smith. Good guy. I really like him. But, he pissed Don off for some nondescript reason and Don just went off. I was driving in the car behind them and for nearly an hour I could hear Don screaming at the top of his lungs at this guy. When we finally got to the shooting location the guy gets out of the car a bit shell shocked and asked me if Don treated me like that. *"Hell no,"* I said, *"I'd kick the shit out of him if he did."* But, here was this guy; my age, healthy, and I'm sure he could fight, but he let Don treat him like that. But, Don behaved like this all the time as long as someone would let him get away with it. Again, Don made a lot of enemies. That's why he always needed someone like me around—someone who was willing to fight. There was more than a couple of times when I had to step in to keep Don from getting his ass kicked.

In fact, near the end of filming *Chupacabra*, it had gotten so bad, as Don was getting so many treats, that we both ended up carrying loaded guns with us all the time. Don had his Smith & Wesson and I had my Glock. I thought then and it makes me think now back to that Rappin' 4-Tay song, *Playaz Club*, **"I don't need a Glock but I bought one just incase some sucka tries to stop me from pursuing my paper chase."** Don was really afraid that someone was going to burst into the office and shoot him. He always told me if that happened to please just shoot the guy and then give him my gun, he would say he pulled the trigger. As you can see, things got very strange, chaotic, and dangerous due to the behavior of Donald G. Jackson during the filming of *Guns of El Chupacabra*.

But, I have gotten off point… Another interesting moment, during the filming of *Chupacabra*, involving Conrad came when we were filming at the aforementioned space of the artist near the L.A. River. One of our crew had brought his girlfriend along. She was a showgirl from Vegas. This being *Zen Filmmaking*, we, of course, offered her a part in the movie. We put her in a scene with Conrad. Now Conrad, any time he had the chance took advantage of it and shoved his tongue down the throat of any actress in a scene with him. Thus, the showgirl got initiated into the acting technique of Conrad Brooks. The crew guy was fuming. I told him to step in and stop the scene. She wasn't my girlfriend and, as such, it wasn't my call to make. But, he did nothing. Thus, Conrad got the kiss, the showgirl got her major motion picture film debut, and the filming of *Guns of El Chupacabra* moved forward.

As stated, Don promised to keep the monster costume in good shape. As we got near the end of this period of filming, this is where my character kills the creature. For those of you who have seen the film you know that, among other things, I shoot arrows into El Chupacabra. That does not keep a monster safe, sound, or intact. Thus, by the time we were done filming with the monster that costume was pretty much trashed.

Don being Don, as we were about to shoot that scene, he told me that he wanted to, *"Fuck up,"* the costume up so that the person who gave it to us could never use it in another film. Not cool. But again, this goes back to mindset and code of conduct that Donald G. Jackson inhabited.

With the completion of this segment of filming we telecined the film, time coded it, and I sat down to edit the movie. Now, this became a very interesting process. Don and I had a full floor of offices in a North Hollywood office building at the time. We set up one of them to be my editing suite. Don rented an editing bay from one of his friends. It was made by Sony and was not dissimilar to the editing controller I used on *Roller Blade Seven.* The problem was, this system had been developed in some weird way, for some weird reason, in that it only worked in reverse. Meaning, whenever I put the various cuts of a scene together I had to do it in reverse. Therefore, every scene in *Guns of El Chupacabra* was not cut editing from start to finish but from finish to start. Believe me when I tell you, that was not easy to do…

During the editing, one of my sweetheart's from Bangkok came to L.A. I took her by the editing suite and showed her some footage from the film one evening. She immediately assumed that Z'Man

(Robert Z'Dar) was wearing a prosthetic jaw. Nope, that's just him... Awh Z'man, you are missed!

I did the first cut and we let the film sit for awhile. The 1998 AFM was still a few months off and we were working on other projects. During that period of time Don and I did *The Rock n' Roll Cops, Lingerie Kickboxer, Mimes: Silent But Deadly,* and a few individual films. As the '98 AFM approached, Don had the idea to add our *Zen Filmmaking* buddy Joe Estevez to the cast which took us to the last stage of filming *Guns of El Chupacabra*. Don envisioned Joe as being the storyteller that comes on and interrupts the movie like in the 1950s and 1960s TV shows in order to narrate and fill in any story gaps. Thus was born, Rocket Ranger Dan Danger.

A funny story here is that Don and I watched the movie and discussed where we needed Joe to fill in the story gaps. I went home and actually wrote out the dialogue that Joe was to say in full screenplay fashion. And, there was a lot of it. I gave it to Joe.

On the day of filming we went to pick Joe up at his place in Hollywood and we headed over to Bronson Cave. Don was doing the camera and I was doing the sound but Joe... Joe didn't learn his lines. He didn't even bring the script that I took all that time to write. ...I am smiling as I write this as it was so amusing. Me, Mr. Zen Filmmaking, writing and giving someone a script and them not even bringing it. *Zen Filmmaking* Forever!!! Don and I did the best we could at feeding him lines that would patch up any story flaws.

Post that, I edited the scenes into the film. We then took the movie to online post. And, that was that, the movie was done. It premiered at the 1998 American Film Market.

Guns of El Chupacabra!

POST SCRIPT:
From the footage we shot during this period of time I was able to construct three individual films making up *The Guns of El Chupacabra Trilogy*. Though the title figurehead of this film group is the most relevant feature, the other films each offer a unique view into the *Zen Filmmaking* legacy of *El Chupacabra*.

A couple of year before he passed away, Don's father died. With this, Don retuned to his hometown of Adrian, Michigan. While there he fell in with a group of Christian zealots who preached, *"A bible in one hand, a gun in the other."* As he was the hometown boy who had made good in Hollywood they heartily embraced him. They even gave him a radio show on their pirate radio station. ...This, until the FCC shut them down and confiscated their equipment. Don was rebaptized and believed he had been cleansed of all his sins. I don't know about that but while he was there he wanted to show the congregation *Guns of El Chupacabra*. The only problem was, there was all that nudity in the film and he believed that the nudity would not be acceptable to a Christian audience. As such, he asked me to edit it out. I did so and sent him that version. This is the PG version of the film that was released much later as, *Crimes of the Chupacabra*. He was very happy with his new group of friends and remained in Adrian for a time until the strain of the relationship with his step mother got too intense and he was forced to leave. I picked him at LAX. This period, and his interactions in Adrian, truly defined the last years of Don's life.

When Don passed away I knew that he was still in possession of the El Chupacabra creature costume. Though I hoped to get it, have it repaired, and do another film featuring it—resurrecting El Chupacabra, Don's wife had discarded it before I had the chance to retrieve it. She did this knowing how much Don disliked the executive producer of Roller Blade Seven whom had given it to us as she had sued Don shortly before his death due to an unfulfilled movie contract. This, in association with the fact that Don's wife and his daughter moved out of the house they had lived in for over twenty years in Canoga Park shortly after his passing, as such they were in the mode of rapidly discarding all nonessential items. Thus, El Chupacabra is lost forever.

FADE OUT.

THE ZEN

Making The Rock n' Roll Cops

Scott Shaw came up with the concept for *The Rock n' Roll Cops* in 1995. Due to other filmmaking commitments, he did not begin filming it until the winter of 1997. Initially, he planned to shoot the entire film in one ongoing take—having the undercover police officers going from one call to the next, with no cuts or edits.

Pre-Production

Shaw was set to go up on the project with his friend Kenneth H. Kim, who had collaborated with him on *Samurai Vampire Bikers from Hell* and *Samurai Johnny Frankenstein* when his *Zen Filmmaking* partner, Donald G. Jackson, asked if he could come onboard, provide financing, co-produce, and perform the cinematography for the film—as he had fallen in love with Shaw's title and concept. Shaw agreed. With this, this film took on an entirely new form. Instead of shooting it without any cuts, the movie was filmed over several weeks and provides many of the bizarre elements noted in Shaw/Jackson productions.

In order to give the movie the true feel of a documentary, the crew filmed several of the scenes with the camera's auto-focus mode. This was done in order to have the primary subjects fade in and out of focus, in certain scenes, as is commonly experienced in documentary films. In addition, many of the familiar faces from the Shaw/Jackson collaborations were enlisted, including: Julie Strain, Kevin Eastman, Robert Z'Dar, William Smith, and David Heavener.

Manic Production

As Shaw/Jackson productions always had their interesting, behind the scenes moments, this was especially the case with *The Rock n' Roll Cops*. In fact, Scott Shaw details that this production was one of the worse case scenarios that he has ever encountered throughout his years of involvement in the film industry.

Shaw explains that for some unknown reason, Jackson was in a manic state of mind virtually throughout the entire production period of this film. Due to Jackson's ongoing antics, Shaw initially wanted to shut down the production and return to his original cast and crew. But, Shaw quickly realized that he could not do this. This was because of the fact that not only had he committed to the project, but also the story and the concept for the film were his idea. He knew that if he left the production, Donald G. Jackson would steal the project and continue to film it—calling it his own. As this was a tactic that Jackson was notorious for doing.

Shaw explains that the craziness of the production began almost the first day when Jackson began doing things like challenging the entire cast and crew to see who could stay awake the longest. Jackson would exclaim, *"Nobody can stay awake for as long as I can. Nobody!"* Shaw ended up being the only one who passed the test—staying awake for as many days as Jackson.

Shaw also tells of how, due to his manic state, Jackson would constantly scream at cast and crewmembers. An ideal example of this occurred when Shaw and Eric Brummer were doing a few scenes together one evening in Burbank, California.

"Jackson was constantly yelling at Eric," explains Shaw. In fact, at one point, Shaw was driving in a car about a block behind the two of them and he could hear Jackson screaming at the top of his lungs, at the actor, over what Jackson believed to be his lack of understanding of, *"Acting for the camera."* Upon parking and exiting their cars, Brummer, a bit dismayed at what had just occurred, inquired of Shaw, *"Does he yell at you like that?"* Shaw replied, *"Hell no, I would kick his ass if he did. Feel free to do so."*

Jackson also exploded, for no reason, at other actors during the production. At one point, Jackson was filming a scene and he screamed at Robert Z'Dar, due to the fact that Z'Dar had missed his *mark,* (the place where he needed to be standing for the camera to see him clearly once he walked into a scene). Jackson screamed, *"I wish I could get a fucking actor on this set!"*

Shaw considers Z'Dar to be one of the best actors he knows and was about to intervene when Z'Dar immediately bounced back and said, *"I take exception to that Donny,"* in his firm and very powerful voice. Z'Dar, a large entity, is no one to mess with and Jackson quickly backed off.

This type of behavior continued throughout the production. As Jackson was the Executive Producer, in association with being the Cinematographer, he was constantly screaming at and/or firing cast and crewmembers. Many of the dismissed crewmembers would come up to Shaw as they departed the set, stating, *"Well, I saw that coming..."* Others, would just storm off of the set.

In one case, a Production Assistant became so upset at Jackson's taunting that he tore the film's production tee-shirt off and stormed off of the set.

The problem was, he was so angry that he walked towards the back of the building where filming was taking place. By doing this, he locked himself in— as there was no way to exit the production in that direction. Jackson insisted that production stop, as he wanted to wait to see the ultimate outcome of the crewmember's decision. Thirty minutes later, after realizing his folly, the man once again angrily crossed the set and went out the front door. He walked off the production while being heckled by Jackson.

The Cinematography

This type of excessive behavior, on the part of Jackson, continued throughout the production. At times, he would become so obsessed with obtaining the precise camera shot that he wanted, that he would re-film the exact scene numerous times. For example, Jackson had Shaw do a driving scene over fifty times, in Shaw's *1964 Porsche 356 SC,* while he attempted to get the exact pull-down from the sky shot that he desired. In addition, Jackson did this with Robert Z'Dar at an ATM machine in the early dawn hours, when he had Z'Dar, and his acting partner, Ann Marie Lynch, do a scene of withdrawing money from the ATM over thirty times.

Shaw, who had worked with Jackson for many years, had come to expect this style of obsessive behavior in regards to Jackson's cinematography. So, this was nothing new to him. In fact, Shaw plans to edit and release a film of Jackson's obsessive cinematic moments someday and title it, *Obsession.*

The Mind of Jackson

In association with the previously sited occurrences, Shaw believes that ideal depictions of the manic mind of Jackson, during this production, occurred in four distinct additional illustrations. This first occurred one night, while the team was filming on a parking lot roof in Burbank, California.

Jackson had hired a personal bodyguard that evening. He did this due to the fact that he was worried that he was alienating Shaw due to his insane behavior.

Jackson always viewed Shaw as someone who would protect him from physical attack if one of his cast or crewmembers were to go out of control. He now began to question this relationship.

During this particular evening, flanked by his armed bodyguard, Jackson was again verbally abusing the cast and crew. He placed his particular focus on one of the cameramen. This man was a Film Director in his own right and was a close friend of Jackson's. In fact, Jackson had helped him to get started in the industry.

Shaw knew that the situation could quickly escalate, *out of control,* this particular evening, as several of the cast and crewmembers were carrying loaded guns. This included the aforementioned Cameraman, Shaw, Jackson, and the bodyguard.

As Jackson continued to taunt the cameraman, Shaw asked him, *"Why don't you just leave? You don't need this."* He answered, *"I am going to prove that I am a better man than he is and stay."* He continued, *"You know why he's acting like this don't you?"* Referring to Jackson. *"He's trying to steal your movie. He did the same thing to me, with one of my films, and I have seen him do this with other people."*

Shaw nodded because he knew Jackson's motivation, which is why he refused to pull the plug on the production and leave the set.

Jackson continued his erratic behavior throughout the evening, into the early hours of the morning. Jackson eventually began to enrage the bodyguard, as well—who began to realize what could happen and how he would be placed in the middle of an unnecessary situation if he remained on the set.

Though the bodyguard had only signed on for a four-hour shift, Jackson kept prodding him with $100.00 bills to stay. The guard *none-the-less* eventually left. Jackson called the bodyguard agency, attempting to obtain another source of protection, but they would not send another guard. Jackson never paid the fee for hiring the guard and was eventually sued by the security company for nonpayment.

As the night wore on, the cast and crew ended up at the *Denny's* restaurant in North Hollywood, California at about 4:00 AM. As if to say he was sorry, in his own manic and distorted way, to the aforementioned Cameraman, when the Cameraman was ordering his meal and requested *French Fries,* Jackson, screamed, *"Have as many as you want! I'm paying! I'm paying for everything!"* And, forced the waiter to bring the man four plates of *French Fries.*

Though this was a gesture of seeming contrition, Jackson's erratic behavior accelerated when the grilled cheese sandwich he had ordered, arrived. For some reason the cook had placed a tomato slice upon the sandwich. Jackson, who virtually never ate vegetables, exploded and threw the sandwich and the plate across the restaurant.

The Turtle Mansion

The second event that ideally depicts the mindset of Donald G. Jackson, during the filming of *The Rock n' Roll Cops,* occurred when B-Movie Queen, Julie Strain and her husband Kevin Eastman, the co-creator of *The Teenage Mutant Ninja Turtles,* were enlisted into the project.

The cast and crew traveled to what Shaw and Jackson jokingly titled, *The Turtle Mansion.* This was the couple's home in Bel Air, California. They did this to film additional scenes for the movie. When they got there, they discovered that Eric Brummer, the cast member who Jackson had yelled at in the car, had already arrived. Shaw began to jokingly tell the story of Jackson's yelling at Brummer to Strain and Eastman. He did this while Jackson continually try to interrupt, whispering to Shaw, *"Don't tell them that..."* Though Jackson felt that this might alienate his relationship with the couple, Shaw felt it was necessary that Jackson be forced to own-up to his actions.

With Jackson's bad behavior having been presented to other people, outside of the immediate cast and crew, Jackson began to mellow. And, the shooting at *The Turtle Mansion* proceeded much more calmly than the previous days and nights on the set and Shaw was allowed to obtain his creative vision.

Another interesting event that occurred on one of the days of filming at *The Turtle Mansion,* that Shaw believes deserves to be detailed to illustrate the reality of Hollywood, occurred when David Heavener arrived on the set. Both Julie Strain and David Heavener are very well known in their own individual segment of the independent film industry. Upon their meeting, however, it was discovered that neither one of them had ever heard of the other, nor did they know about the other's individual notoriety. Shaw, felt that this ideally depicted the truth about fame in the Hollywood film industry.

Call in the Calvary

Another interesting, Jackson motivated, event occurred during production when Shaw remained at the production office, organizing the cast and crew for the evening's shoot, while Jackson traveled to the dilapidated district on the east side of downtown Los Angeles to film some *second-unit* scenes of one cast member driving his 1970s Corvette Stingray. Upon arrival, the cast member's car immediately broke down. Instead of helping him, Jackson simply left the man, in this dangerous area, with no cell phone and no method to contact anyone for help. Jackson simply returned to the production office. Perhaps the most ideally depictive occurrence of this situation was that the man's friend, who had actually introduced him to the production team, left with Jackson, leaving his friend stranded.

A few hours later, the cast member angrily arrived at the production office, with a loaded gun in hand. To amplify the situation, Jackson had locked him out of the building and would not let him in. As the man screamed outside, Jackson called the police, who quickly arrived, finding a man with a loaded gun.

The Bonaventure Hotel

The fourth and final event that Shaw believes deserves to be detailed, regarding Jackson's manic state during production, happened at the exclusive *Bonaventure Hotel* in downtown Los Angeles. Shaw feels that this is perhaps one of the funniest and most telling moments of the film's production.

Shaw explains that what led up to the evening's eventual outcome was also interesting, *in-and-of-itself*. Shaw begins the story by explaining that earlier in the day, from their production office, Jackson had called numerous cast members, from previous Shaw/Jackson films, and told them to meet the crew at the suite they had rented at *The Bonaventure Hotel* in the early evening. Jackson sent a cast member and friend, Collin Gillis, to be the *Cast-Wrangler* at the hotel.

As the evening approached, Shaw and Jackson realized that they did not have any digital tape to film the scenes for the evening. So, they went out to purchase it.

Normally, they would easily pick their DV tape up from very specific locations, such as *Studio Film and Tape* or *Samy's Camera* on Highland Avenue in Hollywood, California. But, this evening, everywhere they went, and they went to every place imaginable, no one had any DV tape—everyone was out. The team surmised that some large production company must have purchased all the DV tape they could find for their production.

Shaw and Jackson drove, searching through all of the industry sales locations. Finally, near 9:00 PM, the two finally located some at a *Circuit City* in North Hollywood. Keep in mind that by this point, the cast members had been waiting in the hotel for several hours, as their call time had been 6:00 PM.

At this point, instead of traveling to the hotel, however, Jackson had the idea that as opposed to filming at *The Bonaventure*, as had been planned, maybe they should film at *The Chateau Marmont Hotel* on *The Sunset Strip*. This, of course, is a very exclusive hotel frequented by high-end industry types. So, the pair drove to the hotel and inquired about the availability of rooms. There were none available.

At this point, Shaw and Jackson proceeded to *The Bonaventure*. En route, Jackson decided he was hungry so the pair picked up the female lead of the film, Ann Marie Lynch, and went to one of Shaw's favorite downtown restaurants, *The Pantry* to have dinner. Upon the completion of their dinner, Shaw, Jackson, and Lynch arrived at the hotel; post the eleven o'clock hour.

Shaw was dumfounded when he saw that instead of checking into the hotel quietly, Jackson was ordering the *Bell Men* around, telling them to first get one piece of equipment out of his trunk, then another, while screaming, *"Be careful with that you fucking idiot! That's expensive camera equipment!"* He behaved in this manner, even though the team had no authorization to film at the hotel.

With their extensive amount of equipment unloaded, Shaw and Jackson headed for the hotel suite. Upon entering the suite, it was revealed that there were over twenty-five potential cast members, hoping to be part of the film, sitting in the room. *As a reminder, this was due to Jackson's calling them.*

The first thing Jackson did was to fire the *Cast-Wrangler* Gillis, for allowing so many potential cast members to enter the suite. Gillis, a good natured man who stands about six foot five and always carries a loaded gun, looked at Shaw, smiled, and said, *"I expected that."*

Next, Jackson rudely sent the majority of the cast home. Some had driven from as far as the high desert community of Palmdale, California.

With the room cleared out, production began. This set the final event, which ideally defined this production, into play.

Well-known actor and Clint Eastwood co-star, William Smith was also one of the cast members awaiting the arrival of Shaw and Jackson. Smith's girlfriend had accompanied him to the set. But, Jackson felt that Smith's girlfriend was a distraction. So, instead of asking her personally to leave, he had one of the Production Assistants tell her that it was Shaw that didn't want her in the suite and that he wanted her to leave immediately. Post the girlfriend being informed of this, she, of course, told Smith.

Smith, hearing of this, approached Shaw. *"What the hell are you talking about? I don't care if she is here,"* was Shaw's response. With this, Smith realized the source of the eviction was Jackson.

William Smith, both on screen and off, is one of the ultimate Hollywood bad guys. He was so upset at Jackson that he grabbed him around the throat and proceeded to strangle him. Though Shaw momentarily intervened, he chose to let the melodrama play out. Smith, while his hands were around Jackson's neck, remembered his long-standing friendship with Jackson and cooled down. His girlfriend ultimately left the suite to wait in the hotel bar as Smith's scenes were filmed. The rest of the evening's filming proceeded very well.

Shaw explains that with this event, Jackson's attitude immediately changed. And, from this point forward, Jackson was no longer an *on-set* problem. Shaw directed the remainder of production with no further cinematic interference. But, Shaw also details that the negative occurrences that took place in association with this production ideally depict what can happen when you allow someone to bankroll your film. For this reason, post the completion of this production, Shaw never again allowed any of the concepts or ideas he has for a film to be financed by anyone but himself.

Cinematography

With the completion of each day of filming, Jackson, as the cinematographer, would take home the footage. As Jackson tended to be a less than organized individual, when it came time to edit the film, he could not find all of the footage. Thus, the edit of the movie was put on hold. Shaw actually felt that this was a good karmic cooling down period, as Jackson had infuriated so many of the cast and crew members of this movie, due to his manic state of mind, during filming.

Completion

It was not until 2003, when Jackson checked into the U.C.L.A. Medical Center, for the last few months of his life, that he insisted that Shaw go to his home and acquire all of his film footage. With this, Shaw was finally able to find all of the footage for the *The Rock n' Roll Cops.* Shaw edited the film. When it was complete, Jackson watched it from his hospital bed and was blown away by what they had created.

Hollywood P.D. Undercover

In 2001, prior to this edit taking place, Shaw had met Richard Magram. Magram was one of Shaw's filmmaking students at U.C.L.A. The two hit it off and decided to make a film together. Shaw had always wanted to go back and film his original concept for the one-take version of *The Rock n' Roll Cops.* Thus, production was set in motion.

Just as they were about to begin filming, Kenneth H. Kim contacted Shaw and he too came onboard the production. Though it was decided it would be too difficult to actually film the movie in one continuous take, due to the novice actors and crew they had in place, *none-the-less,* the movie went up and Shaw was able to create his original vision.

Distribution

As Shaw thought he would never be able to acquire all of the footage for the original, *The Rock n' Roll Cops,* when he initially edited and released the film he shot with Magram and Kim, he used the title *Rock n' Roll Cops*—minus *"The."* This version was released solely on VHS. So, there are a few collectable copies of this film out there with the title *Rock n' Roll Cops.* This film was eventually retitled and re-released on DVD as *Hollywood P.D. Undercover.* This is a similar case with the actual film, *The Rock n' Roll Cops.* In this period of transition, it was titled *Rock n' Roll Cops 2: The Adventure Begins* and was initially released only on VHS. So, if you can find a copy of this version of the film, it too is very collectable.

The Rock n' Roll Cops
The Story of the Production

Fade In:

Over the past year or so I have written three, *Stories of the Production*. With the completion of each one, I receive tons of asks to do another movie profile. That's great! I'm glad you like them and find them informative. *Zen Filmmaking!*

I first began with one on *Max Hell Frog Warrior*. Then, I wrote one about *Guns of El Chupacabra*. Finally, I did one on *The Roller Blade Seven*. Each one spells out the details of the film in a free flowing, stream of consciousness manner. The one thing that all of these movies, (including *The Rock n' Roll Cops*), have in common is that I made them in association with Donald G. Jackson. For those of you who have read the previous *Stories of the Production* you will understand that working with Don was always chaos in the making. The fact is, this is probably the *last Story of the Production* I will write as the production of the films I have made without Don were very, (for lack of a better term), boring. Aside from the occasional asshole crewmember or ego-driven castmember, things on my sets generally go off without a hitch. That's just who I am and that's just how I make my movies. Thus, writing about them would provide the reader with very little suspense or melodrama.

This being said, *The Rock n' Roll Cops* was a crazy chaotic mess. Why? One reason, Donald G. Jackson. He used to love to rile people up. I guess that provided him with some sort of a sense of misguided power. I don't know? I do know that of all the films I made with Don, *The Rock n' Roll Cops* was probably one of the shortest in-production pieces we ever did together. We shot it pretty fast. It was only up for a few weeks. We shot it between 11 November and 12 December 1997. None-the-less, it was, without a doubt, one of the wildest and craziest.

As I mentioned in association with the other *Stories of the Production,* if I went back into my production notes I could provide you with an exact date-by-date, play-by-play of everything that took place. But, I'm not going to do that right now. Maybe I will do that at some point in the future.

For the record, there is a chapter in my book, *Zen Filmmaking* that tells the overview account of the creation of this film. In that piece the literary emphasis is placed on a distinctive set of sentiments and events that is different from this essay. So, you may want to check it out. Here, with this piece, I hope to provide you with a more personal understanding of the actual what-went-on during the creation of *The Rock n' Roll Cops.*

Okay… Here we go…

Guns of El Chupacabra
The Rock n' Roll Cops went up directly after *Guns of El Chupacabra.* Don and I had been working nonstop on film-after-film for a few years. *Guns of El Chupacabra,* as was the case with several of the other films he and I created, took a very long time to complete. As stated in *Guns of El Chupacabra: The Story of the Production,* there was one point when Don and I realized we had been filming that movie for over a year and we were not even done.

In any case, to tell a little bit of a backstory, as is referenced in one or more of the previous, *Stories of the Production,* Don loved to promise people one thing or another but he never delivered.

From this, he created a lot of enemies. Though Don would promise people producing, writing, and director positions, at best he would allow someone to write a script, critique it, and then never speak to them again. One-on-one he would often say to me, *"Let them go find their own money to make a movie. Why should I pay for it?"* Thus and therefore, there was a lot of negative energy being focused our direction from people who were mad at Don so we had to go armed pretty much everywhere we went as Don was receiving a lot of death threats. And me, because I was seen to be his friend, a lot of people wrongly included me in their equation of hatred. Combine this with the fact that Don always talked shit behind the backs of people, as he loved to create havoc in interpersonal relationships whenever possible, thus and therefore by the time we filmed, *The Rock n' Roll Cops,* it is hard to believe the amount of pandemonium that surrounded us.

Pre-Production

Due to Don's feelings about financing the films of other people, it came as kind of a shock to me when he told me he wanted to do my film, *The Rock n' Roll Cops.* I had previously told him about my idea for the film and he brought it up one day when we were having lunch out of nowhere. We certainly had co-directed several films together, but when he asked me to solo direct this film with him shooting it, I was very surprised. Though knowing Don as I did, I knew it was not going to be as simple as all that.

The one thing I had going for me, and Don knew it, was that I didn't need him, (or his financing), for me to do my own films. As the digital age was taking hold, I had become the master of the team, as I was the only one who possessed the knowledge of computers, digital editing, and the like. But, what actually made Don ask me to step to the forefront, I guess I will never know. But, none-the-less, he did and so we began pre-production.

As stated, we were just coming off of *Guns of El Chupacabra,* and several other films, so we had a large talent pool to choose from. Throughout all of our filmmaking endeavors over the years, we were constantly casting, so we were always meeting new people to bring into the fold.

We went up fast on this film. At the time Don was having legal issues with the company that had been providing him with film financing, so he had ventured off on his own, setting up a film finance company that romanced those people with a lot of disposable income. Hand-in-hand with this came a lot of additional people that wanted to be in the film business in one way or another. From this, we found additional compatriots.

One of the amusing events that occurred just prior to shooting *The Rock n' Roll Cops* was when one of the high-end money people came over to our production offices to discuss possibly financing a film. At that time, Don was very interested in getting the bumpers of his '62 Plymouth Belvedere powder coated. Instead of even talking to the guy he let him sit there as he made phone call after phone call discussing the powder coating process. I could not help but smile watching this guy, who I am sure had never been treated like that before, sit there uncomfortably in disbelief. But, that was Don...

For the record, I want to be a little carful in some of the names I use in this piece because I do not wish to make anyone regret that they are mentioned here. ...Because a lot of shit went down during this production and I don't want those people to be reminded of a negative experience. Anyway... Just keep that in mind.

Back to the storyline...

My vision for the film was to do the camerawork very much like the television series *Cops*. Not staged or set up in any manner. Just in your face cinematography. And, I think we achieved that. I suggested to Don that he mostly shoot in autofocus mode so that the focus would fade in and out like it does on *Cops*. And, to some degree, he did that.

For the camera, we used the then, just on the market, Sony VX1000, Mini DV Camcorder. For the sound we used a Sennheiser ME66 Microphone, predominately on a pistol grip, plus clip-on lavaliere microphones for many of the dialogue scenes.

In terms of casting, as stated, we had a large talent pool to draw upon.

There is something that most people who are not involved in actual Hollywood filmmaking do not understand. That fact is, if you are a production company, actually making movies, there are a lot of would-be stars and starlets hanging around with you all of the time desiring to get on screen. Not to mention all of the people who are constantly calling you to remind you of their existence—also desirous of being on screen. ...Some, with fairly big industry names. Don and I certainly had our fair share of people who made up that category. So, doing our casting session for *RnR Cops* was pretty easy.

I will say, here at the outset, that we did cast a new face in this film, Ann Marie. We had a casting notice running in Dramalogue, the primary indie film casting newspaper at the time, and she was one of the hundreds-upon-hundreds of submissions we received. As I remember, she was a newly arrived transplant to L.A., from Boston, who had come here, like so many others, to find fame and fortune. Unlike so many others, however, she was a truly talented actress and very nice person to work with. She put up with all of the shit that Don dished out without a whimper and was a great-great asset to the cast.

So, with a virtually endless cast in place and plans for filming *The Rock n' Roll Cops Zen Filmmaking* style, we had boundless locations. Thus, the movie went up.

In Production

For our first night of filming we brought in a couple of porn stars we had previously worked with as female femme fatales. We got a limo from one of our castmembers who used to own a limo service. We were set to go.

Don suggested that we use David Heavener as my costar, which was fine with me.

David is an interesting guy. He had set out on his own several years the previous, found financing for his films, and made some high-end indie productions with some big-name players. Like Don, however, he had a lot of enemies in the industry. In fact, even my ex-brother-in-law had a beef with Heavener believing that he should have made money from a movie of his that Heavener was distributing. Heavener's side was that he gave the guy ten thousand dollars to finish the film and that was payment enough. Even my sister-in-law would call me up and say, *"Please don't work with David Heavener."* But, David was the same age as me, we had worked together before with no issues, he had never done me wrong, so I was all-good with the suggestion. He was a talented guy and had a big name in the industry at the time.

The first shot of the first night was the limo pulling into the parking lot behind our North Hollywood production offices. Don being an obsessive cameraman did trip on that pull-in shot a bit, making the limo drive around the block and pull in several times. But, the numerous takes, as always, equaled one shot that was eventually used in the final cut.

The next shot was David and I, with the beautiful porn girls, interacting in the limo.

In terms of improv and *Zen Filmmaking*, David was always great. He had his acting chops well-honed so with just a minimal amount of story guidance, he was good to go.

The problem with David, as an actor, is that he is a bit of a ham. Meaning, he likes to try to steal the scenes. For me, that was never an issue, however. I really don't have a big ego in that department. As a filmmaker, if someone has something worth saying, let 'em say it and we can work it out in the editing room. The girls, on the other hand, they were a little stiff. But, they were very pretty so it was all-good with me. Finally, after probably three hours with the girl both clothed and unclothed in the limo, and Don obsessing about his in-limo camera work, the scene was shot.

In is kind of funny/interesting to be describing this process in so few words because at the time it drove me nuts how much Don obsessed about him getting the shot just perfectly. For a big film, there is a reason for that kind of enhanced, over-shoot process. But, for the camera-based freedom I hoped to embrace in this production; well, it was not going the way I had hoped. But, Don was the camera guy, my co-producer, and my financier so I had to let him have his say.

We finished up the evening at about 2:00 AM or so with my character and another actor, who had been in *Guns of El Chupacabra,* doing a scene together. After we were done, he complimented me how much he liked the naturalness I emulated in the scene.

...Different from my character in *Chupacabra. "That film was deep cult,"* I explained to him with a smile. *"This film is me on the streets..."*

The Problems Begin

During the production of this film, we shot it almost exclusive at night. I wanted to give it a very urban feel and I think we achieved that.

For the second day of actual production, Don and I showed up at the office around 2:00 PM and begin to plan out the next evening of shooting and whom we were going to call into the process.

The second night of production is where the problems began. Along with a few actors who never made it on screen... ...Don loved to do that to people. Bring them along for the ride but then never film them... But, we had also called in a very good guy named Eric. We had worked with him before, he had a great look, and was a talented actor. He wanted to play his character as a black-influenced white guy. Being an open to input director, I liked what he was doing so we ran with it.

The only problem was, he had another movie set to be on later that evening. One which featured the great actor William Smith who was also in *RnR Cops* and I will speak of him in a bit. Don, loving to fuck with people, kept Eric from going to the other set. We filmed some stuff in Burbank and aside from being asked to not film in front of a movie theater, all went well. But, Eric had to leave. As we had driven him to the set, his car was back at our offices, so he couldn't leave. Don fucked with him and fucked with him until I finally stepped in and had this one actress, who was being unused, drive him back to the office. With Eric on his way, we continued to film scenes late into the night in Burbank.

A day or so later we decided to film again. We decided that we should establish the relationship between Eric's character and mine. It was Sunday, so we knew there would be very little traffic over in the junkyard section of the Valley. We drove there in the afternoon, got some daylight car drive-by shots, which I eventually used as a backdrop for the front-end credits of the film, and then set up the scene where Eric's character attempts to steal my '64 Porsche 356 SC. Though Don did have his share of camera obsessions that day, in that period of the shoot-day, it was not too bad. We got the shots. I also did the gag where Eric is driving off and he hits my character and I roll off of the window and the hood of the car. We then shoot me jumping into my car to give chase to Eric's character. All-good.

A funny side-story here is that we did not shoot the actual, in-car, through the window angle on that gag until late in the evening that night. As the original scene was shot in the late afternoon, the shots did not match at all. We jokingly explained it to each other as we filmed it, *"Filmmaking is the suspension of belief."* But, I never actually used that angle in the final edit.

Anyway, it was time to move on. Then, there, Don goes ape-shit nuts.

We are set up to do a driving scene. Don is in the car with Eric, filming him discussing my character and what just took place. I gave Eric some basic instruction about what to talk about and I am following them in my car. The rest of our crew is following me. Watching the footage, Eric did a very good job. He's a good talker. But, that is not what was weird. Maybe fifteen or twenty minutes into it all, I hear Don begin to yell. Keep in mind, I am in the car behind them. So obviously, Don was yelling very loudly. We drove for maybe another twenty minutes. The entire time I can hear Don screaming at Eric at the top of his lungs. Telling him what a stupid fuck he is and stuff like that. I mean, flat out, I was in disbelief.

We ended up in a parking lot and Don angrily gets out of the car, massively agitated. He is going off about how Eric is a stupid, fucked up actor and he is a complete moron. What set Don off, I do not know. I went over to Eric who was standing there obviously shell-shocked. He asked, *"Does Don talk to you like that?" "Hell no! I would kick his ass."* The fact is, I am surprised Eric didn't do just that. I guess it was a combination of surprise at Don's behavior and maybe that he must have been trained to have respect for his elders or something like that, because he certainly could have kicked his ass if he wanted to. He was a young, healthy guy.

This is something that I first realized about Don when we were doing *The Roller Blade Seven*. Don would go off of the deep end at people, especially and pretty much only when he knew that he had someone around that would protect him and fight his fight for him. But, in the case with Eric, that would not have been me because Don was totally in the wrong. Moreover, Don always pushed people to see how far he could get with them. Obviously, he realized that he could treat Eric like shit and get away with it. Thus, another example of why Don had so many enemies.

After that, I sent Eric home with one of the other crewmembers. Don and I set out to film my side of the car chase conversation.

If you look at the *Zen Documentary* I did titled, *Cinematografia Obsesion,* you can see the obsessively insane nature of Don's camerawork. We shot me doing the same scene over-and-over-and-over again maybe thirty times or more times as we drove through the Valley. Even me, a normally very calm guy, was getting pissed. Again, this obsessive style of camera work may be necessary for some high budget productions, but I just ended up using one of those takes in the final cut. What a waste of time!

The Turtle Mansion

The next day of production we were scheduled to go to the Tuttle Mansion as we called it. This was the Bel Aire home of Kevin Eastman, (Co-Creator of the *Teenage Mutant Ninja Turtles*), and Julie Strain.

Sadly, just last week, I did an interview regarding Julie and our film work together. She is apparel suffering from severe dementia and is not long for this world. Very sad, she is not that old. …Younger than me.

In any case, we did a lot of work with Kevin and Julie around this period of time. Both great-great people! Like I told the interviewer last week, it was not unusual that Julie would call up and say, *"Let's make a movie."* So, Don and I would go over to their house and do just that. …Julie loved to work from her home and as they had this beautiful house with a gigantic backyard and pool, it was a really great setting to film movies.

On that day, it was our plan was to shoot in the afternoon. But, I get a call from Don at about 10:00 AM. He says that I must rush over to Kevin and Julie's house right away as Eric was on his way.

Eric, was a filmmaker in his own right, and Don, being the very paranoid guy that he was, became worried that Eric would go over there and ask them for money. So, I get in my car and drive, in a rush, from Redondo to Bel Aire. Though Kevin and Julie were happy to see me, we sat around staring at each other for a couple of hours before I get the call that Don had got in touch with Eric and demanded that he come to the office instead. Thus, Don, Eric, David Heavener, and a couple of other people were on their way. Again, another mind game played by Don for no good reason.

A couple of interesting things happened on that day of filming... First of all, this was one of those times when I provided a fuck you to Don—done so for Don being Don. When the cast and crew arrived, I begin to tell Kevin and Julie the story of Don yelling at Eric in the car. It then became like one of those things that happens in a sitcom where Don was standing over to one side shaking his head, *"No, don't let them know I am an asshole and I treat people like shit."* I smiled at him and I continued to tell the story. I figured if you are going to treat good people in that manner, your actions really need to be called out.

Another interesting thing that occurred on that day was the meeting of David Heavener and Julie Strain. It was the strangest thing... They were two of the biggest names in the indie film world at the time and neither one of them had heard anything about the other person. They both went blank when I introduced them. I guessed that was just ego. They were both so self-involved with themselves and their own careers, why should they care or even know about anyone else?

Overall, the filming went very well that day. My character had a fight with Eric's character and threw him in the pool. We established Kevin as another key co-star to the story. And, we filmed that great dance scene with one of Julie's female friends.

Though we filmed a couple of days of *RnR Cops* at the Turtle Mansion, this was undoubtedly the most productive of those shooting experiences.

An interesting, telling event, happened near the end of that day of filming. It had begun to rain and I was doing a scene outside with this lawyer that Don had met via his new film finance company who was also interested in being an actor. Good guy. We called him, *"Law Boy,"* as he looked so young. Also, Rain is a great, free special effect, so to all the filmmakers out there, I suggest you don't run from it but use it in your scenes whenever you can.

Anyway, I had gotten totally soaked. We left right after that to go and regroup at the office before we went out for a night shoot. But, my clothes were saturated and due to the fact that I was carrying a lot of equipment in my car, I didn't have room for the backup suitcase filled with clothing that I normally carry with me. I decided to stop off at the mall and pick up some additional clothing. I was in the department store disgruntled that I was not finding anything to buy that I felt would fit my character and I begin to receive page after page, phone call after phone call. Finally, I answered my cell and it was Don completely freaking out that I was not yet at the office. I guess he thought that I got pissed and bailed. And, Don begin Don just couldn't do anything by himself. I explained I would be there in a bit and he calmed down...

Praising Doctor Praisewater

It was about at this point that Don began to become the worse version of himself. I guess he became jealous at my control over the film. He deicide that hand-in-hand with *RnR Cops* we would shoot another film that he had the idea for, *Praising Doctor Praisewater*. This was to be a semi-comedic film about a sketchy doctor who was supplying people with illicit drugs.

This whole concept of doing two movies, side-by-side, didn't really bother me because we had done stuff like that in the past. I did observe, however, how this process provided Don with the tools to become a bigger asshole to the cast and crew and attempt extend his control over both projects.

On the high side, as we were using the same cast, it allowed the desirous talent the ability to get more on-camera screen time. Me, I went along for the ride.

To be honest, however, this was the first point where Don began to try to steal *The Rock n' Roll Cops* from me. But, I can be a stubborn person. I was not going to let that happen.

To skip ahead a few years in the future, after Don had passed away, a man who Don had apparently sold the rights of *Praising Doctor Praisewater* to, contacted me. Though the movie was never finished and I told the investor that fact, he asked that I send him the footage, which I happily did. When he received the footage he became very upset as I guess Don had really sold the guy with the fact that the film was something much more than it was. When, in actually, it was nothing more than a jumbled messed of random scenes. That was Don...The investor was obviously pissed. Even though this was the case, the investor, knowing my reputation, asked if I was seeking film financing and offered to finance my next film. I explained to him that is not how I created my movies.

Regarding *Praising Doctor Praisewater,* had I been allowed to keep the footage I probably, with minimal addition pick-up shots, could have put the movie together and released it. But, the footage is gone. Thus, *Praising Doctor Praisewater* is lost forever.

Darkness Falls

It was during this period that I really began to witness a shift in Don. Anger could be seen brewing in his eyes. If you want to see an ideal example of this (on film) look to the scene where Don's character does a scene with Ann Marie's and my character on the stairs of an outdoor parking lot. This is where his character says, *"Did Jake tell you that he's a Rock n' Roll Cop."* This is the one of the few times that I actually felt like I was going to have to knock Don out as the aggression level in him was insanely high and I really thought he was going to take a swing at me in the many-many takes of that scene that we shot. But, I guess he knew what would happen if he did, so nothing ever happened. But, it was intense!

I long believed that Don had an undiagnosed case of bipolar disorder. Combine that with the no sleep, the large amount of prescription drugs he was taking, and possessing the mindset of a spoiled child who is only happy when he was getting his own way and there was a constant chance of everything going South.

As production continued, things got worse and worse. For example, we were filming with David Heavener. We started out in the early evening and did a great scene at a restaurant as we were having dinner. We then went to Los Angeles Union Station. We did a great scene with David having a breakdown in a wheelchair as a nurse pushed him through the train station. Like I said, he was a bit of a ham when it came to acting so I just let him run with it… The scene played great.

We shot some other stuff but as the night wore on it was getting really late. For me, I have no problem staying up all night. For David, however, around 3:00 AM he began to say, *"Come on, Don…"* As Don was obsessing majorly about his camerawork, he yelled out. *"Fuck you. You're getting paid!"* Here was David, one of Don's longtime friends, yet he said that to him. I couldn't believe it. Though the backstory is, Don always had a troubled relationship with David. Maybe it was jealousy? Maybe it was spite? Maybe it was power tripping? I don't know? But, more times than I can count David was the target of Don's distaste.

The next night we were shooting at Jay Burgers. …One of my all-time favorite burger places. Sadly, it closed a decade or so ago but I went there from the early '70s forward. On that night is where Don and I did that great scene where he blows up a blow-up globe and, *"Offers me the world."* The scene played great. But, this was a public burger stand, on the wrong side of the tracks, over in East Hollywood. A lot of gangbangers hung out there.

Now, growing up where and how I did, I know that most Latin gangbangers are not going to give you any shit if you don't come at them. Which is exactly what Don did to this one guy.

Here was Don, a fifty-six year old man, (but looking much older due to his leukemia), and there was this young gangbanger with a couple of friends. Don begins telling him to shut the fuck up and get the fuck out of the shot. Obviously, the guy came at Don.

Again, I guess Don thought that I would step in. But, I didn't create this mess. Had the guy actually attacked Don I guess I would have had to intercede. But, Don apologized and stuck out his hand to shake the others guy's hand. Which he did not do but at least a fight was avoided.

The Shit Hits the Fan

Undoubtedly, the worst night of production came when we decided to bring in my *Zen Filmmaking* brother, Z-Man, Robert Z'Dar into the cast. The shit really hit the fan on that night.

Hand-in-hand with Z-Man, we had the largest cast and crew that we had throughout the entire production. But, in this case, it wasn't just Don who was in a pissy mood, it was several other people who were grinding their teeth due to the behavior of Don. I remember going into production that night with an actual concern about what was going to come next, as pretty much everyone was pissed off, strapped, and ready to fight. By the time we got to the set I stuck my Glock under the seat of my car as if bullets stared flying I didn't want to be the one to blame. I know that sounds melodramatic but that was the kind of emotional intensity that was surrounding the movie by this point in time.

For our set, Don had the idea that we shoot some scenes on the roof of this parking structure in Burbank. That was all fine and good with me but, like I said, we had a large cast and crew, so I was concerned. As Burbank is one of the hubs of the industry, the cops are very aware of guerrilla productions and quickly shut them down. I've actually had helicopters zone in on my productions while filming in that city. None-the-less, never one to back down, we staged for the shoot.

On location, immediately, Don went off. Instead of going off on Eric, he focused in on a guy named Robert (not Z'Dar) who we brought along as an additional cameraman.

Robert was an interesting guy. I first met him when I was first working with Don on the never competed, *Roller Blade 3*. Check out *the Zen Documentary* I made about that film, *Roller Blade 3: The Movie That Never Was,* if you want to see some behind-the-scenes of early DGJ. Previous to that, Don had hooked him with a production company and Robert had directed his first movie at the age of nineteen. He even directed Z'Dar and me in the movie, *Divine Enforcer.* Though he was very hands-off. Though Don constantly pitted Robert and I against one another, by making false statements about what we said and stuff, I never let that kind of BS affect me. I always judge a person face-to-face and I had no problems with Robert.

Anyway, Don went off at Robert screaming some of the most demeaning things at the guy. I was in disbelief. Like Eric, Robert was a young, healthy male. He could have torn Don apart. I asked him that night, *"Why don't you just leave?"* I mean, he only lived a mile or so from the location and could have walked home. But, he said, *"I want to prove who is the better man."* Wow, I would not have reacted that way.

In terms of Z'Dar, Don just went after him, as well. At one point he screamed at Bobby, *"I wish*

I could get a decent actor on the set." "I take exception to that Donnie," was Z'Dar's only reply. I mean, I don't know how Don could say that to Z-Man, he was a GREAT actor!

After that, Don goes into this whole yelling discourse about how he is in a lot of pain. Which I do not doubt that he was. A side note is that Don was on a lot of medication due to his leukemia. Apparently one of those medications was very destructive to human cartilage and Don had no remaining cartilage in his right hip. This caused him to walk with a pronounced limp and use a cane. Plus, it caused him to eat a lot of Vicodin. So, I am sure that he was in pain. But, that was no reason to take it out on Z-Man.

Side note: We actually incorporated that part of Don and him needing pain medication into the storyline of *RnR Cops*.

Anyway... Don kept pushing and needling and trying to take over the evolution of the scenes and the movie. But, I would not back down. Robert said, *"I've seen him steal movies like this from other people."* My initial thought was maybe that was why Don wanted to do this film in the first place. He was a horrible confiscator of other people's ideas. Maybe he liked my concept and didn't have any ideas of his own. He thought that I would get pissed and bail. But, that's not me. The more you push, the more I push back.

Around 1:00 AM or so we had shot all we could shoot at that location and Don decided he wanted to eat so we headed over to the nearby *Denny's*. Again, it was a crazy chaotic mess. Don had this crazed look in his eyes.

Don, Robert, Ann Marie, and I were sitting at one table. Z-Man and the rest of the cast and crew were at other tables. I guess Don realize he had been treating Robert badly and he asked him what he wanted to eat. Robert told him he just wanted some fries. *"Give him three plates of french fries,"* screams Don at the waiter. Don then ordered a grill cheese sandwich for himself.

Denny's used to have these great grill cheese sandwiches. Right at that point, however, they had begun to change their recipes. Don found a tomato on his sandwich which caused him to pick up his plate and literally throw it across the room. I could not believe it. I truly thought that they were going to call the cops. But, for whatever reason, they did not.

Another interesting thing that took place that night was that after I ordered coffee, so did Don. The weird thing about this was is that Don never drank coffee. He hated it. Then, he went into a rant about how could stay up longer than anybody. He could film for days and not stop. The man was obviously losing it.

Shortly after that we sent most of the cast and the crew home. With Z-man and Ann Marie we continued to film until the early morning. What changed, I don't know, but Don began to back off about moving in on my position as director.

Again, in *Cinematografia Obsesion,* you can watch as Don obsesses about filming a shot where Z-man goes and gets some money out of an ATM.

The night and the day of production were done…

The Armor Shop

During the filmmaking of *Guns of El Chupacabra* we had met these people who operated an armor shop where they created some great medieval armor for cosplay, enactments, and… We introduced the team to Julie and they were enthralled. You can see some of their armor in *Chupacabra*.

In any case, they had a shop in Burbank and we contacted them. They were more than happy to let us shoot there. For a price, of course…

We had a pretty big cast and crew that evening and Don was not in a good mood. In fact, he was behaving like a total bitch. But, this was my film so I had to hold onto it tightly. I wasn't going to be driven from my set.

He was treating David like shit. *"Could you get in the fucking shot,"* and stuff like that. The real focus of his anger that evening was on this PA named Dennis that we had hired a week or so the previous. A good guy, who was new to L.A. In addition to being our PA, I put him in the film and his acting was spot on.

In any case, Don went after him and went after him hard. He was ruthless. At one point, we were dressing the guy in some armor, so he was shirtless. Finally, the PA had enough, and he walked off of the set without his shirt. The only problem was, he walked towards the back of the shop. From which, there was no way out and onto the street. For a long time, literally like an hour, I wonder what happened to him but then he stormed through the set and walked out of the front door, still wearing no shirt. And, this was the winter. It was not warm. So, he had to have been cold.

Like I said, a good guy. A good guy who Don fucked with for no reason. We lost a lot of very talented people over the years by Don behaving in that manner.

We did the shots in the armor shop that night and moved on.

I guess this is as good as a point as any to mention this. Yes, on the set Don was behaving like a total asshole. But, when we were together during the day, planning the next shoot, he was totally normal. We would laugh and joke like we always did…

Let's Play Some Music

During the filming of *Guns of El Chupacabra* we were introduced to this guy who had a large warehouse space over by the L.A. River. We filmed the Kevin and Julie in armor scenes at that location. You can also see some of that guy's great gothic artwork in the background.

In any case, we needed an interior location to further develop the story. So, we contacted the guy and returned to his space. There, among other things, we planned to film a jam session with David and I.

David was a country western singer who had a couple of albums on the market. But, he didn't have access to an electric guitar. So, I packed up my '64 Gibson Trini Lopez for him to use and I took my Gibson, Kris Derrig, Les Paul for me to play. I would have like to have brought some of my Marshall stacks to use as amps but there was no way that I could fit them in my Porsche. So, all I had room for was my '57 Fender Deluxe. One of the other castmember brought a practice amp for David to use.

Maybe someday one of you people out there with a lot of CGI experience can put a wall of Marshalls behind us. But, that was all we had to actually work with.

What really surprised me when we got down to filming the scene was that I thought that David and I were just going to jam with me playing lead. But, David had actually written an entire song titled, *The*

Rock n' Roll Cops. Wow! He really went all in and that was highly appreciated.

In the final cut of the film I didn't use the song, however. We had spoken about actually going into a recoding studio and recording it right. But, that never happened. As, the audio from one Sennheiser ME66 microphone just did not do the song justice, it never made its way into the film.

Shooting Continues

We shot some interesting stuff over the next few days. I don't know how much Don had been sleeping, or what he was taking to stay awake, as he was also doing *Praising Doctor Praisewater.* ...A film, by this point, that I didn't want to have anything to do with.

In any case, I showed up at the office as we were set to go out that night and film. I had gotten to the offices in the late afternoon and Don and/or no one else was there. I hung out for a little while and Don with his cast and crew barrels in. He was mad and agitated. What had apparently occurred is that the castmember, who owned the limo, and provided a great character in *RnR Cops,* was also doing *Praising Doctor Praisewater* with him. Remember, people want that screen time... As I was told, the guy's limo had broken down in this really sketchy part of ghetto L.A. but instead of helping him out Don just told the guy to fuck off and figure it out for himself. Don and the crew just left him there. I mean that is really messed up.

The backstory about that guy was, he was a former gangbanger and a current drug dealer. The guy was always strapped with one of those large, Dirty Harry, Smith and Wesson 44 Mags in a shoulder holster. So, he was no one to mess with. As

Don drove off, the guy was obviously pissed off big time and was hitting Don with some serious threats. Can you blame him?

Anyway, back at the office, Don and his people all pull out their guns awaiting the arrival of the guy. I mean, what bullshit melodrama. All for nothing. Again, I am left in a state of total disbelief. Don then calls the cops and tells them that he is being threatened by this guy and the guy is on his way to kill him. Unbelievable…

Some people love all that style of adrenaline filled bullshit. Don always did. But, not me. I just don't need it.

I guess the guy got his car started and just as he was showing up the cops arrive. I couldn't even watch what was going on. I went to my office and sat around talking with this one actress who had not been involved in the melee. Luckily, they didn't arrest him, they just told him he had to leave. But, Don should not have done that. Plus, he did that with the full support of the cast and the crew of *Praising Doctor Praisewater*. I refused to let of them film any more scenes in association with *RnR Cops*. Me, I would have stayed there and helped the guy out if his car had broken done. Not Don, he loved the melodrama. Bad, bad, bad…

The Final Scene

Though we shot for a few more days, the final scene of *The Rock n' Roll Cops* involved the great actor, William Smith.

I don't really remember where or why we decided to do it but we chose the famous Bonaventure Hotel as a location for his scenes. Don and I went there early in the day and rented a hotel suite. We then went back to the office where Don proceeded to call this insane amount of castmembers to meet us in the room—promising all of them a big part in the film.

We then had a core group of people meet us at the office and Don sent this one guy to the hotel as the Cast Wrangler.

Now, this guy who was also in the movie. …A very good guy and a great actor. He was the brother of an Academy Award winning director. He predominately worked as an extra while he wrote scripts hoping for one to break through. He was given the key to the hotel room and was told to keep everyone in the room and not let them wander the halls.

Don and I then left the rest of the central cast and crew in the office and set out on our day.

I knew what Don was doing. He loved to fuck with people and he just wanted to see how long he could make them sit around doing nothing. We went out and had lunch and later dinner. That tells you how long we were out.

Out, we were also planning to buy Mini DV tapes for the evening's shoot. The thing was, there was none to be found. We literally went everywhere. And, I mean everywhere around Hollywood and the Valley but they were all sold out. Apparently, some big production company had just discovered the format and bought everything. We searched and searched until we finally found some at an electronics store. That was a strange experience and a good lesson to filmmaker; i.e. make sure you have your film stock before you schedule your shoot.

Then, Don had the idea, why don't we film at the Chateau Marmont on the Sunset Strip instead of the Bonaventure? We went there. Don boldly exclaiming that we wanted to film some scene that evening in a suite for this great film we were making. *"This is the director, Scott Shaw,"* he exclaimed. Again, I could not believe his actions. Whether or not it was true, they told us they were fully booked. By now, it was about 9:00 PM so we headed for the Bonaventure, calling the people who remained at out office and telling them to meet us there.

The next thing that shoved me into disbelief was the way Don encountered the staff of the hotel. We pull into the underground parking lot of the hotel and instead of being cool and casual he boldly tells the bellmen how to unpack and load up all of this massive amount of film equipment he had in his very large trunk. I mean, we didn't have a permit to shoot at the hotel or anything like that and I expected the management would come down on us. Don literally had the bellmen unpack two full hotel carts of equipment and take them up to our suite. It is hard to even explain what I was feeling.

Next, we go upstairs. We walk in the room and see that there were at least fifty expectant castmembers sitting around. All of them stuffed into this two-room hotel suite. These were all people that we had worked with before. Don goes off, *"Get them the fuck out of here! Why did you let all of them in here!"* Don yells to our Cast Wrangler. In disbelief, people try to speak to me, as I am the nice one. I just ignore them and walk away. It's all too insane for me. There is nothing that I can do. As was always the case, it was Don who made the phone calls and set all of this into motion but it was Don who tried to blame someone else.

Next, Don goes after the Cast Wrangler. He starts screaming at him for not maintaining control over the people. A very nice guy, he looks at me and said, *"I guess I should have seen this coming."* He inquired as to his pay but I told him that was Don's department. He left. But, at least he didn't hold a grudge against me.

Talent on the Set

About 10:00 PM the great actor and Clint Eastwood Co-Star William Smith arrived with his girlfriend, (who later became his wife). Don was immediately pissed that he brought her along. Me, I had no problem with her being there at all. While I was setting up some lighting, Don apparently told Bill that I did not like her on the set and that she had to leave. Which she did. I was told she went down to the hotel bar.

A few minutes later, I asked Bill where she went. He told me Don said I wanted her gone. *"I never said that,"* I exclaimed. With this, Bill goes into the bedroom of the suite, where Don was getting the camera ready, and joking put him in a chokehold. As they were longtime friends, I knew there was nothing to worry about but it was fun to see how the tables had turned on Don in an instant and he was totally incapacitated by a truly tough, take no prisoners, sort of guy.

The next strange thing that occurred is that Don completely stepped back from any interaction onto how I was going to guide the scene. There was no input about camera or otherwise. I talked to Bill to tell him exactly what I wanted him to do. Don said nothing.

Now, this was not the first time Don had done this over the years. On more than a few occasions, Don would leave our sets altogether. But, due to the way Don was behaving over the past week or so, I did not expect it.

In any case, Bill wanted to play the charter with a Russian ascent. Sure. I was good with that.

So, I guided Bill, Ann Marie, and Don through their scenes and that was that. Bill was paid and he went home.

We stayed around the hotel until the early morning hours of daylight shooting filler stuff with Ann Marie's and my character. The noteworthy thing was, Don was totally brazen. He had us shooting all over the hotel, in the elevators, and even in the lobby. This, as stated, with no permits. Ballsy, I thought.

At one point, the hotel security guards even came out and took a look at us. But, they said nothing and just walked on. So, we got the shoots while fully utilizing the Bonaventura Hotel with no permits or anything like that.

And, that was that. Those were the final shots of the film.

The Aftermath

Upon completion of *RnR Cops,* I assumed Don would hand over the footage to me and I would edit the film. We had an editing room set up in our offices where I had done several other of our films and I thought this film would follow the same pathway. It did not.

Almost immediately upon rap, Don returned to his usual, more or less normal, self. I will leave it to you psychology majors to figure that one out. Plus, he also gave up filming *Praising Doctor Praisewater.*

We filmed *RnR Cops* in January of 1998. The American Film Market was rapidly upon us and I created a poster for the film as we were going to offer it for sale and international distribution.

One of the weird things that went on during that AFM was that there were people outside actually protesting David Heavener and passing out flyer bagging on him. Thus, Don wanted his name removed from the cast. I thought that was a bit messed up, as Don knew whom he got into bed with when he hired David, but I played along. So, there are a couple of different credit lists on the poster out there.

Though there was a lot of interest in the film from buyer, we didn't have a trailer or anything to show them, so the film went nowhere except for the fact that I was interviewed by Rolling Stone Magazine and a few other media sources regarding the film.

But, that was it. Though Don and I talked about the film over the next few years, as I never had the footage, there was nothing I could do to make it become a film.

In 2002, I was teaching a class at U.C.L.A, *The Art of Independent Filmmaking,* and I got to be friends with one of my students, Rich Magram. A great guy, we decided to make a film together.

For that film, what I hoped to embrace was that same feeling of the TV show, *Cops* that I hoped to capture with the original *RnR Cops*. I wanted to it to be in your face cinematography. As I believed I would never possess the footage for the original *RnR Cops,* I titled this new film, *Rock n' Roll Cops.* We shot it very documentary style, like I had hoped to do with the original film.

Filmed and edited, it was then released.

Very soon after this, in 2003, Don became very ill and asked me to take him to the hospitable. His time was almost up. Knowing this, and knowing that I was the only one who would keep his

261

filmmaking legacy alive, he made sure that his wife gave me all of the footage to all of his and our movies. There was literally hundreds of hours of uncut footage. Immediately, I located the *RnR Cops* footage and began editing the movie. But, Don passed away before I could finish.

One of the first things that I noticed when I began editing the film, and something that I did not previously realize, was the fact that we had shot a lot of very usable scenes. Some of these played out very well for a very long period of time. For me, as a viewer, I don't really like movies that stretch on for more than ninety minutes, however. So, there were a lot of scenes that I substantially cut down and a number of intact scenes that I did not use in the final cut. I believe that there is enough unused footage that I could actually create another full-length movie. But, unless there is a reason, I doubt that I will do that.

As I had already released a movie with the title *Rock n' Roll Cops,* I released the original film as, *Rock n' Roll Cops 2: The Adventure Begins* on VHS.

During that period of time, DVD was rapidly taking over video and I said, *"Fuck it, I am going to retitle and rerelease things as they should be."* Thus, *Rock n Roll Cops* became *Hollywood P.D. Undercover* and *Rock n' Roll Cops 2: The Adventure Begins,* became *The Rock n' Roll Cops.*

Thinking back, as I write this, I don't actually know how much *The Rock n' Roll Cops* actually cost to make but it was not cheap. All of the established talent had their day rates and we paid the other castmembers about one hundred dollars per day and the crew about two hundred dollars per day. Me, I was on a five hundred dollar a week retainer plus four hundred dollars a day for each day we were in production. Don, I am sure, was making way more than that. Plus, a few of the locations we actually rented and that was not cheap. So, this movie did cost some money to make. The exact amount, I will never know.

As to the *Zen Filmmaking* legacy, Don and I always felt we made two masterpieces as a team: T*he Roller Blade Seven* and *Guns of El Chupacabra*. But, I would add *The Rock n' Roll Cops* to that list. Even though it was a crazy, mind-bending experience due to the behavior of Don it, none-the-less, is a true embodiment of *Zen Filmmaking*.

That's the story… The story *of The Rock n' Roll Cops.*

FADE OUT.

THE ZEN

Donald G. Jackson and The Demon Lover

To understand the creation of the film THE DEMON LOVER one must first look to the paradox that was Donald G. Jackson (1943 - 2003). Reverend Donaldo, as he was affectionately known, was born in Tremont, Mississippi, but grew up in Adrian, Michigan. His mother had returned to her hometown to give her first-born a proper southern birth.

First and foremost, Don was a lifelong Christian. He could instantly detail to you the order of the books of both the Old and New Testament, and could exactly quote scripture.

He was a Christian, but only a close-knit group of his closest friends were aware of this fact. Most were exposed to the other Donald G. Jackson— the one who was prone to yelling and screaming at inept cast and crew members, the filmmaker who hated a person one minute but loved them the next, the man who was married for forty years but frequently seduced the new starlet on the set, the man who was known to trip on mushrooms and ecstasy, the man who loved the music of Elvis Costello and Kid Rock but was a consummate folky. Perhaps Fred Olen Ray described Don best when he placed a notice of his death on the Fangoria website, *"Of all the independent low-budget/no-budget filmmakers I have known throughout the years, I can say, with a completely straight face, that Donald G. Jackson was one of the few true artists of the genre. Never cowing to the pressures and demands of financiers, or straying from his course in order to please others, he stuck with his vision through hell and high water. In doing so he created some of the most bizarre films of recent memory, films that often left the viewer scratching their heads in disbelief. Whether you 'got it' or not, Don truly had his own vision and he never gave up on it. I knew Don for 27 years and I'm pleased to say he was my friend."*

Don possessed the desire to create a feature film long before production on *The Demon Lover* ever began. As Don grew up, he was in love with the Republic Serials of the 1930s, 1940s, and 1950s. He was also an avid comic collector. With action-adventure super heroes, and the good guy always prevailing over the bad guy as a backdrop, he was forever shaped by his early influences.

Don first began shooting 8mm, then Super 8, and finally 16mm in his adolescence and early twenties. Though he wanted to be a filmmaker, like so many other would-be creative people, he was locked into the grind of the nine-to-five. He worked at a factory that produced auto parts for fifteen years. Ironically, it was at this factory that Don meet the man who would helped to get his first full-length feature film, *The Demon Lover*, off of the ground. That man's name was Jerry Younkins.

Younkins, on his first day of work, at the same factory where Don was employed, had his finger chopped off by a machine. This accident was to equal $6,000.00. Younkins decided that the money would best be spent on making a movie with the budding filmmaker, Donald G. Jackson—a movie in which he would star.

Prior to meeting Younkins, Don was already in motion towards making his first feature film. It was to be a film about an African-American Private Investigator named, *Lincoln Green*. This was also to be the title of the film. Younkins, on the other hand, was much more influenced by the horror genre of the era. As he had the money, Don's focus was shifted to making a horror-style feature entitle, *The Demon Lover*.

Though Younkins wanted to make a straight-ahead demonic, horror film, Don, as a Christian, changed the focus of the film to a parody. Whether or not this was by accident or decision, Don would never say. But, by the time the feature was complete, it was so bizarre, a parody was all that it could be called.

The ironic things about all of this was the fact that by the time everything was in place to make the movie—Younkins had spend all of his money. *The Demon Lover* was, therefore, financed by Don taking out a mortgage on his house, getting a loan on his car, and borrowing money that eventually drove his family into bankruptcy. By the time the creditors came calling, Yonkins, claiming poverty, was nowhere to be found. Don would often lament, *"I wonder what would have happened if I had made the movie I wanted to make..."*

The Demon Lover had at least two strikes against it from its inception. One, the majority of the actors had absolutely no experience in acting for the camera. And two, the script was written as a high-budget feature that could never have been made for the small amount of cash that was actually possessed by the filmmakers.

Many may think that simply attempting to make a movie in Michigan would be hard enough. This was actually not the case. The Ann Arbor Film Festival was one of the most influential festivals of the era. In addition, many seasoned filmmakers lived in the area. Though this was the reality, the disorganized wildness that was the cornerstone of Don Jackson's filmmaking career lead the film down the road to becoming, for lack of a better description, *"An art film."*

The man who would later rise to rock star status as, *"The Motor City Madman,"* Ted Nugent, actually signed on to do the music for the film. In the late sixties and early seventies, Detroit was the Mecca for hard rock. Nugent lived close to Don and Yonkins and signed on for the gig during a period of time when his band, The Amboy Dukes, was going through a period of reorganization. Soon after this, however, Nugent got a new record contract and shot to superstardom. Don claimed many of the songs intended for *The Demon Lover* were on Nugent's album, *Cat Scratch Fever*.

Pre-Production on *The Demon Lover* took almost two years before any film actually began to roll in the camera. Once filming was completed, it took another two years to be edited and released. As is so often the case of the filmmaker, Don made virtually no money on the film, even though it was released to the then very lucrative drive-in theater market, and was also eventually released on video under a number of titles.

Though Don was an active participant and an outspoken proponent of the film, he never liked the final content of the movie. He would often detail, *"A lot of negative things happened in association with making that movie. Things that I do not believe would have happened if it was not about such a dark subject. I really made a mistake letting Yonkins talk me into making that movie."*

Though the movie was never the feature Don wanted to make, and he regretted it ever since its inception, Don was given a gift in association with *The Demon Lover* that few first-time filmmakers will ever receive. That gift was a documentary about the making of the film entitled, *The Demon Lover Diary*. Though *The Demon Lover Diary* was made over twenty years ago, it continues to show at film festivals and receive extensive publicity in newspapers and film magazines to this day.

Joel DeMont and Jeff Kreines made, *The Demon Lover Diary*. Don had initially hired Jeff to be the cameraman on, *The Demon Lover* and agreed to allow them to make their documentary, financed by AFI, The American Film Institute.

For those of you have seen, *The Demon Lover*, it is obviously a one-sided attack on Don, which does not really depict the true essence of the film, nor the knowledge of filmmaking that Don possessed by that point in his life. This being stated, *The Demon Lover Diary* did more to immortalize the life and the filmmaking career of Donald G. Jackson than anything to date.

In 2002, *The Demon Lover Diary* was screen to a sold-out crowd at *The Director's Guild of America,* in Hollywood, California, in association with The Los Angeles Film Festival. Just prior top this, there was an enormous amount of press about Donald G. Jackson and *The Demon Lover*. Several newspapers ran long articles and full-page photo spreads on Don and the movie. This was a great passing gift to the filmmaker, as he died less than a year later.

PART III
ASKED AND ANSWERED

Donald G. Jackson: The Final Interview

Guillaume Richard

Could you briefly introduce yourself to our French readers?
Well, I am filmmaker who grew up in Michigan during the 1950's. From my early years forward I was in love with the magic of comic books and movies. I loved music, as well. I was a great participant in the folk music era and to this day love some of the great music that came out of that period: like the Kingston Trio, the Whiskey Hill Singers, etc., etc., etc.

Is it your early love for comics and serials which led you to be a filmmaker?
Well actually, I first became a filmmaker when I was a teenager and began working for this guy who owned a photo shop. In association with dealing with still cameras, he also used to film the local high school football games with a 16 mm Bolex camera. One day he asked me to go and film the game for him because he wasn't feeling well. Instead of filming from the sidelines, like most sport photographers, I was on the field getting right in the middle of the action. Though the coaches got really mad at me, when they saw the intimate nature of my photography, they knew I was on to something. And that was the beginning of my becoming a no-rules filmmaker.

What are your favorites comics and serials? Do you still collect comics? Is there a recent comic title that you enjoy and buy regularly?
Some of my earliest comic favorites were some of the more obscure comic books like, Doll Man, Robot Man, Sub-Zero, Fighting Americans, and onto some of the more well know one's like The Avengers, Flash Gordon, and Tarzan.

I have been collecting comic books since I was five years old and still love to collect them. Though I have not been drawn to any of the new, major release comic books, I always keep my eyes open for something new and exciting. Just as in my youth, it always seems to be the more obscure comic artists that are the most creative and inspirational.

As a comic fan, what do you think of the recent bunch of comics transpositions to the big screen (like Blade, Spider-Man, Daredevil, The Hulk...)? If you had the opportunity, which comic title or hero would you like to adapt as a movie?

Some of the movies are Okay. But, I have not seen any that has really done the character justice. I don't know if it is the casting of the lead character or just the overall presentation of the film. But, in all cases, I have been left unsatisfied.

All of my movies are filled with Super heroes. Whether it was Sam Hell in Hell Comes to Frogtown or Jack B. Quick Space Sheriff in Guns of El Chupacabra, there is always a super hero element to my films.

You declared that The Texas Chainsaw Massacre changed your life. In which way?

Basically, it allowed me to understand that as a filmmaker I could make whatever style of movie I wanted and there would be an audience to see it. I mean, The Texas Chainsaw Massacre pushed the boundaries of what was acceptable to the film going audience at that period of time and it accomplished that fact for a very small production budget. It inspired me to go and make a movie!

Could you tell us about the making of your first film, The Demon Lover? And could you contradict this insane rumor telling that your partner Jerry Younkins had to cut one of his finger off in order to finance the film with the insurance money?

The Demon Lover was a movie I should never have made. As a Christian I was really against the subject matter and the content. I have always wondered what my life would have been like if I had gone with my original idea of making a movie call Lincoln Green — about a black private investigator. It was really Younkins who pushed for us to make that movie. And, a lot of negative things went hand-in-hand with the making of the film. I have always been sorry I made it. But, it is one of those situations that once something is set in motion, there is no way to stop it. So, all I could do was make the movie the best that I could.

Regarding his finger: Actually, it is true to a certain degree. Younkins came to work at the factory where I was employed. On his first day, due to his careless behavior, his finger was cut off by a machine. Though he promised we would use the settlement money the factory gave him to make the film — which is why I said, "Okay," to Demon Lover. But, by the time we were ready to shoot the film, he had already spend all the money. So, the film was financed by me taking out a loan on my car and on my house.

Was it the interest in the 70's for movies about the devil (The Exorcist, The Omen and many others) that led you to choose this kind of subject? Have you done some research on demon worshipers or cults (like the California based Church of Satan) to prepare this film?

No. As I said, I am a Christian and I really don't like the subject matter of those films and I never want to associate with people who are not walking on the path to light.

How did Gunnar Hansen become involved with this film? What is your relation with him nowadays?

Texas Chainsaw Massacre was inspirational. So, when it came time to shoot Demon Lover, I contacted Toby Hooper and he put me in touch with Gunnar and we got him in the movie. After we finished filming, Gunnar and I did not speak again until just a couple of years ago.

A funny story regarding Gunner is that my friend and filmmaking partner Dr. Scott Shaw was doing a film in Texas in 1994 where they were going to use Gunnar as one of the actors. Before they were even introduced, Gunnar walked up to Scott and immediately began insulting me — as he knew we had worked together. Scott just laughed it off. It wasn't until 2000 that I saw Gunnar again, at the San Diego Comic Convention. Scott and I walked up to say, "Hi." I asked him why he was mad at me and all he could tell me is that I owed him $5,000.00. Actually, the deal was if the Demon Lover ever made money, he would get $5,000.00 in addition to the $5,000.00 he was paid for acting in the film. Though the movie probably did make money, I never saw any of it. I never got paid. So, I could not pay Gunnar.

I really think it is so sad when people like Gunnar hold on to negativity. I mean this movie was made thirty years ago. And, all Gunnar can still focus on is a "Maybe" agreement. How sad his life must be if he stills care about something like that.

How was the film was received by the audience? What kind of distribution did it received at the time? Was it a wide distribution?

Demon Lover was received well by those who saw it and understood it — meaning that some people understood that we were poking fun at horror movies and horror filmmaking in general. It premiered in New York City and then was distributed to Drive-In theaters. Later, when the video revolution hit, it was distributed under several different titles. The problem is, as is so often the case, is that we, the filmmakers, never saw a dime of this money.

At this time, were you connected to others filmmakers based in Michigan (like Sam Raimi or others)?

Actually, I came along before Sam. When Sam and Bruce Campbell were making Evil Dead, Sam contacted me and told me that I was one of his major influences for becoming a filmmaker. He asked me some pointers about Independent filmmaking and I guided him the best that I could. I guess it worked, as he has obviously become a very successful filmmaker.

You arrived in a transitive time for independent filmmaking and B movies, right between the last hours of the drive-ins and the dawn of the straight-to-video industry. Many local filmmakers who worked in the 60's and the 70's haven't been able to retrain as easily as you and were forced to give up filmmaking or change their activities. What do you think about that? Do you have a theory about these sudden changes?

Mostly, it is about money. Back in that period when everything went straight to movie theaters or drive-ins, it was very expensive to get your product seen. I mean, for every theater there had to be a print made of the film — which was, and is, not cheap. The Video Revolution allowed everything to be made more cheaply.

I think the reason that many of the earlier filmmakers did not make the transition is that they were, for lack of a better word, "Snobs." The felt that their product should only be seen on the big screen, either in a theater or in a drive-in. From this, they robbed themselves of an ongoing career, as they didn't accept the fact that times change. As a filmmaker you have to be willing to adapt to change if you want to move forward.

Tell us about the infamous Demon Lover Diary? When did you understand what was the real motivations of the film maker? What was your reaction at the time? Nowadays what's your point of view on this movie?

It's funny, Demon Lover Diary still shows at film

festivals across the U.S. and maybe the world. Just about every year, it is showing at some theater or at some film festival. Last year there was a big presentation of Demon Lover Diary here in L.A. It showed at the Director's Guild of America and several newspapers did articles on me in relation to this film. This is funny, because this film was released over twenty-five years ago.

The reality of it is, however, the people who made Demon Lover Diary were just out to make me look bad. Every scene they used in the film was an attempt to make me look incompetent and all of their comments and narration during the film are very negative and for the most part, not true. They took scenes where I am nice to them and turned these scenes around to make me look like I didn't know what I was doing.

If you watch the movie, you will notice that they were staying at my mother's house while they helped out with the filming of Demon Lover. They were so noisy and rude to my mother, and so dirty, that my mother had to finally throw them out. Of course, that fact never made it into their movie.

In response, all I can says is that I went on to make more than fifty films since Demon Lover, whereas these filmmakers are still attempting to make a name for themselves from one film they made about me twenty-five years ago. Overall, however, I think documentaries are a great art form. I have turned all of my years of behind the scenes footage and all of my film masters over to Dr. Scott Shaw. Next year he will be began to make the true documentary about the filmmaking career of Donald G. Jackson. So, if you want to know the true story about me as a filmmaker, that one will be the one to watch.

At one time you were thinking of doing a sequel called Return of the Demon Lover. Could you give us details on this project? What the story was? Was it supposed to be a direct sequel? Is this project lost?

This was one of those projects that someone submits an idea to you and you toy with it for a little while but then ultimately reject it. There is a lot of fans of Demon Lover, particularly in Michigan — where the film was made. There was a group of people who wanted me to approve the project and put it together. They even had a couple of the original members of the cast who were willing to appear in it. So, I thought about it.

For a time I thought, if I were to Produce a second version, maybe I could make a more positive contribution to the horror film market and erase any of my bad karma I may have received from making the first Demon Lover. I wanted Scott (Shaw) to go and Direct it. As he would have been the only person I could trust to bring the essence of the film together. I was going to say out here in L.A. and Produce it. But, Dr. Shaw wasn't interested in the subject matter. And, that got me thinking of how another Demon Lover is just not the kind of movie I want to be involved with. So, I put an end to the concept. If anyone in Michigan goes ahead with this, it will be against my wishes and my legal rights — as I am the person who owns all Rights, Title, and Interest to the film and the title.

Was it your own idea to make a movie starring wrestlers? Were you familiar with this universe? Could you tell us about Ringside in Hell, was it supposed to be more of a fictions movie with real wrestlers than a kind of docudrama like I Like to Hurt People?

In the Midwest, were I grew up, Wrestling has always been one of the lifeblood's of sports. Every month or so there would be a big wrestling match planned at one of the local arenas and the matches were on local television every Saturday and Sunday. I loved wrestling from the time I was child forward. The wrestlers were like comic book super heroes. So, I really wanted to make a film about them.

What I began doing was to take, first my 8 mm, then my Super 8 Camera, and later my 16 mm Bolex to matches and I began to put a lot of wrestling footage together. The idea for both Ringside in Hell and I Like to Hurt People were both born from that inspiration.

Tell us about I Like to Hurt People. How did you met The Sheik ? Why did you choose such a controversial character like The Sheik to a more likable one like Hulk Hogan or the French wrestler André the Giant? What was The Sheik like on the set? Do you have anecdotes about the wrestlers on the making of this movie?

André the Giant is in the film. But, Hulk Hogan was and is a superstar wrestler and you just couldn't touch him. He was under very strict contacts — every time he was photographed or filmed, those images had to be approved by his manager and the wrestling federation. What I loved about The Sheik is that though he was a well known wrestler, he was his own man. I went up to him at a match one day, told him what I wanted to do. And, he was the nicest guy. He gave me full access. He also introduced me to many of the other wrestlers, who allowed me to film them, as well.

Tell us about this project of movie you had with the TV horror host The Ghoul? Why this project didn't get made and what the movie would have been like?

The reality of filmmaking is — there are a million great ideas. But, getting them all made is impossible. And, that was just one of those projects.

The problem with filmmaking is, there are so many people involved in every project. So many egos. Sometimes projects just happen easily and naturally — while others you try and try and they just do not happen. As a filmmaker, you have to be willing to accept that fact and move on and not become obsessed and stagnate if you realize that a particular project is not going to get made.

Why, when, and in what circumstances did you choose to move from Michigan to California? How did you get in touch with New World Pictures and find yourself implied on the making of Galaxy of Terror? What was your role on this movie? Is it on the making of this movie you first met James Cameron?

I sent New World a copy, they liked what they saw. So, they purchased and distributed, I Like to Hurt People. That financed my move to Los Angeles in 1981. Once here, I needed a job. New World was hiring, so I went to work. I became the Assistant Camera for the Special Effects photography for Galaxy of Terror. That is where I met Jim Cameron — as he was the 2nd Unit Director of this film.

Can you tell us about your experience on The Terminator?

Though there has been a lot of stories told about the making of The Terminator, most of them are not true. They are just Public Relations from the Studios. My involvement in The Terminator came on the 4th of July 1983, (American's Independence Day), when Jim (Cameron) called me up and asked if I would like to shoot something for him. He was not happy with The Terminator and wanted to shoot some additional scenes. As the money from the production company had stopped coming, he had to pay for this out of his own pocket. What ended up happening is that I shot the opening scene where Arnold Schwarzenegger comes to the past and is naked at the Observatory in Los Angeles. I also shot several other scenes in the movie.

One funny story is: At one point, the union crew was due for their lunch and didn't want to keep lighting the scene. Jim was worried about having to pay Arnold overtime. So, he asked me if there was anything I could do. We got a small portable light, known as a "Mini Cool," out of the truck of my car and I had Jim hold it and pan it as Arnold walked through the scene. We got the shot, Arnold got to go home without being paid overtime, and the movie was completed.

For me, Cameron's Terminator is nothing but a smart and ambitious B movie, in the sense that it doesn't differs much from others B movies from that time. You knew James at the beginning of his career, how do you explain he evolves so fast from the status of a B moviemaker to one of the most valued Hollywood director? Are you still in touch with him?

Sure, we are still friends — even though, due to his massive success, he lives in a very different world than I do.

What explains his success? I don't know? What explains anybody's success in Hollywood?

The first thing you learn about success and filmmaking in Hollywood is that talent has nothing to do with anything. So, the people who come here who think they are talented and expect to be successful can forget it. In the case of Cameron, his success was based on a combination of hard work, luck, good karma, and being at the right place at the right time. God bless him, he is one of the few who truly, "Made it."

Could you tell us about your many collaborations and your friendship with Fred Olen Ray? Do you prefer him as a wrestler or as a director (laughs)?

Fred is a great guy and a very successful indie filmmaker. Funny story, since you mentioned him as a wrestler. Fred had asked Scott and I to come and film one of his first public wrestling matches. We thought this would also be a great place to get some footage for one of Scott's films we were working on, Rock n' Roll Cops. So, cameras were rolling and Fred came into the ring to start his match. BAM! Fred gets thrown to the ground very hard by his opponent and we notice that his foot is turned completely sideways. He had broken it very badly. So, obviously the match was over. But Fred, refusing to give up the sport, as soon as it healed, he was back in the ring. He is a true wrestler.

Regarding our collaborations: Fred makes a very different type of film than I make. His are more directed towards the mainstream audience and mine are more geared towards the art crowd. Which is probably why he has made a lot more money than I have. Whenever we have worked together, it was out of friendship — when he needed a little help doing something — when he can't find somebody else, he may ask me. (Laughs).

Tell us how New World came up to finance Roller Blade?
Roller Blade was not financed by New World. Roller Blade was shot on 16 mm and was financed by my credit cards. The total shooting budget was $5,000.00. New World picked it up, gave me some completion funds, and distributed it. This occurred at a time when the video market was just beginning to take off. Roller Blade was hyped by New World as, "The First Straight to Video Feature Film." Roller Blade made New World over one million dollars. Which is why they financed Hell Comes to Frogtown.

What was your inspiration for this movie and how did you come up with the idea to associate a post-apocalyptic environment with girls on roller skate?
There is no one single inspiration for Roller Blade. But, I have long had a love affair with the samurai sword and the Japanese samurai films. Combine this with the fact that roller skating was so popular here in L.A. — you would see beautiful girls skating down the street all the time. From this I came up with the idea "Roller," for the skates and "Blade" for the sword.

Just a note here: I came up with the title long before the Roller Blade style of skate were released. I always wondered if they saw the movie and if that is where the got the idea for their name?

Do or did you use to roller skate yourself? (PS: personally, I was pretty much into skateboard from the end of the 80's till the middle of the 90's)

No, I leave the roller-skating and roller blading to other people.

Tell us about the cast of Roller Blade: Michelle Bauer, Suzanne Solari (a recurrent actress of your Roller Blade saga), Shaun M. Davidson (was she a roller champion?), Lisa Marie (Tim Burton's wife?), Terri Cameron (related to James?), Barbara Peckinpah (she was in a couple of pornos), Pat McClung...

They were all very nice people. I had put a casting noting is a industry newspaper, that was around at the time, here in L.A., called Dramalogue. I meet them all from the submission of their headshots. None of them were related to anyone famous — they were all just very nice girls and they all wanted to be in an independent feature film.

In a way can we consider your post-apocalyptic movies (The Roller Blade and the Frogtown sagas) as your own Star Wars saga?

No. I see each of my films as whole and complete onto itself.

Except your own films do you have a favorites post-apocalyptic movies? Following the success of Mad Max there have been many post apocalyptic movies made. Do you know about the Italian film of Enzo G. Castellari or the Filipino film of Cirio H. Santiago. They were post-apocalyptic movies? What do you think about them? (PS: this issue of Trash Times will feature a huge article on post-nuke films from around the world)

No. I'm not really into any of those films and/or filmmakers.

The reason I embrace the Post Apocalyptic world in several of my films is that it is very freeing. As a filmmaker, if you let your audience know that the film is Post Apocalyptic, the backdrop for the scenes can be anything. For who is to say what the world would look like. It can look like anything you want. The environment can be as wild or as sane as you wish to make it.

Could you give us details on your obscure UFO: Secret Video? You said it could be compared to an early Blair Witch Project, why?
I came up with the concept for that movie in the 1970s and began to shoot a little bit of it on Super 8. Then, other projects came up, so I let it go for a while. It wasn't until the 1980s that I actually began filming it again. The reason it is like an early Blair Witch is that it is shot on video. This is long before the DV revolution hit — where everything now is shot on video. I shot this movie on standard VHS. So, I was one of the first people to actually go out and shoot a film on video.

This movie has sat around in my closet for years — waiting for the right time to be released. About two years ago, I decide that it would be great if I shot a few more scenes for it — as I am still friends with one of the lead actors, Jeff Hutchinson (Hutch). So, Scott and I got one of the new actresses we were working with, went up to Bronson Cave (The Bat Cave from the T.V. Series) and shot a scene with Hutch, as his same character, almost twenty years later. How many films can claim that length of time — still in productions (laughs).

As with most of my footage, I have turned it over to Scott and he will be editing it together in the near future and it may finally be released.

Tell us about the genesis of Hell Comes to Frogtown? Where did you find the inspiration for frog mutants ? What kind of deal New World proposed to you? And how do you feel about that afterward?

There is a section of Los Angeles known as Frogtown. The story goes, that back in the 1940s this area was overwhelmed by a large invasion of Frogs — which is why it got its name. I had a friend Sam Mann, who was one of the actors in Roller Blade and lived in this area. We were driving along one day and he came up with the title, Hell Comes to Frogtown. From there, I ran with the idea and that is how the movie developed.

New World had made so much money on Roller Blade they offered to finance Hell Comes to Frogtown. My original plan was to shoot the movie with Sam Mann and Suzanne Solari (both from Roller Blade) as the leads. I was going to shoot it on 16 mm, with my Bolex — as I had done with Roller Blade. But then, New World decided they wanted to "Up" the budget. The problem is, the minute you let the devil in the door, the devil is going to take control over you. And, that is what happened with New World and Hell Comes to Frogtown. They decided that they wanted to cast name talent and take over the production of the film. So, the movie evolved from being a 16 mm art film, to a relatively high budget 35 mm cult movie. Sadly, my friend Sam didn't get to play Sam Hell and Suzanne was only given a small part in the film.

Were Roddy Piper and Sandahl Bergman your firsts choices for the roles of Spangle and Sam Hell? What were they like on the set?

No, as stated, my original plan was to shoot the movie with Sam Mann and Suzanne Solari as the leads. But, New World wanted to use Roddy Piper as he was a very famous wrestler at the time — and this was going to be his first movie.

As a fan of wrestling, I was happy to have him. But, as you can understand, what occurred was not fair to my friend Sam. I think I may have made the wrong choice by not standing by my friend Sam, who actually came up with the title and the idea for the movie. But, I spoke with him and he seemed Okay with what was happening. Though Hell Comes to Frogtown is, no doubt, my most famous feature, by my accepting New World's offer, I believe it did set a lot of bad karma in motion.

Regarding Sandahl Bergman: She had just finished Conan: The Barbarian, and they wanted to use her for her name power, as well. I had very little to do with any of the casting of the film. Again, this is the problem when a large production company becomes involved in a project — the actual filmmaker is allowed very little creative control. Which is why I have never again worked with a large production company. But, Piper and Bergan were both very nice people to work with.

Anything to say on Cec Verrell (Centinella)? (I had a crush on her watching this film — laughs)

No, just somebody cast by New World. Also, very nice

The "Dance of the Three snakes" scene didn't really stand its promises? Did Sandahl Bergman have something to do with that?

In the script, Bergman's character was to be naked in this scene. On the set, she would have nothing to do with nudity, however. So, it was one of those power struggle things happening between the actor and the director. Due to New World's influence and decision, the actor won.

William Smith is one of my favorite actors. How did you get in touch with him? He would have made a perfect Sam Hell too, don't you think? Are you still in touch with him?

Yes, Bill is a great actor and a great friend. He has been around the film industry forever. And, I have known him for a lot of years. I put him in my films whenever I can.

Nicolas Worth is also brilliant, even under his heavy make-up. A very talented actor. Did you notice him from his creepy performance in Don't Answer the Phone (1980)?
No, he was cast by New World.

The makeup of the Frogmen are excellent, could you tell us about that?
Steve Wang who went on to direct films like Kung Fu Rascals, The Guyver, and Drive was the main force behind the frog masks and make-up. He is a great guy and has gone on to do a lot of special effects work for a number of very big feature films.

There's always comedy coupled with eroticism and sexual content in your movies that remind me of the films of Russ Meyer. Do his films form part of your influence?
Some of Russ's stuff is great. Particularly when you think that he made them without the help of any of the big studios. But, he has never been an influence to me. It was more the avant-garde films from the 1960s like Dr. Chicago and Chinese Fire Drill that really inspired me as a filmmaker.

I think you're also a car lover and "Hell Comes to Frogtown" showcases two amazing cars, were they part of your own collection?
Yes, I am a big fan of classic cars. I love the cars made in Detroit from the 1950s and early 1960s. One of the cars in Frogtown is a 1962 Plymouth Belvedere. I found and purchased two at the same time. One, we customized for the film and the other one I customized to my own specification and have driven ever since.

R.J. Kizer, the guy guilty to have shot the useless and ugly new scenes of the American version of The Return of

Godzilla is often credited as the co-director of Hell Comes to Frogtown. Why? Was it imposed to you by New World? Why? What was your relations with him on the set? Of which part is it exactly responsible in the final cut of the movie?

Like a lot of people in the film industry, I sometimes say things, trying to soften the reality of what actually occurred in a particular situation and trying to make it more understandable for those who have never made a film. But, now is the time for me to spell out the truth.

Hell Comes to Frogtown was my baby. Though I have been the one to get the most press from the film, regarding Kizer, again, New World took over the project and said that was part of the deal — Kizer was going to be the co-director of the movie. Even though I was the creator, my complete creative control was taken away. New World became angry at my desire to maintain control over the project and I was eventually removed as the director and banned from the sets. There was never any collaboration.

Regarding the final cut of the film, New World handled it. Though I watched some of the editing — they didn't like my flaring temper, when I didn't like something I didn't like. Again, this is why I have never worked with another big production company. Because it just takes all of the creativity away from the filmmaker.

Hell Comes to Frogtown is your one and only film to be released in France (on video under the weird title "Transmutations"), but it seems you always had a great following here with magazines frequently noticing your projects. How do you explain that?

Wow, that is great to hear. I believe there is a certain type of individual who truly enjoy offbeat art films. And, that is the kind of movies I make. So, I guess these people seek them out.

Now, with the Internet, everything has changed. Now, it is much easier to learn and found out about everything. So, this has really been a big help to my career and getting people to notice my films.

You have to understand, I am from a different generation. We use to publish small fanzine to get the word out about films and music. In the 1960's there were hundreds of these small magazine out there. And, we would all try to track them down to find out what was new. Now, everything is instantaneous on the Internet. And, this is great!

You know French people are known in the world for eating frogs? In your Frogtown movies, did you never consider to have a French character feared by the frogmen for his cooking tastes? What do you think about that? (Laughs)

Next time... I have assigned all rights to the Frogtown series to Scott (Shaw). So, when he makes the next one, remind him, and he can add a French (Lead) Character to the film. Preferably a beautiful girl.

Did you have other projects planed next with New World before the studio closed its doors?

No, not really. By the time we finished Frogtown — they hated me. Because I am a very hands on Director. The downfall of the relationship all stared at one point, the first day of shooting, when they had an art director creating one of the sets. When he finished, I checked it out and it all look too clean and pretty to be a part of the film. I told him about it, but he didn't listen. He had all the arrogance of an art director and felt he had to answer to no one. So, when he stormed off of the set, I got a few can of spray paint and went and spray painted graffiti on the wall of the set. When he came back, he freaked out. He complained to the powers at New World and they had a talk with me. They told me, "Everybody has their job on a studio film. Yours is to direct the actors." So, that was the beginning of the end. I never wanted to make another movie for them.

In 1989 you shot the second chapter in the Roller Blade saga: Roller Blade Warriors : Taken by Force. However, this picture isn't a direct follow up of the adventures of the Sisters in Roller Blade. Why? What happened to "Roller Blade Part 2: Holy Thunder." the movie announced at the end of Roller Blade that was supposed to be a direct sequel?

The reason it isn't a direct follow up is that I realized I had completed the concept and the idea I had for the first film and it was time to move the story onto new realities. This is exactly what Scott Shaw and I did with Roller Blade Seven. Though the movie was based on the same premise, it was time to take the concept to the next level — which we did.

Regarding Holy Thunder: What I was doing was like at the end of the early James Bond movies — announcing the next movie to be released in the series. But, like I've discussed — in filmmaking there is a lot of ideas and some of them just do not get made. That was the case with Holy Thunder.

Roller Blade Warriors is my preferred entry in the Roller Blade saga: very fast paced and entertaining. It seems to me there's many references to (spaghetti) westerns and samurai films as well. Are you a fan of these genres? What are your main influences (directors, movies) in these genres? Leone, Peckinpah, Kurosawa?

Sure. This was very intentional. Sergio Leone and Akira Kurosawa are two of my biggest influences. As we filmed the entire movie in a very spacious outdoor environment, I was allowed to pay tribute to these two directors and add my own style to the mix.

Anything to say about the cast of Roller Blade Warriors: Kathleen Kimmont (Lorenzo Lamas ex-wife... later be well known for her role as the Bride in Brian Yuzna's Bride of Re-Animator... her mother was actually in RBW as well?)

and the lovely Elizabeth Kaitan (once again my type of gal-laughs). How did you meet them?

All very nice people. I used to hang out with Kathleen a lot — which is how I met her mother, the famous Abby Dalton.

Elizabeth, again, just an actress I cast through Dramalogue. Obviously a great asset to the film.

Roller Blade Warriors was your last collaboration with Randall Frakes? Do you plan to work with him again?

Randy has remained a good friend. Though we have discussed working on projects together over the years, nothing has really happened. He is so busy writing scripts for other people and I have been so busy finding financing and making movies that we have never teamed up again. Maybe in the next life...

What lead you to work for Troma on the making of Class of Nuke'Em High 2: Subhumanoid Meltdown? Was it a good experience? What do you think of this independent company?

Mostly it was my friendship with Eric Louzil. He asked me to come and help out on the films. So, I was happy to do it.

I think Troma is a great company. Lloyd Kaufman has brought some very bizarre films into the mainstream. But, do I like these films? No, not really. They are just not the kind of films I like to make. They are too story driven. I like to make more abstract movies that allows the different members of the audience to draw their own conclusion as to what is the true meaning of the film and the storyline.

How do you met Scott Shaw and how do you come up with the idea of the Zen Filmmaking? Could you explain what exactly is the Zen Filmmaking to our French readers? In a sense Roller Blade Seven was your first Zen film, right?

Meeting Dr. Shaw was one of those strange karmic events, that was destine to change history. I was casting a movie and somebody sent me a headshot of him holding two samurai swords. To this day we don't know who it was who sent the photo: his manager, another director, or a fan. We don't even know where the person got the photo.

Since I first became a filmmaker I had been looking for a Caucasian guy who actually knew how to use the Samurai Sword. Scott had spent a lot of years in Asia. So, when I saw the photo, I was very intrigued. The guy who was helping me cast the movie, looked at Scott's photo and said, "You can't call him, he'll get all the girls." I called him anyway. I met Scott that afternoon at the Gower Gulch in Hollywood, where all of the old Cowboy actors used to hang out. I climbed into his 1964 Porsche, along with two of my actresses, and we have been friends ever since.

Zen Filmmaking came about due to the meeting of the minds of Scott and myself. Scott came up with the title and I had the years of low-budget experience. The basis of Zen Filmmaking is "Spontaneous Creativity." We don't use scripts because this would limit the instantaneous nature of Zen Filmmaking. This does not mean it is improve. It is not! What occurs is that we study our cast and location like an empty canvas that we want to create a painting upon. We sense the energy and then move forward guiding the actors to say the right things and do the right actions — which ultimately construct a form of cinematic art.

I think that most filmmakers could not do what Scott and I do. They need structure, which is why they rely upon scripts. But, at our heart, we are both spiritual artists. This is why we have worked so well together and have created a few great movies. I really see us as spiritual brothers — when we work together it is like we have one-mind.

Roller Blade Seven was much an art film — kind of experimental in a way (any references in this domain?) —

than the usual B movie. Do you think that the audience that enjoyed your previous movies misunderstood this one, that the public "slept" on its artistic values? Which was the audience's reception of this film in the United States and in Europe?

I have found that people who enjoy art films, vivid cinematography, and intense editing really like it. Those who want to be negative and judgmental can find all kinds of things to criticize. But, that is only because they really don't get it.

I mean, Scott and I spent a long time filming that movie at a lot of very beautiful and spectacular locations. We used the dam from Escape from New York, the Observatory used in Terminator, and tons of very beautiful desert location in California and Mexico. We also invented a new type of cinematography, in association with this film, known as, "The Roller-cam." This is where we had a masterful skater film many scenes while skating around the actors using my Bolex. This gives the film a very spiritual sense of nonstop movement.

The problem is, people want to criticize movies. They all want to claim that they can make a better movie. Well, I say, "Let's see it." I would like to see anybody do a film with as many spectacular locations and with as many interesting camera movements as Roller Blade Seven. Particular with the very limited budget which we had to make the movie. Only about $30,000.00. And, this film was shot on 16 mm.

Most people never know how hard it is to make a full length feature film. So, I say, "Stop complaining. Get off your butt, and let's see what you can do. Then, you can talk."

The main thing to remember about Roller Blade Seven is that we intentionally created an art film. Just like Dr. Shaw always says, "Some people love Picasso, some people hate his work but you can't say it isn't art." This is the same with The Roller Blade Seven — you can love it or you can hate, but you can not say that it is not art.

Can you tell us about the great cast of Roller Blade Seven? Karen Black (the homage to her role in Easy Rider is very smart), William Smith (excellent as always), Don Stroud (very funny role! was it his own idea?), Frank Stallone (difficult actor?), Joe Estevez, Rhonda Shear...

When we first began pre-production on The Roller Blade Seven, the Executive Producer, Tanya York, said we needed two "Name" talents in the film. We agreed upon Don Stroud and William Smith. As time when on, she kept wanting us to add more and more "Name" talent. So, this is why the cast continued to grow. All of them were great. We met Joe (Estevez) through this process and he has remained a close friend that both Scott and I have used in several films. William Smith is, of course, a good friend. Karen is great. Don was excellent. And Frank, well Frank was Frank...

Regarding the character development. We just spoke with each of them before filming. Karen we told that we wanted to do a tribute to Easy Rider and, as you can see, she was great. She wanted some ideas for dialogue, so we gave her two of Scott's books: Essence and Time, which were made up of spiritual aphorisms, and she just choose her dialogue from them.

With Bill, I wanted to do something different, something he had never done before. So, we put his character in a wheelchair — claiming the character was hurt in a skate boarding accident. I think it worked great. I mean, we took one of Hollywood's badest, bad guys and had him do something he had never done before — act from a wheelchair. I think he made the character of Pharaoh, great. It couldn't have been played any better.

Don, we just let him run with character. He wanted to pay his bongos in the film. So, we went out to the California High Desert, and we moved forward from there.

We needed a diabolical character in the film, so we

gave Joe Estevez, (Martin Sheen's brother), the name, Saint Offender. He was great — he also choose most of his dialogue from the same two books, written by Dr. Shaw.

Frank, was a last minute addition. I am sure he expected a big cast and crew when he showed up on the set — as he was the brother of Sly. But, the only crew was Scott, myself, and later a Camera Assistant.

Though it wasn't really intentional, I think we really messed with him when he arrived and we gave him this rubber Knight suit to wear. You could see the expression in his face. He was embarrassed. But, ultimately it looked okay on film and that was all that mattered.

You know, he really wasn't a bad guy. He obviously had an ego because of who his brother is, but he did his lines, we paid him his money, and he went home. We never heard from him again.

There's also two well known actresses from the adult scene: Jill Kelly and Jade East. Can you talk about them?
This was Jill Kelly's first film. She was a friend of one of my friends, who is now known as Tiffany Million. Tiffany, Jill, Scott, and I met one day in Burbank. Went out to a Mexican food restaurant and got drunk on margaritas. We all just clicked. Jill wanted to be an actress, so the next day she was in the film. The rest of her acting career is history.

Jade East was a friend of Robert Z'Dar. He suggested her for the film as she wanted to do some non-porno roles. At the time Scott and I put her in the film, we didn't even know she was porn star. But, she was very nice and we were happy to have her on the set.

Is it true that Traci Lords, David Carradine and Eric Estrada were supposed to be in this film? In what roles? And why they couldn't be in the film?
Scott and I often discuss how it was a great loss to

not have had Traci in the film. She would have really given the film the extra boost that it needed to get it more out into the mainstream. Traci and Scott became very close during the period when Scott was teaching her how to use the samurai sword for her role in this film. Traci is a very nice person and was set to do the film. The Executive Producer, Tanya York, wanted her to sign contact that she could use the footage we filmed for RB7 any place, any time, in any movie. Traci wouldn't sign it. Smart girl. So, we lost her.

Eric was going to play the Great Celestial Mechanic in the film. Scott and I went up to his house to discuss his role. All he could say was, "I don't give a fuck about my career. All I care about is the money." Sadly, money is what kept him from the movie. He wanted $10,000.00 to do the film. And, Tanya would only offer him $9,000.00. This was just to mess him with. So, he didn't do the film.

Scott was the one who courted David Carradine. I think he had worked with him a couple of times before. But, he was just about to start filming the T.V. Series, Kung Fu: The Legend Continues and it was the contract, (the same one that Traci wouldn't sign) that kept him away, as well.

How did the actors of Roller Blade Seven reacted to the fact there was no script for the movie. Did they understood and get along well with the concept of Zen Filmmaking without making problems?

Most were just great. I mean the real actors in the film — the one's who actually spoke, were all very talented and experienced actors. So, they had no problem not using a script. Whenever someone wanted some dialogue to memorize we would give them the two books by Scott that I mentioned. These books were made up of Spiritual Aphorism. So, this really kept the film focused on the spiritual essence of life — which is really what I wanted. In fact, near the end of the film when my character, Father Donaldo performs the wedding ceremony for Hawk (Scott

Shaw) and Stella Speed, I read the introduction from Scott's book Time. So, it was really a lot of fun using those two books as a guideline.

Scott Shaw is very talented in martial arts and sword fighting but he did not seem to be at ease on rollers. In certain plans where his feet are not seen, one would say that it simulates roller skating...

That was one of the jokes of the film — that Scott, Hawk as he was known in the film, really hated to skate. If you remember one scene, his character keeps falling down off of his rollerblade and he says, "I can't believe she made me wear these skates."

Roller Blade Seven is full of amazing and eccentric characters: Kabuki (was her look was inspired by the gang of the "Baseball Furies" in Walter Hill's The Warriors?) the Banjo Man, Fukasai Ninja (nice armor, who designed it?), the Black Knight, Madison Monk. Can you tell us more about these characters (who got the idea, what was the inspiration)?

The way these character developed is the essence of Zen Filmmaking. We never had any plans for any of these character. In fact, just the opposite. We asked the girl who played Kubaki to come up with a custom idea and she showed up on the set like that. I mean, how magical is that? And, no, though I love many of Walter Hills' films, RB7 was not inspired by The Warriors. The other character happened the same way. We gave the people a little guidance and they did the rest.

The costume for the character Fukasai Ninja was just something our art director, Mark Richardson had lying around. He tuned it up a little bit to better fit the movie — so an actor could roller skate in it. And, bam, the character became a big part of the film.

Do you enjoyed playing the role of Reverend Donaldo in this film and his sequel?

Sure, it was fun. And, that's why I did it — to have fun and have some fun with a character. Like Scott and I always say, "Fun is what it is all about."

Return of the Roller Blade Seven was shot back to back with Roller Blade Seven? What was your relation with the producer of the two films? What exactly is Legend of the Roller Blade Seven?

I really don't want to talk about Legend of the Roller Blade Seven. The Executive Producer, Tanya York, broke all of the contracts with Dr. Shaw and myself and reedited Roller Blade Seven and Return of the Roller Blade Seven making it one very bad movie. If you see the original film, some of Scott's edits are magical. They set trends long before that style of flash cut and repeat cut editing ever came to MTV and Music Videos. And, this was the first movie he ever edited. He had never edited before! But, he just somehow understood how to make movie magic! Tanya came along and decided that the two movies were too weird. So, she wanted to make them more normal. All she did was take the two films and have some moron reedit them into one feature and totally destroy our vision.

The funny story about Tanya is that I was one of the people who helped her break into the film industry. I had hired her as a Make-up Artist (I used to call her a Cake-up artist) on Roller Blade Warriors. One day I got really mad at her and was about to fire her. But, I didn't. Keep in mind, she was only about sixteen years old at that point in time. So, by the time she was the Executive Producer of Frogtown II and Roller Blade Seven, she was only about twenty years old. What happened is that after I finished Roller Blade Warriors, I introduced her to David Heavener. She went on to help him produce Twisted Justice. Then she wanted to make her own films. I suggest she put an ad in the newspaper looking for investors. She found a millionaire who was interested. So, due to my long credibility in the Independent Film Market, I went with her to the initial meetings. And, it was my reputation and track record which convinced the man to invest in her films. So, it was very unfortunate when she screwed me over more than once regarding my film projects. She has also screwed over a lot of other people. Today, she is one of the most successful independent producer and distributors in Hollywood. So, that tells you something about karma. What, I don't know.

In retrospect, are you fully satisfied by these two films and by your films in general?

Scott and I believe that we have made two masterpieces as a team: Roller Blade Seven and Guns of El Chupacabra. So, am I happy with Roller Blade Seven and Return of the Roller Blade Seven — absolutely! Could we have done more if we had more money? Of course, that is always the case. But, I believe these films will stand the test of time.

Frogtown 2 is a very funny sequel to the original movie. Is it really Tanya York of York Entertainment who co-wrote the story of this film (is it the same person who gave you troubles with Roller Blade Seven and Return of the Roller Blade Seven?

Tanya York never wrote anything. As she was the source of financing for the film, she wanted screenwriter credit and took it. The truth is, once financing was in place, I went home and wrote the entire script for Frogtown 2 in eleven hours.

What was the budget of Frogtown 2 compared to the original film? Did you have to face problems you didn't encounter on the making of the first film?

The budget for Frogtown 2 was $180.000,00.

Whenever you work for somebody else there is problems. One of the people who worked for Tanya on this film really wanted to be the Director. As it was my idea, he couldn't do that. But, he tried in every way to get me fired. When he couldn't make that happen, he just made the cast and the crew miserable. He had no sense of camera work or of timing. So, he would throw impossible demands at the cast, the crew, and at me. It was really a miserable time shooting that film. But, I believe that it turned out Okay.

The only problem that I had when I watched this sequel is that the two protagonists (Spangle and Sam Hell) seem to be perfect strangers. Why are some of the background elements of the first film wiped out?

Most of that was caused by the tension that the previously mentioned person brought to the set. This film was Dennis Duff's first movie and I am sure she felt the pressure more than most of the seasoned veterans. That may have caused some of that lack of chemistry. But, she was very nice and Z-Man, as I call him (Robert Z'Dar) has long been, and still remains, a close friend.

Like I stated in regard to the Roller Blade series, it was just time to move the story forward and create some new elements. And, that is what I did.

Frogtown 2 is mild compared to the original, there's not much sexual elements as in the first film, why? Does the PG13 rating was imposed to you?

Sexuality is really not my first focus in filmmaking. If it works, it works. But, the reason there is much more sexuality in the first Frogtown is that Randy Frakes was the primary screenwriter. And, sexuality is his style. He wrote the rape scene into Roller Blade Warriors and I was totally against that. I just don't like that kind of stuff. But, that is the problem when you work with scripts, you are locked into what the production company and the actors expect is going to happen.

Does your inspiration for the "Texas Rocket Rangers" come from the old Republic serials (like Commando Cody)? What is your favorite serial (of the rocket men saga)? Are you familiar with the Dave Stevens comic: Rocketeer? And what do you think of the movie adaptation?

Absolutely! In fact, in Guns of El Chupacabra we introduce a character, Rocket Ranger Dan Danger into the film, played by Joe Estevez. This character is a direct throw back to television shows of my childhood when a commentator would come on and give you a play-by-play scenario of what was taking place.

Regarding Rocketeer: I have meet Dave Stevens and know about his Rocketeer. But, I was never a really big fan. To me, the character just seemed redundant to many of the comic book characters from the 1950's.

Can you tell us about the cast of the movie: Charles Napier, Robert Z'Dar, Denise Duff, Don Stroud, Brion James, Lou Ferigno (what was his reaction when you told him he had to paint his face green for the most part of the role? — laughs)...

There was a lot of people being considered for the film. Lorenzo Lamas and Katheline Kinmont wanted to do it. But, Tanya said, "No." She was very sorry when Lorenzo did his very successful television series Renegade a year or so later.

I was for Z'Dar, as the lead, all along. I mean, with his jaw he looks like such a super hero. In fact, I really wanted him to play the film like Dudley Do Right, the comic book and cartoon character, who is a Canadian Mountie. I though if he spoke like that, it would be so funny. But, ultimately that idea didn't happen. Once Z'Dar was locked in, then I wanted Dennis as she also had the big jaw. The same with Napier. I wanted the movie to be a battle of the jaws... (Laughs).

Brion James came on board and he did the character better than I could ever have hoped for. I told him, he could move the dialogue wherever he wanted — say what ever he wanted to say. But, he wanted to stick to the script. So, he said the word that I wrote.

Lou was brought on board, due to his obvious association with the Hulk. So, he was used to being painted green. (Smiles). Lou was a very nice person to work with.

Tell us about Toad Warriors. Why has it been edited into a 30 minutes feature called Max Hell Comes to Frogtown ? Will it be possible to see the 90 minutes cut of Toad Warriors in the future? Do you really consider making a Frogtown TV series? Does some networks are already interested in this project?

The unfortunate reality of filmmaking is that distributors want 90-minute movies for distribution. So, a lot of times, in the world of Independent filmmaking, you have to put a lot of filler in a movie to make it long enough.

Scott and I made Toad Warrior as not so much a sequel to Hell Comes to Frogtown but a project that drew from its influences and could stand on its own merits. When we got to editing it, we found that there were some great scenes in the films, but a lot of footage we really didn't like. But, due to the fact that the distributor wanted a 90-minute film, we had to leave a lot of the footage in that we really did not want to. This is not to say that it is a bad movie. It is just longer than we felt was actually necessary.

The full-length version was released in Malaysia, Indonesia, The Philippines, and Japan.

Earlier this year, Scott took the incentive and did something we had been talking about for a long time — editing the film down to just the scenes and storyline that we felt were the best. Thus, Max Hell Comes to Frogtown was born. It is about 30 minutes in length.

We call this a Zen Speedflick — taking the essence of a full-length film and breaking it down to its most essential elements.

When Scott reedited the film, he didn't even go back to the original source material. He just took what was already edited, cut it down, and made it a 30 minute movie — which we both feel is a far better version. The story gets told, with none of the unnecessary footage.

Regarding the ongoing nature of Frogtown: There has been a lot of talk over the years about making it a T.V. Series, a cartoon, or a comic book. One of the biggest problems with Hollywood is that there is always a lot of talk. So, nothing has happened yet.

On some of your recent films you used the pseudonym of Maximo T. Bird. Why and where this pseudonym come from?

I use that when I don't want to take credit for certain of my films because they are so bad or the investors wants their money back. (Laughs).

No, not really. It is just my alter ego. Just a fun name...

Was the goal of making cute films such as Little Lost Sea Serpent, Baby Ghost and Rollergator to touch a family audience?

At the time I made these films, I was financed by a company who wanted Children's films. So, what I did, was give them the Donald G. Jackson version of a Children's film — weird. These films were all script based. I would come up with the story and they were written by Mark Williams. I believe they all stand on their own as interesting little pieces of art. They are not necessarily my favorite pieces of work from my library. But, none-the-less, they are out there for the world to see.

You shot in many formats, which one do you prefer?

Right now, I love DV. I mean when I stated out, everything was so expensive. Even 8 mm! You had to buy the film, develop it, and then try to edit it together. If you scratched or messed up the negative, or if you needed another shot, it was so expensive to go out and get it. And, the price went up with each step: Super 8, 16 mm, 35 mm. I even shot in IMAX for a while. But, with DV, you are so free. You can do anything. You need another shot, you can just go out and get. You can bring it in to your computer and put it anywhere in the movie you want it.

If this format were around, even ten years ago, I would have been a rich man. Because, for my entire adult life, I have spend all of my money on making movies. And, this has cost me a lot. Even though I was one of the first people to shot movies on video — it was still expensive in the early days. You still had to transfer it to VHS or SVHS with time code to edit, and then output it to Beta. But, now that has all change. DV has changed filmmaking forever. I don't even believe there is a reason to shoot on anything else.

Can you talk about your collaboration with Julie Strain and Kevin Eastman? How did you met them?
I first met Julie back in 1986. She auditioned for Frogtown. Then, I met her again when she audition for Frogtown 2. I first worked with her on a film that was never released, called, Queen of Lost Island. And, we have remained friends ever since.

Kevin, I met through Julie — as they are married. But actually, my relationship with Kevin goes back many years. He created the Teenage Mutant Ninja Turtles. When I was doing Frogtown, I wrote him a letter and he answered. I still have the letter.

Like Julie, Kevin is a very nice and very creative person. We even got him to begin acting in films. He has a great role in Guns of El Chupacabra.

Scott and I did several Zen Films with the two of

them — some of which have not yet been released. So, there is still a backlog of our work that the world will hopefully see someday.

Can you tell us about the amazing Guns of el Chupacabra? What led you to the idea of using this creature from the recent Mexican folklore?
Dr. Shaw and I were interviewed on a National T.V. show while we were shooting Guns of El Chupacabra, we told them a tall-tale about how we were driving in Mexico scouting locations for a movie and we actually had an encounter with a Chupacabra. But, as discussed, sometimes in Hollywood the truth gets a little stretched. But in actuality, I was surfing the internet one day, and saw an article on the Chupacabra and it just hit me — I need to make a movie about this creature. I called up Scott. And, the rest is Zen Filmmaking history.

Guns of El Chupacabra is another of your Zen film made in collaboration with Scott Shaw. It's very subversive, funny and disorienting even if it starts like an usual B movie. What was your point with this film?
The point was to present, as in all the other films Scott and I have created, that good overcomes evil. That the world is a spiritual place. Certainly, we have fun in presenting these facts in an abstract manner. But, if you read between the lines, and look to the true essence of the film, it is easy to see what we are attempting to say. Be good, be spiritual, be happy, have some fun, and you will be victorious and some good things will come to you.

In your career you directed straight B movies (like Hell comes to Frogtown, Roller Blade Warriors) and more experimental films referring from your Zen philosophy (like Roller Blade Seven and Guns of el Chupacabra). What kind of movies do you prefer or feel more conformable with? Do you consider yourself much as an independent B moviemaker or an experimental artist?

I am an artist first and foremost. Which is why I am probably not rich. Had I wanted to go the traditional route, I probably could have been rich. But, it was just not in me.

Like I always say, "If I wanted to make money I would never have gotten into the film business. I would have opened a hamburger stand." (Laughs).

Do you plan to make other Zen films in the future?

No, probably not. Scott has continued to make Zen Films. Dr. Shaw really is the essence of Zen Filmmaking. He has really taken the art form to the next level. He has shot all of his recent Zen Films in both the U.S. and Asia and they are really great. Me, I have been focusing mostly upon making documentaries for the past few years.

From your experience and point of view as an independent filmmaker what is your opinion on the recent movies and the current movie industry (on both sides, independent and major studios)?

Most independent films have just gotten boring. Most of them are doing nothing new. They are just presenting the same story we have seen a million times before. The problem is, most indie filmmakers think they have created gold — when they have just shot the same movie that was made better twenty or thrifty years ago. On the other hand, some of the Lars von Trier stuff is really cutting edge. He has taken a style, based in Dogme 98, and continued to move it forward. I think Time Code, by Mike Figgis was a masterpiece. How the hell did he do that!

So, there is still some very creative, cutting edge stuff being made. Some of the big films are Okay. I mean with big budget you have so many more options. Some of the Michael Bay stuff is great. You can sit there and count and every five seconds there is a cut and a new angle is revealed. Actors like Vin Diesel in Triple XXX are a lot of fun.

What kind of movie would you do if a major studio would give you a big budget?

The same things I have done in the past. I would just go out there and make a very big Don Jackson movie on a very big scale

Are you connected with filmmakers of the current independent and B movie scene?

As mentioned, I am friends with people like Fred Ray, Randy Frakes and, of course, Scott Shaw. But, for the most part, Indie Filmmakers are too full of themselves. They bore me with all of their self-involved nonsense. So, though I know a few filmmakers, who I consider friends, I try to stay away from most of them. They have nothing to offer me, and I have nothing to offer them.

What would you say, what kind of warnings or advices would you give to a young independent filmmaker?

Do what you love. Don't make a movie just because the subject matter is popular. Go out and make a film that you have a passion about. Even if the film is not received well, you will still be able to be proud of it and you will have begun to define yourself as a filmmaker, with a specific style and point of view.

Music always had a big place in your life. Do you still host a country music radio show?

I did that up until just recently. Sadly, the FCC (Federal Communication Commission) came in a shut down the radio station. They said what we were broadcasting was too subversive. Not my show, anyway... But, I guess some of the other DJ's were saying some pretty provocative things.

What are you working on right now?

Well, right now I am in the hospitable and I am fighting for my life against Leukemia. So, this will probably be the last interview I will ever give.

The project I was about to begin working on was a documentary about the folk music of the 1960s. But, I guess I will have to pass than on to the hands of somebody else.

What are your projects? Do you plan to make follow-ups to the Roller Blade and Frogtown saga? Does your project called Wheelzone Rangers is connected with the Roller Blade saga? What is Horny Toads? Is it a serious project or only a joke?

Horny Toads was a joke. Dr. Shaw and I toyed around with doing it — make a very serious movie about a very dumb subject — just to mess with the audience. But, we let that idea go. Wheelzone Rangers was a sequel to Roller Blade Seven that Scott and I came up with in '94. So, if Scott wants to pick up where we left off in Return of the Roller Blade Seven, he has my blessings. Scott tends to make a different type of film than this, however. You know, the student becoming the master and all that. So, I don't know if he will ever move forward with the concept. But, I have assigned all rights to him. So, you never know...

Where can your fans find and order your movies, especially the more obscure ones?

Well, there is basically two places: my website: zendance.com — which, I don't know how long it will be up if I move onto the next world. And, Dr. Shaw's website: www.scottshaw.com. As he is the chosen keeper of the library and legacy of Donald G. Jackson, and I have assigned all the rights to all of my films and tapes, both edited and not, to him, he is probably the best long-term source for the works of Donald G. Jackson.

One last world for the French reader of Trash Times...
Get out there and "Do it!" That is what life is all about.

Max Hell Frog Warrior: The Facts and the Fiction

James Kim

Max Hell Frog Warrior holds a unique place in cult film history. It is both loved and hated, revered and shunned, praised and harshly criticized. There have been reviews, critiques, analysis and evaluations. It has been shown in movie theaters in Japan, the Philippines, and Malaysia, it has played at film festival in the U.S., the U.K., Russia, Ukraine, and Australia. There have been countless showings of the movie in screening rooms and at makeshift backyard and bar film events. It has been bootlegged and released via a stolen Beta Master. It has been illegally downloaded thousands of times from offshore websites. There have been articles written about the film. It has been referenced in numerous books and publications. It was even mentioned on the HBO television series The Newsroom. There has been gossip, misnomers and lies told about the film, the filmmakers and the filmmaking process used in the film's creation. The one thing that no one has done in the twenty years since this film was created is to talk to the last remaining filmmaker of Max Hell Frog Warrior, Scott Shaw about what truly happened during the creation of this movie.

Max Hell Frog Warrior was initially released in its original edit form as Toad Warrior. It was later reedited, retitled and rereleased. The focus of this interview will be to hopefully remove some of the speculation and misconceptions about this film and get to the bottom of what actually took place throughout the entire creation of this movie. I hope to present the truth and remove the fiction from the facts about Max Hell Frog Warrior.

Nice to meet you Dr. Shaw.
Great to meet you and please call me Scott. I'm not a formal sort of guy.

Okay Scott. You know why I'm here. I want to talk to you about Max Hell Frog Warrior.
Finally.

That's what I think too. Why has nobody ever interviewed you about this film?
Truthfully I don't know. Everybody asks me about The Roller Blade Seven, Guns of El Chupacabra, Undercover X, Vampire Blvd., Killer Dead or Alive, Vampire Noir, the Rock n' Roll Cops and movies like that. I know people talk about this movie a lot but no one ever asks me anything.

I have seen a lot of things written about Max Hell Frog Warrior on the web. Have you seen any of that?
Yeah, I've seen some. I'm really not one of those people who wastes my time on the internet seeking out that kind of stuff. I'm really too busy. I'm all about creating new things, not about reading what someone thinks about stuff I've created in the past. But some of the stuff has been brought to my attention.

Is it correct?
Mostly what I've seen out there are a lot of people's opinions. As they are people's opinions, I guess from that point of view they are true. But nobody has asked me. Nobody asked Don. All people do is see the movie, think they know what's going on and talk about it. From that point of view nobody understands anything about what really took place in

the creation of this film and this has been going on for a very long time. I mean we finished Toad Warrior in 1996. That's twenty years ago. Before it was ever released I sent a screening copy of it to a friend of mine who ran a magazine and he gave it to one of his reviewers. The guy wrote a review and tore the movie apart saying that we were trying to make a copy of Hell Comes to Frogtown. The guy was so stupid that he said we were using cheap imitation Frogtown masks. But those were the same masks actually used in Hell Comes to Frogtown! He tore up the directing making a bunch of insulting comments. The guy didn't even know that Maximo T. Bird was Donald G. Jackson, the creator of Hell Comes to Frogtown. How stupid is that?

Did that review bother you?
     No. It made me laugh. It really pissed Don off though. I mean the guy did compare me to a low budget Kurt Russell. So that made me smile. The thing is I don't really care about reviews. Love it, hate it, that's your choice. The thing I don't like is when someone presents their opinion as fact when their fact is wrong.

Has that happened a lot with this film?
     Oh yeah. On the internet people can say anything they want. True or false they don't even care. The sad thing is people have come to believe that people's opinions are the truth and just because somebody is saying something it must be true. I think that's really sad. Before you believe anything, find out the facts.

Yes, I agree with you. Do you think bad reviews have hurt Max Hell Frog Warrior?

I don't know about that. In some cases, I think people watch a film like Max Hell Frog Warrior because of the bad reviews.

Why do you think some reviewers attack a film like Max Hell Frog Warrior?

Who knows? People do what they do for any number of personal reasons. What I do think is that before anybody becomes a film reviewer they should get out there and actually create their own film, which takes a lot of time and energy. Then they should go through the process to find distribution for it and see how they feel when people tear it apart. Talking about a film is easy, creating one is very hard. If someone has never actually made a movie they have no idea about what is involved so they shouldn't be saying anything unless they have walked down that road. Moreover, I believe that you have to look at a person's motivation for reviewing anything at all. You have to ask why are they doing it? In the case of reviewing films on the internet it is usually that they are trying to make a name for themselves without actually doing anything. My opinion is everybody has an opinion but your opinion only matters if it adds to the greater good. Telling people your opinion means nothing unless it makes everything better. Negativity only equals negativity, just as positivity only equals positivity.

That's deep.

Not really. It's just common sense.

Let's get to the inception of the movie.

Let's go.

Why did you decide to make this movie?
That was actually kind of a long process. I hadn't seen Don for a few years after we finished Roller Blade Seven. I got pretty screwed over during the making of that film. In fact, the very first thing Don said to me when he got into my car when I drove him to the hospitable shortly before he died was, I'm really sorry about what happened to you with Roller Blade Seven.

If I can interrupt. What happened?
It was basically a financial thing. Don got paid a lot. I got paid zero for all of my time and involvement with that film and in many ways I did way more than Don.

If I can interrupt again?
Sure. This is your show.

I understand your books gave words to the dialogue and you did the acting, editing and the music.
Yes. All that and a lot more.

What actually happened?
Well, the executive producer totally cheated me, broke our contracts, reedited the film for U.S. release, pulled my screen credits, and the list goes on. But Don continued to work with her and get financed by her after we finished Roller Blade Seven. So it was basically a backstabbing sort of thing. I walked away from that film beyond broke after not getting paid of months. Someday I'm going to write a book about the Roller Blade Seven and I'll tell the whole story as so many things took place during the filming of that movie both good and bad.

That's nice he apologized. It must have been on his mind for all those years.

Yeah, I guess. But by then I was so over it. Had he apologized ten years earlier it probably would have mattered more to me but by that point it didn't really mean anything anymore.

So what brought you two back together?

Don called me out of nowhere. He had continued to make films. I had continued to make films. The thing was I had pretty much given up on acting and I didn't want to do it anymore. My plan was to get fat and just produce and direct movies.

Get fat. That's a strange desire.

Yeah, I guess it is. For me it was just a way to put out to the world the new and different space I was living in. I wanted to be seen differently.

What happened when Don called you?

We set up a meet and he immediately threw out to me that he wanted to make another film with me as the star. I gave in.

Why do you think Don called you out of the blue?

I don't realize it then but I think what it was is that he found out he only had a few more years to live as he was dying from leukemia. He remembered how well we worked together and that I was one of those people who gets things done. I think he wanted to leave a legacy and without someone like me that wasn't going to happen.

Why?

Don was one of those guys who had a million great ideas but he couldn't get things done. He would start something and never finish it. He had to pay a lot of people big money or all his projects would just fall away. The fact is, that's why so many more of his films were released after he died than while he was alive. When he was on his death bed he finally gave me all of the footage and I completed the films for him. The truth be told without me all of Don's films and his legacy would have been lost.

How did you two come up with Max Hell Frog Warrior?

That's a complicated and long story. It really took us quite a while. Once we decided to work together again we toyed with several ideas. The main focus was we hoped to rekindle what we had achieved with Roller Blade Seven because by that point in time that film was already a big cult hit in Europe. We were getting fan letters and later emails all the time. There were several ideas we played around with but we finally decided upon a film called Hell Comes to Hog Town.

What was the story?

Basically I was going to ride in on my Harley with an electric guitar over my shoulder and do battle with the bad guy who was referred to as The Hog. There was going to be a lot of music, me playing guitar, fighting, etc.

Why did you change your minds?

We realized that it was just going to be too hard to do. Too Big. We wanted motorcycle gangs, bands to be playing in an old western town and stuff like that. All that would cost a lot of money. A lot of money we didn't have.

It was budget that had you make a smaller film?
Yeah, I guess you can say that.

So what caused you to focus on Frogtown?
Don never liked the previous two Frogtown films he made. His creative control had been taken away from him on both of them. One day it was like an epiphany we just decided to make Frogtown the way we made Roller Blade Seven, no script, just go out and do what we do. Keep the whole process really simply and really pure.

Once you decided on the film you were going to make how did you cast it?
We had our offices in North Hollywood. We put out casting notices and did all that traditional nonsense. We found a few good people. We also knew we wanted to work with Joe Estevez and Jill Kelly. Don brought in a couple of girls he had worked with previously and I brought in Roger Ellis who had been in Roller Blade Seven but I had used him in much bigger roles in Samurai Vampire Bikers from Hell and Samurai Johnny Frankenstein. I wanted my friend Ken Kim to be in the film as well. He was also in RB7 and we had made a couple of films together since then but he came in one day right before we started shooting and remembered how much he hated Don and walked out.

Why did he hate Don?
Don rubbed a lot of people the wrong way. He really messed with people. He made a lot of enemies. Basically he was a complete asshole unless he liked you, feared you or wanted something from you. A total power tripper.

Which one of those were you?
   guess a little of all three.

It sounds like you two had a crazy relationship.
   To put it mildly.

Did you pay your actors?
   Oh sure. Joe and Jill were professionals so they had their established day rates. The rest of the cast varied but the average was about $100.00 per day plus food and gas and that kind of stuff.

Did you get paid this time?
   Oh yeah. I had learned by lesson.

When you started filming did you have a script?
   Nope.

Did you have any idea what you were going to do when you started shooting?
   Not really. We just knew that we were going to start the shoot and lay the foundations for the film at our offices. We had the whole second floor of a building so we put together some makeshift sets.

How do you work? I have read a lot about Zen Filmmaking but can you tell me about the process?
   The main thing to know is to never hold yourself to a preconceived notion. Just let it flow. If you have an idea, great. If you have no idea, great. Just do it. Get it done. Start out, get the cast doing what they are doing and let whatever happens be captured on film.

That is really mindboggling. How you make movies with no idea about what you are going to do?

Is it mindboggling? Think about this, how many bad movies have you seen? I'm not just talking low budget, I'm talking high budget as well. Everyone of those movies had an idea. The filmmakers knew what they wanted, had a script and tried to get what they had in their mind on film. Maybe they tried and tried again. You hear stories of people shooting thousands of feet of footage just to get one scene the way they want it. I remember Dennis Hopper talking about working with Francis Ford Coppola on Apocalypse Now. He said Coppola shot as much footage trying to get the first scene with Hopper as Hopper had used in making the entire film Easy Rider. Apocalypse Now is a great film but do you need to go to that extreme? I don't think so. Yes, you can make each scene as good as you can make it. But it is only going to be as good as it is going to be. Free yourself and art takes hold and the magic takes over.

What do you mean by magic?
For example, in the opening scene of Max Hell where my character flies in on an ultralight, we had no idea we were going to do that. We just drove out to the El Mirage Dry Lake Bed with our cast and crew planning to film. When we got there we saw this couple with their ultralights and we asked them if we could use them. They said yes and the rest is history. That ultralight scene really added a big beginning to the film and we had no idea that we were going to do that.

That is magic.
Yes it is. That's Zen Filmmaking.

What was your crew like?

There was Don and me. He shot most of the film, I shot some of it and we had another great cameraman Jonathan Quade. We had a few production assistants and that was pretty much it.

What kind of equipment did you use?
We started out filming with a Canon L1. That's a Hi8 camera. The DV revolution hit right about the time we were making the movie so we bought a Sony VX1000. Our mic was a Sennheiser ME66. In terms of lighting that's kind of an interesting story. On the first day of the shoot I went to my storage unit to pick up my lights. When I got there I found that someone had cut a hole through the wall of the storage unit next to mine and had stolen all of my lights, my c-stands, my extension cords and a bunch of my amps and guitar equipment. So we ended up shooting most of the movie with available light. We did have two very low end Smith Victor photofloods that Don owned and a couple of his minicool lights for the outdoor night shots.

That was it?
That was it.

That's impressive what you captured with that limited amount of equipment.
You gotta know what you're doing, then the doing is easy.

In terms of actors, with no script how did you do the character development for the movie?
It's really very simply, we let people be who they are. If they have an idea for a character that will play into the film, we use it. Most newbie actors need more guidance so we give it to them. We had a bunch

of wardrobe so if someone needed something, we suited them up.

Was there a reason that you didn't have the people who played the frogs fully covered in frog costumes? You can see their hands in some of the scenes.

That's funny you say that. Fred Olin Ray said the exact same thing when he saw the film. It was just one of those things, we did what we did. Suspension of belief that's what going to the movies is all about, isn't it? Let the audience slip into the realms of the abstract. In a movie like Max Hell Frog Warrior why do the frogs need to be completely frogged out anyway?

I know everybody asks you this but when you have no script how do your actors know what to say?

As the years have gone on I now only work with people who are great at improv. but back then if someone didn't know what to say Don or I would feed them their lines. They would say it and we would shoot it a few times until they got it right and we felt the camera captured the scene correctly and that was that.

Did you tell Joe Estevez what to say?

Not really. Joe's a great talker. He's a great improvisational actor. You just give him a little direction and he runs with it. Same with Roger Ellis. Another great talker.

With no script did you know where you were going to shoot?

Yeah, of course. We wanted to reference some of the locations we used in Roller Blade Seven plus add a lot of new locations we had discovered. When we were planning to shoot exteriors we always had a destination in mine but sometimes we would find new places en route.

How did you come up with your character Max Hell?

Don and I had talked about it and we really wanted to bring back some of the essence from Roller Blade Seven. I still had the rollerblade elbow and knee pads from RB7. I had a black suit and a sword. My character was born.

If you wanted to reference Roller Blade Seven, why wasn't Donald G. Jackson in the film?

He didn't want to be.

How many days did it take you to film the whole movie?

It actually went on for a few months. We would meet at our offices everyday around 11:00 AM and do what needed to be done. We continued to do casting sessions, we had lunch, drank beers with our friends, went to other people's sets, hung out with other filmmakers, scouted locations, and went out to music clubs at night. We filmed when we felt like filming.

So you were not like a formal movie production team?

Yes and no. The number one rule of Zen Filmmaking is that fun is what it's all about. So our main focus was fun while make a movie in the process. The thing to understand is the minute Don and I started working together again it wasn't just about Max Hell Frog Warrior. Though that was the first movie on the schedule we immediately began to make several more films as well. Hand in hand with Max Hell we laid the foundations for and began filming Shotgun Blvd., which later became Armageddon Blvd., Ghost Taxi and several others.

Let's go scene by scene and talk about the film.
    Let's go.

In the opening scene Jill Kelly is running from the frogs. How did that scene come about?
    It was just a thought we came up with in the moment. We got out to El Mirage very early in the morning. We did the ultralight scene and then we needed to introduce Jill's character. There has to be tension in every film so it was an obvious choice that Jill had to be chased by the frogs. We needed to set the storyline in motion so we had them take something from her, the frog serum.

During that scene is where you first introduce martial arts into the movie. Did you choreograph that?
    No, not really. That was just a spur of the moment thing. That was the thing with Don as the cinematographer, he would become so obsessed with filming certain scenes over and over again. I document his cinematographic OCD in the Zen Documentary Cinematografia Obsesion. For scenes like fight scenes he just didn't care. So there was only like two quick takes of each kick. As an editor that kind of stuff really drove me nuts. One of things that did happen when I was kicking a frog with a jumping side kick is that Jill was standing right there to be in the shot and due to the lack of any forethought my sword smacked her right in the teeth. She had just gotten her teeth caped so she was obviously a bit worried but luckily no damage was done. She was way nicer about that than she should have been.

After the frogs gets away you and Jill Kelly get into a truck and ride off. What was the inspiration for that scene?

No real inspiration. Just Zen Filmmaking. One of our people on the set had the truck. It just happened. The guy wasn't a professional actor, he just had a good look and a cool old truck. I had to feed him every line over and over again. He was so nervous he couldn't remember anything. I sat in the bed of his truck with the rear window open and told him what to say one sentence at at time. Jill was fine. She's a pro.

You had a fight scene in the back of that truck. Was that frog a stunt man?

No. He was actually a production assistant. Nice guy. All he cared about was getting paid his $100.00 cash at the end of every day and he would happily do anything. He actually was a frog in several scenes throughout the film.

After those introductory scenes you started to introduce other characters into the film. Tell me about the early Joe Estevez scenes.

We actually shot the stuff with Joe and Humphrey Bullfrog on the first day of production. Joe's a great actor. We pared him with a girl named Sandra Purpuro who played the character Cricket. Her and her boyfriend had just moved to L.A. from New York and were looking for some roles. We had cast them through Dramalogue. I think we cast them that same day. They were both very talented actors. Sandra went on to have a great career.

How did you set up the scenes on that fist day of shooting?

Totally off the cuff. We started with the Bullfrog character and then built on the storyline with Joe.

How did you come up with the name Mickey O'Malley for Joe's character?

That was totally Joe. Don actually hated that name but he didn't want to offend Joe so he just let it ride.

I too thought that was a strange name for the character. Who is the crazy guy in those scenes with Joe Estevez speaking Japanese?

He's a great guy from Japan named Tom Tom Typhoon. Whatever happened to him I have no idea. Don had met him at a casting sessions a little bit before we had started working together again and he pulled him onto the film.

Did you tell him to be that dynamic?

Oh yeah. You know he spoke some English but he didn't speak it very well so his character speaking in Japanese was the obvious choice. I communicated with him in Japanese. But he was just one of those great guy who could really take that style of insane character to the limit and really sell it. I kept telling him bigger, bigger. He went bigger.

In the progression of the film, after those initial scenes you start to introduce other characters into the movie. One of the first things I notice is that in Toad Warrior there is a scene in a laboratory with a woman talking about the fog concoction. In Max Hell Frog Warrior that scene is all but gone. Why is that?

To tell you that story I'm going to have to take you away from your scene by scene analysis a little bit. I never edited Toad Warrior. I had gone to Thailand to prepare for a documentary I was going to shoot in Cambodia. The film needed to be done so Don gave the editing to his friend named Chris Roth. Chris is a great guy and a professional editor. The thing is, both Don and I never really like the final cut of the film. It was a little too normal for our tastes. In fact, one of the documentaries I did about Don shortly before he died shows Chris in Don's office and they are talking about the editing process for the film. Don was saying that I should probably reedit the movie. Chris said if I did that it probably wouldn't make much sense. Don said that's probably better. That's the mindset Don and I came from. Though Chris did a great job of making sense out of the footage when there was no script and he also did a good job of trying to reference some of the editing elements of Roller Blade Seven in the movie but he just approached the editing from a different state of mind than Don and me. He came at it from a mindset of formula and normality. Don and I liked the abstract. To answer your question, I didn't like that scene so it was gone.

But you did edit Max Hell Frog Warrior?

Yes and no. What I did was to go back into movie take out some scenes, add a few more, and shorten or elongate others. I never actually started from scratch for the edit that became Max Hell Frog Warrior.

I have read that you plan to reedit the entire movie at some point.

Yes. That's true. The fact is over the past ten or fifteen years I have started to do that three or four times. I get maybe thirty minutes into the film and stop. Then I eventually dump it.

Why?

I don't really have an answer. There is so much great footage that wasn't used in the original edit that really should be. I need to do it but for some reason something has stopped me. Hopefully someday I'll do it.

Where did you film that laboratory scene?

That was at the home of one of our actresses. The blonde girl Elizabeth Mayer. Her character's name was Dr. Trixi T. She's a great actress and a really nice person. She also a great musician.

Though this is jumping forward a little bit there was a great scene with her and Joe Estevez where they break into a dance and do the hooky pokey.

Yeah, that's a scene I really don't like. It's just humor for humor sake. I hate that kind of stuff.

If you don't like it how did a scene like that come about?

That's the problem when you let actors step away and develop their own story ideas. I don't really let that happen on my sets anymore. I maintain story control. Back then it was different and it was Joe Estevez. We always gave him the benefit of the doubt. Who knew Elizabeth and Joe would come up with that? He was Joe so we let the cameras run and that's what we came away with.

I think I need to explain something here and this is all part and parcel with the evolution of Zen

Filmmaking. Back then we did that. We needed filmed footage as our movies had to be a minimum of 82 minutes to get international distribution. Now I don't care. I own my own distribution company and I make film art the way I see film art. A full length feature or a short film, it just is what it is. I let it become what it becomes. I just let it be perfect onto itself. Yes, my films are based on improv. But it is guided improv. As long as I like what's going on I let the actors run with it. If I don't like it then I stop the scene and readjust the flow and the direction.

Trixie T. also has a fight with another actress over your character when they are in a jail cell.

Yes. That was a scene she did with Camille Solari. Another great actress. See there's an example of how the two girls went off and created what they created all on their own and it worked great. No direction needed. So as you see, when that style of unguided improv. takes place it can go either direction. It can work or maybe it doesn't.

One of the other main charters in the film is Overload War Toad.

Yeah, that was Roger Ellis.

That is really a strange name. How did you come up with that character?

It was combination of letting an actor be who they are and then giving them just a bit of direction. We choose the name and Roger ran with it. Roger was a West Point grad who rose to the rank of Lieutenant Colonel in the Army, retired, got into the Native American movement, grew his hair long, and came to Hollywood to be an actor.

That's crazy.

Yeah it is. But that's the story I was told.

Did you give him his dialogue?

Some. But like I said before he was one of those guys who was just a great talker.

Speaking of talking. He has a female sidekick in the film who keeps trying to talk but he continues to tell her to be silent. What is that about?

That was just a little inside joke. In acting everybody wants to talk. They think that's what acting is all about. But real acting is far more than that. This was Don and my way of telling the actors to just shut up and be. I think those scenes play really well.

On the set you called the Bridge of Broken Dreams your character also keeps a girl from talking.

Yeah, same deal. That's the thing when you make a Zen Film. You can get the scene while having fun and adding a little philosophic commentary to it.

Tell me about your scenes with Conrad Brooks. He was in Plan 9 from Outer Space wasn't he?

Yeah he was. Conrad is a great guy. Love him. He's one of those guys that comes out of a different era in acting where the acting was really big. It's great. I love that style of what some would now call overacting. We tried to reference that style of acting in Roller Blade Seven.

How did you meet him and start working with him?

Conrad's career had been stagnant for many years after the passing of Ed Wood. I think it was Fred Ray who pulled him back into the game and then his career really took off. I mean he's done a million movies. I think Don met him through Fred. Conrad used to say that his comeback happened a little too late as his face had gone. Meaning he had gotten old. But at least he had a great comeback as so many people do not. He's still going strong in his 80s.

In one scene with him you had the same creature character that was in Rollergator.

That's true. Conrad was one of the stars of that movie. In fact, he played the same character that he was in Rollergator, the Swamp Farmer.

Why did you bring his character back and put it in Max Hell Frog Warrior?

It's a movie about amphibians isn't it? The truth is we wanted to do something with Conrad and it was just a natural choice.

You do an outside scene with Conrad Brooks where you encounter two frogs. They latter go off and then they transition between frogs and two pretty girls. How did you come up with that?

Kind of by accident. We wanted the frogs to do some dialogue but when they were inside the masks their dialogue was really muddy. So initially we had them take off their masks and do their dialogue so it would be clear when we mixed the soundtrack. But then all of a sudden we had the realization that we have two beautiful young girls let's have them transition between frogs and who they really were. I think it worked really well.

That's Zen Filmmaking?

That's Zen Filmmaking.

You also have some interactions with a frog on a motorcycle in a couple of scenes. How did that come about?

Actually that's two different people on two different motorcycles. The first one we shot the same day as we did the outdoor scene with Conrad. We just saw a guy ridding his motorcycle along the path we were on and we went up to him. He completely freaked out when he saw people in frog masks. We were shooting in the area of L.A. known as Frogtown. Right there by the L.A. River. There is a serious gang over there called Frogtown. He thought we were with that crew. When he found out we were just shooting a movie and when we gave him $100.00 to put on a frog mask, ride his bike, and let Max Hell talk to him, he was all good. The second one is kind of a more interesting story. We were casting and this girl came by and told us she was a major motocross rider. She said she had a bike and all of the equipment. We immediately wanted her for the film thinking we could do all kinds of things with that character. We had her meet us up at the dirt road section of Mulholland Hwy. She arrived on her bike wearing all her gear. But the minute we started filming she fell off. We started filming again and she fell off again. This time breaking her clutch lever. We realized she had a bike and all the gear but she didn't know how to ride and this was way too dangerous for us if she got hurt. As I'm a rider we decided it was better if I asked her to borrow her bike and then we filmed me riding it. We didn't want to waste the shot or the fact that we had her bike on set.

What happened to her?

After that we never saw her again.

You did have a lot of interesting exterior locations in the movie. How did you find them and did you have to pay to shoot at them?

We would find them just by looking. Pretty much anywhere you live there are interesting locations if you keep your eyes open and seek them out. In terms of payment, no we never paid to shoot at any of them. We just showed up and shot the scenes. It's not really in the rules of Zen Filmmaking but it probably should be, no filming permits, no location rentals.

Let's talk about a couple of the recurring scenes throughout the film.

Okay.

In three different screens you have the same interaction with three different girls where they kiss you and say they've been hurt. How did that come about?

Just Zen. We actually did the interior shot of that scene first and I really didn't like it. I thought we wouldn't use it. So we did it again later, outdoors with Camille. A bit later in the filming we needed a scene to do with an actress Robin Kimberly and I was really tired. I had been up partying all night the night before and it was getting late in the day. I just grabbed at something to do. So we shot it again. At the time I figured when we put the movie together we would choose between one of the three. It was actually Chris when he was editing Toad Warrior that he put all three of the scenes in the film. I thought that was genius.

There are also several times in the movie where you face off with an opponent and you charge at each other with swords on top of a hilltop at sunset. Why was that scene used multiple times?

First of all, check it out, that is not always the same scene used over and over again. There were several takes of that scene. That's the thing about Zen Filmmaking there is always tons of subtle elements that you really need to look for if you hope to truly understand the movie. In terms of why we filmed that scene it was a combination of a tribute to Kurosawa and a throwback to Roller Blade Seven where we have that great scene where my character charges towards the ninja and once I cut him he spurts all that blood high into the air. The reason why the scene is used multiple times is that it was a great transitional element between other scenes.

There is the scene where Sergeant Shiva interrogates a frog and then two of your female costars. Where was that scene filmed and what made it come about?

The cameraman I mentioned Jonathan Quade had a studio set up in his garage. That's where the scenes were filmed. Sergeant Shiva was an actor named Kent Dalian. He was the boyfriend of Sandra Purpuro that I mentioned earlier. In terms of dialogue we just gave him a bit of direction and let him run with it. He was another great actor.

Where did the comments about your mother come from when he asks Agent Banner about where she got the information?

When I grew up it was one of those ongoing jokes to insult a person's mother. It just came out of nowhere. They were just looking for an exchange of dialogue and I gave that to them and they ran with it. That's a great and very amusing exchange I think.

I notice that the three primary female leads in the film are named Agent Star, Agent Spangle and Agent Banner. How did that come about?

The star spangled banner. That's pretty obvious.

Does that have a meaning?

The star spangled banner, man. Don't you love America?

When your character breaks the girls out of their captivity you get into a car. I think it was a Porsche. How does that tie into the storyline? Isn't this movie set after the apocalypse?

Yeah. That's my baby, a 1964 Porsche 356 SC. To your question, why do things have to make sense? This is Zen Filmmaking. Things don't have make sense. A scene just has to be whole and complete onto itself. People really need to stop thinking so hard when they see a Zen Film. Just let it happen. Just let it be what it is.

I have one more question about your scenes. It's about the spanking scene. In Toad Warrior it's just a quick flash. In Max Hell Frog Warrior, it's much longer. Why is that?

That's a fun scene don't you think? Robin Kimberly was a great sport, really fun to work with. Great girl. When Chris edited the film I think he wanted to tone down on that kind of stuff. Make it more of a kid's films. Me, I love presenting something that you don't see in films everyday. That's why when I went for the reedit I added most of the footage that we shot for that scene. It's just for fun.

I would like to talk to you a little about what happened to this film after it was finished.
Sure.

How was it originally released?
Don had a company that sold films that he created and that he purchased. It was called Donald G. Jackson and Company. I always thought that was a little bit vain. Anyway, back then the internet was not the primary source for independent film distribution as it is today. You had to go to formal functions like the American Film Market. Back then it was a major event held once a year. People came from all over the world. If you made independent films you'd paid a lot of money to rent a room at the hotel on the beach in Santa Monica where it was held. The buyers would come, see what you had and maybe buy the rights to one of your movies for distribution in their country. As I told you Don and I never really liked the final edit for Toad Warrior so it was for sale but we weren't really pushing it. We got a lot of offers but we only took the ones for theatrically only release in Japan, Malaysia, and the Philippines. The market came and went. Don took all of the money we made from Toad Warrior and our other films and spent it on himself almost immediately. Again, he screwing me over financially and that was that.

He sounds like a real jerk.
Yeah, he could be.

Then what happened?

We buried the movie and went off and did other things. A few years passed, Don got sicker and sicker. I had reedited the film down to a Zen Speed Flick called Max Hell Comes to Frogtown.

What's a Zen Speed Flick?

Basically taking a movie down to its most essential elements. Don loved it. He wanted me to get back into the footage and redo the whole film but it never happened before he died. As we talked about it still hasn't happened. Though I did do the reedit of Toad Warrior into Max Hell Frog Warrior and that was the one I wanted released.

When was Max Hell Frog Warrior released?

In the late 1990s. It first came out on video tape. Remember those? Then the DVD revolution hit and it was released on DVD and later via download.

You never planned to release Toad Warrior?

No. But then somebody somehow got a hold of a Beta Master and released it on a compilation DVD.

Did you have to sue that company?

No. They were very cool about it. After I contacted them and they found out that I had the copyright and that I owned all the rights, title and interest to the film they took it off the market. But the damage had been done. It was out there.

You released Toad Warrior as well?

What else could I do? I don't like the cut. Don didn't like the cut. But to kept that unauthorized version from being the only version of Toad Warrior out there I had to release the authorized version.

I know there has been a lot of websites offering Max Hell Frog Warrior for free download? They are not authorized to do so, are they?

Nope. That's the nature of the world everybody wants to make money off of the creations of other people. Personally, I think it's really sad. I mean I certainly realize that everybody wants everything for free these days and they make all kinds of excuses and justifications to themselves for why they should get it. But the fact is the big studio make major dollars off of their films, independent filmmakers like myself do not. When people download movies off of these free sites they really are hurting the independent film creators. I know nobody cares but that is the fact.

Can't you do anything about those companies?

Here's the thing, I have always been an outspoken advocate about stopping copyright infringement and intellectual property theft. Some people don't like my opinion but I believe if you are the actual creator of something, that you really care about, then you do understand. You care about your creation. If you are just somebody out there who doesn't give a shit about other people or what happens to them as long as you get what you want for free then you obviously don't care. Here's the fact, if a person makes one cent off of using anything you created then they are in volition of international copyright laws. You can sue them and you will win. But these companies are all offshore. If they were in the U.S. you could go after them but how can you even find them? If they were in the U.S. the FBI would shut them down. The main thing for everybody to remember is that these supposedly free download companies are making money. If they weren't they wouldn't be doing what they're doing. They are just doing it by stealing the creations of others. So what are you going to do? You just have to believe in people and hope that they will make the right choices.

Max Hell Frog Warrior has remained one of the most talked about cult films. Did Max Hell Frog Warrior become all you hoped it would become?

That's a hard question and you may not like the answer. Did we create what we hoped to create when we set out to make the movie. Yes, kind of. Did it become the movie I hoped it would become when we first began production? No. Do I like the movie? No, not really.

Oh my god that's scary.

You asked. I answered.

In closing can you tell me any funny stories that occurred during the filming of Max Hell Frog Warrior?

Don and I generally had a lot of fun when we worked together. Could he be a self-centered jerk? As we talked about, yes he could. As I say there was always a price to pay in association with anything Don. But mostly we had a lot of fun. Overall the making of Max Hell was a fun process. I guess one story that comes to mind is that he used to love to set call times really early so we could catch the golden hour light when the sun came up in the morning. On one of those shoot days we met at the office at like 4:00 AM. We went to Camille Solari's house to pick her up. It was cold and the heater in my Porsche didn't work, plus it is a really small car. Don's car wasn't running well so we decided to take Camille's car. It was really early, she hadn't gotten much sleep, and she asked if Don would drive so she could sleep in the backseat. We took off to pick up Jill at her house in Simi Valley. We're driving along on this windy road and Don falls asleep at the wheel and almost trashes the car. Camille obviously freaked out. Me, I've been so close to death so many times I thought it was funny as nothing actually happened. But Camille begged that I drive. Don didn't want to let go of the wheel but he finally turned over the keys to me. We got to Jill's house. Don nicely paid Camille her $100.00 and told her to go home and get some sleep. We got into Jill's car and went out to the desert to film. I've never seen Camille again.

I don't know if that was the kind of funny story I had hoped for but this has been a great interview.
No problem.

Let me ask you one more question.
Sure.

I have heard that you are going to film another Max Hell Frog Warrior movie. Is that true?
Yeah. I actually filmed most of it a couple of years ago. Some weird things started to happen in association with Max Hell Frog Warrior and I begin to question if I wanted to do another one as I had really begun to shift my focus to creating non-narrative Zen Films. So it's basically there. It would just take a couple of more shots to finish it up. If I get the right inspiration I will probably finish it someday. If not, it can just be one of the mystical Zen Film lost in never never land that no one will ever see like Lingerie Kickboxer.

Thanks so much for this interview Scott.

Thanks for doing it. You wanted to know the truth about what took place and the kind of things that took place, I think you actually got it.

Yes, I did. Thank you.

The High Priest of Zen Filmmaking

Kelty O'Bannon

Scott Shaw, the creator of *Zen Filmmaking,* has continued to change the way filmmakers view their process of creation. He has been writing about this style of filmmaking for the better part of twenty years and has taken-in many converts to his realms of understanding.

Shaw is much more than a filmmaker with a unique set of ideals about filmmaking, however. In fact, he came to the art form of filmmaking rather late in life—at the age of thirty. Prior to his emersion into the craft, he was a well-known martial artist and a well-published author on the subject of eastern religion. Each of these factors helped Shaw to create a unique and new understanding of the art and craft of filmmaking.

Though Scott Shaw was not the first film director to employ improvisational acting as a tool in the creation of a film, he was the first to formalize a method where each filmmaker can embrace the most natural elements of *improv* and Zen Buddhism and then integrate them into a method where they can utilize these foundational assets and create a truly unique piece of filmmaking. He has created this new style of filmmaking with such precision that many noted filmmakers have borrowed from his ideology and integrated this method into their own.

For this article, I speak to Scott Shaw in a restaurant in Beverly Hills, California. Beverly Hills is a city that flanks Hollywood. We sit at a table surrounded by many of the Hollywood A-list players, who are having lunch. Due to our surrounding, I cannot help but be motivated to ask Scott Shaw my first question.

What do you think of Hollywood?
I think it's all bullshit.

What do you mean?
If you are referring to the generic term, *"Hollywood,"* where all the films are made and all the people get famous, and everyone thinks this is the place to be, then it's all bullshit. Most people who come here to be famous leave very disappointed. Hollywood has nothing to do with art. And, fame has nothing to do with talent.

What does it have to do with?
Luck and who you know.

Why then did you get involved in the filmmaking profession?
Like I always say, I hope to be a beacon of light in a sea of darkness.

What do you mean by that?
Well, first of all, I didn't come from a family based in the Hollywood industry. I didn't grow up rich. And, I didn't have friends who could walk me though the door and get me inside the industry. So, I had no easy way in. Plus, I wasn't a pretty girl or a man willing to fulfill the desire of other men to get whatever I wanted. And, believe me that is the ticket that many successful actors, actresses, and filmmakers have used to become successful in the industry.

So, what did you do?
    I simply embraced my art.

What do you mean?
    When I first started out, I had the same aspirations as most of the people who come to Hollywood to get into the industry. The only difference with me was, I was born here. Just like everybody, I hoped to be a star overnight. Which caused me to turn down a lot of roles that probably could have actually helped my career. But, I was also lucky. I got my SAG card really quickly. Actually, I was cast for a role in a union film on like my second audition and I began to move my way through the industry.

What happened next?
    I quickly saw that most of the industry, particularly the independent sector of the industry, where new actors get their feet wet, was full of a lot of *wanta-bes* who waste everybody's time making promises about films they will never complete.

What happened to you next?
    Well, I met Donald G. Jackson and I created *Zen Filmmaking.*

Wow, what a jump
    Yeah, I guess it was. But, you have to understand, all of life, not just being in the film industry, is based upon foundations. By the time I met Don, I had been a serious photographer for almost twenty years. I had been very involved in eastern mysticism virtually my whole life, and martial arts since I was six years old. I had my photographs shown in galleries around the world and

used in tons of publications. In addition, I had made several documentaries in Asia. So, when Don and I started working together, I was ready.

I have to ask you because I have seen it written in several places. Is it true that you were a monk?
Yes, it is. I was first a *Bramacharaya* and then a *Sanyass (a Swami)* for several years.

How did that affect your life?
It is pretty simple and straightforward—though I no longer wear the orange robes, the essence of who that person was has never left me. I simply am more interactive with modern society.

Your early filmmaking is closely linked to Donald G. Jackson. How did you two work together? Was it a democracy?
No. A democracy indicates that there are two or more points of view. This was not the case with the films Don and I created. We worked together as a single-minded team. Sometimes he would have the idea. Sometimes I would have it. But, we never doubted each other's end results.

Some people refer to Donald G. Jackson as your mentor. Is this true?
Creatively, we were an equal team. But, when I first met Don, he certainly had much more experience in the independent film industry than I did. So, in that regard, yes, it is true. In fact, when he was living the last few months of his life in the hospital, before he died, he would introduce me to all of his doctors and nurses as his son. So, I guess he viewed me as a son. But, in reality, I was the computer guy. So, when the digital age hit, it was me

who was guiding the ship. But also, if you look at my life prior to meeting Don, what I had accomplished stands clearly on its own merits. Plus, the minute Don and I finished the first two films we made together: *The Roller Blade Seven* and *Return of the Roller Blade Seven,* I immediately went off to make my own films. So, I see the early time of our collaboration as Don was the technical end and I was the creative and spiritual side—as he always would turn to me for spiritual advice. Later in his life he would always say about me, *"The student has become the master."* So, make of that what you will.

There have been many critics of Donald G. Jackson. Was there a downside to working with him?

Yeah, there were many. To put it kindly, Don was a complicated guy. But, he always treated me with the utmost respect. And, we made some great films together. So, even though there was always a price to pay that was attached to working with him, what we created would not have been created had we not teamed up.

Where did he get inspiration for films?

In regard to filmmaking, he had an interesting characteristic. Some may call it undesirable. In that he was a lot like Quentin Tarantino. He could view previously created projects—whether they be comic books, movies, or whatever, and then reinterpret them to suit his own ends. Don was notorious for confiscation, or at least attempting to confiscate, other people's ideas. He tried to do that with me a few times.

What happened?

No comment.

How do the films you made with Donald G. Jackson differ from the films you have made without him?

    Don was a comic book orientated guy. Much of his inspiration came from that genre. Me, I am an urban kid. I was born and raised in some of the worst parts of L.A. So, that's my inspiration. I love the abstract beauty of the inner city and the stories the city has to tell.

What is the symbolism of the Happy Face emblem that is seen in the films you made with Donald G. Jackson?

    That was basically Don's creation. You have to look back to the 1970s to see the inception of this. In the 1970s the Happy Face was everywhere. So, Don took this and made it a commentary on society and a signature in his films. It was one of those things that each of us, as we get older, hold on to in order to remember a specific era that meant something to us. And, that was Don's.

In virtually all of your films, there is at least one image of the Buddha. How does that tie into your overall filmmaking message?

    Don had the Happy Face, mine is the Buddha. It is just my way of subtly suggesting that the audience stay conscious and embrace the mystical.

You have filmed several of your movies in Asia and virtually all of your films, at least partially, in Hollywood. What can you tell us about that?

    That is my yin and yang. I was born in Hollywood and grew up in South-central L.A. and Hollywood. Hollywood is the center of the universe for filmmaking. But, Asia is where my heart is. Asia's abstract mystical nature, its beauty—that is who I am. So, I film there whenever I have the chance and then come back to Hollywood to add the structure to the story. The other side of it is, I am from Hollywood, and so I know it inside and out. But, the rest of the world does not. They see Hollywood as this grand illusion—the place to be. In my films I try to show the more gritty side of Hollywood, to illustrate the true nature of this city.

There are certain people, other than Donald G. Jackson, that have worked in a production capacity with you on several of your films, most noticeably Hae Won Shin, Kenneth H. Kim and Kevin Thompson. What can you tell us about that?

Well, Hae Won has worked with me since I first got into the industry. She has helped me in many ways—in virtually every capacity. She has a degree in photography, so she has been my cinematographer; she has helped me in production and has been an actress in my films when I need to fill in the storylines. Ken, I met early in my emersion into the industry. In fact, I met him when we were actors on one of the first films I was cast in. After that, he helped me put some of my early projects together and we did another film together a couple of years ago. I was introduced to Kevin when I was about to begin production on *Undercover X*. We needed one final lead-actor and Richard Magram, who was producing the L.A. portion of the film with me, suggested Kevin. And, he was perfect. Kevin is one of those people who just, *"Gets it."* He completely understands my style of filmmaking. I call him up and tell him I am putting a new project together. He doesn't even ask what his character will be. He just asks, *"When and where."* He is a great guy and a great actor to work with.

Do you think it is important to work with people like that?

Absolutely. I think every filmmaker; whether they are in the low or the high budget side of the industry finds cast and crewmembers that they work with over-and-over again. By working with someone you know, you understand what to expect and this just makes every project easier and better.

It seems that your early films were martial art orientated. That has seemed to change. Can you tell the readers about that?

You have to understand, I have been a martial artist since I was six years old and watching people beat each other up on film has just gotten boring. But, more than that, most martial artists who are actors have really bad attitudes. I just don't want to deal with them anymore.

Another thing I have noticed about the evolution of your films is that you have begun to use much smaller casts.

Yes, that's true.

Can you tell us about that?

Again, it has just been an evolution for me. I used to like to add a lot of character-driven texture to my films. That meant there were a lot of people in my films. Some had large parts and some roles were much smaller. Now, I see my films much more as intense character studies. So, I keep the number of cast members way down.

What is next on the horizon for Zen Filmmaking?

Zen Filmmaking will forever evolve. It is not a static entity that cannot move forward or be reinterpreted. Each filmmaker who uses *Zen Filmmaking,* as a basis for their filmmaking, will find and evolve their own method of using it as a foundational factor for a freer style of filmmaking.

What advice do you have for filmmakers?

Drink a bottle of Italian red wine every night. Go out and a have a *latte* or *cappuccino* at least once a day at a coffee house. Workout in a gym several times a week. And. Live. Because this is where all the inspiration for filmmaking comes from—living!

Big Sister 2000 and Women in Prison Films

Hans Becker

How did you become involved working with Donald G Jackson?

Don Jackson and I met in 1990. Somebody sent him a photo of me holding two samurai swords. We never found out who sent that photo to him. But, he had always wanted to meet a westerner who had extensive martial arts experiences to put in his films. Prior to my emersion in the film industry, I had spent a lot of years in Asia and I have been involved in the martial arts since I was six years old. So, after he received that photo, he called me and cast me as the lead in a film he was about to create. But, the film fell apart. About a year after that, he got financing for another film and we made our first movie together, The Roller Blade Seven.

You Co-Directed Big Sister 2000. How did that come about?

Anytime Don and I did a film together he wanted me to take co-director credit. Sometime I accepted, sometimes I did not. In regard to *Big Sister 2000,* there are various versions of the film in release. In some, I have Co-Director and Co-Producer credit, and in others I used a different name or took no credit at all.

The reality is, I did not and do not like the movie. Initially, I didn't want my name associated with the film. There were a couple of reasons for this. *Big Sister 2000* film was based on an idea Don had. Then, a friend of Don's, Mark Williams, wrote a script for it. The problem was, this script took Don's original idea in a totally different direction.

As you may know, I never use screenplays for my films. In fact, I am completely against using them. That is the essence of *Zen Filmmaking*—No Scripts.

On the first day of shooting, Don knew I didn't like the script that had been written so he told the actors to forget the script and go ahead and improv their lines. But, they had memorized their dialogue, so all they said was what was written in the script.

I really felt the subject matter of the script was far too negative for my tastes. So, I left the set and pretty much had very little to do with the actual filming of the movie. I directed a few scenes that were eventually added to the movie.

I am in possession of all of the original footage for the film, however, and someday I plan to go through it, reedit it, shoot some additional scenes, and produce a movie more based upon Don's original idea.

Was it difficult to produce that movie?
It was actually a very easy movie to produce. When you already have all of your locations and you work with actors and crew that you know, production is very easy.

Your filmography is big, would you like to make a real Women in Prison (WIP) movie?
No, I do not like women in prison movies. They are far too negative and I do not like the physical and mental abuse that takes place in them.

As I mentioned, I have spend a lot of time in Asia and I have known some women who were actually in prisons. When you hear about the torture that takes place in those places, you do not want to glorify it on the screen.

My films are always about good overcoming evil and people overcoming adversity. They are about the Good Guy (or Good Girl) winning. I do not make exploitation films.

How did you get the idea to make a WIP movie merged with Sci-Fi? (Maybe from the movie Star Slammer / Prison Ship by Fred Olen Ray)?

I know Fred and he is a great filmmaker. You have to understand, however, his movies have fairly high budgets, where I find it much more artistic and artistically challenging to make a movie with little or no budget. So, the style of movies Don and I made are very different and, no, *Big Sister 2000* was not based upon a Fred Olen Ray film.

The reason *Big Sister 2000* has a bit of a, *"Sci-Fi,"* as you put it, or a Post-Apocalyptic theme is that many of the early films that Don and I made together revolved around this theme. The reason is that when a filmmaker uses this theme, the movie does not have to be based around current reality—anything can happen, which really frees you up as a filmmaker.

How did you cast Julie Strain?

Julie originally auditioned for a part in Don's film, *Hell Comes to Frogtown.* She also auditioned for, *Return to Frogtown.* Though she didn't get a part in either of those films, Don knew her and simply called her up and asked her if she wanted to be in the movie. She did. In fact, since *Big Sister 2000,* Don and I did several films with her and her husband, Kevin Eastman, the co-creator of, *The Teenage*

Mutant Ninja Turtles—though they have recently divorced.

Do you think WIP movies are typically fantasies for men?
Yes.

What do you think about the genre WIP movies?
As stated, I don't like them.

What souvenir do you have of the shooting of Big Sister 2000?
A weekend with one of the actresses in the film. I'm not going to say which one.

Have you any anecdote to relate me?
Perhaps the most interesting anecdote is that after making *Big Sister 2000,* and seeing the final edit, Don also realized that it was a very negative subject matter and he never wanted to make another movie like *Big Sister 2000* again. And, until his death in 2003, he did not.

Donald G. Jackson:
The Filmmaking and the Filmmaker

Jim Acton

Thanks Scott for agreeing to field my questions. I had hoped to get these to you sooner but life has been so crazy lately. As a quick reminder, these questions pertain to several films: Little Lost Sea Serpent; Baby Ghost; and Rollergator, as well as your filmmaking style, and that of Mark Williams and Don Jackson.

First, can you talk a little bit about your anti-script approach to filmmaking? I know it's your preferred method, but can you identify any drawbacks to that style?

  Zen Filmmaking is really about freedom—it's about freeing up the entire process of filmmaking and allowing the inspiration of the moment to be the only guide. As Donald G. Jackson and I both agreed, *"All the stories have already been told,"* so why bother attempting to tell a story, with a limited budget, that has been far better depicted in a high-dollar film? But, more to the point, to go into a filmmaking project with a formalized script leaves the filmmaker left simply trying to reenact what is written upon the page instead of allowing spontaneous, true artistic creativity to be the guide in a film's creation.

  The downside to *Zen Filmmaking,* (if you can call it that), is that there is little story structure. Some finished *Zen Films* end up with a much more coherent storyline than others. But, story structure is not the sourcepoint for creation in *Zen Filmmaking*. As a *Zen Film* is formulated at the editing stage, you are never quite sure what you will end up with. For some filmmakers they love this freedom. But, for the average filmmaker and for the typical movie going audience, they may not.

Zen Filmmaking is about art and spiritually-based artistic expression, while waiting for those moments of cinematic satori. It is not about structure, nor is it about catering to what a particular member of the audience may be expecting or looking for. Zen Filmmaking is cinematic freedom created by capturing moving images.

How well did you know Mark Williams? What was he like as a person and filmmaker?

Personally, I met Mark Williams through Donald G. Jackson. As you may know, he played the character Heavy Metal in the film, *The Roller Blade Seven.* So, we spent a lot of time together during the period of filming RB7 and its sequel *Return of the Roller Blade Seven.* Don met Mark through Steve Wang who created the frog masks for the original *Hell Comes to Frogtown* and the sequels: *Frogtown II* and *Max Hell Frog Warrior.* Mark Williams and Steve Wang were friends from the San Jose region of Northern California. They had both moved to L.A. to pursue their film careers. Like Steve, Mark was also an SFX guy and, as such, was pursing a career in that field when he met Don. From this, he helped us with some of the costuming and makeup on RB7 as well as bringing his pet snakes onto the set for the scene where Stella Speed's (Allison Chase) character is covered with them. He was also instrumental in all of the SFX of Don's children-based films.

After *Roller Blade Seven,* when Don and I went to work on separate projects, Mark became an essential element in the filmmaking of Donald G.

Jackson, beyond simply the SFX. Don would provide Mark with the concept for a film and Mark would go home and write the entire script in one evening.

Mark, like Don, was a highly comic book influenced individual. So, they worked well together as a creative team; at least for a time.

As a filmmaker, Mark did not possess the intense work ethic of say filmmakers like Donald G. Jackson and myself who were willing to go for hours upon hours, even days upon days, without a break to get a film created. In all fairness, this may be because Mark was internally very ill and did not know it yet. (But, I will address that issue in a moment). Mark saw himself, at least in terms of the films of Donald G. Jackson, as the screenwriter and an actor. Thus, he would come on the set and simply hang around and provide script based story direction. This, in association with the fact that Mark began to smoke cigars constantly, (Don hated smoking). Plus, Mark became dependent upon money from Don; this is something that Don hated when people took this path. In fact, Don became his only source of income during this period of time. All this eventually caused Don to violently dismiss Mark. Thus, their relationship ended.

At this point, Mark went on to find other jobs in the film industry, primarily in SFX departments. He also created a comic book that was financed by Rikki Rockett, the drummer for the band Poison. The last time I personally saw Mark was about a year before his passing. Don and I were at the San Diego Comic Con and we discovered that Mark had a booth for his comic book. I spoke with him but Don refused to.

After this, Mark followed his path of occasional film work and comic book creation.

Sadly, Mark passed away from complications from prostate cancer at the young age of thirty-nine. Though Don had not spoken with him since their parting, he, I, and Joe Estevez, (the star of the movies you have asked about), did attend Mark's memorial, held at Dark Delicacies in Burbank, where Don kindly spoke about their relationship to the gathering.

As someone who I've read was a bit of a wild guy (and who also had experience working on sci-fi and horror films) why do you think he was drawn to making monster/creature films for younger audiences, such as the ones mentioned above?

At his heart, Don was a comic book guy. He loved the characters created within those pages. As such, he made films with that as his focus.

What drew Don Jackson to get involved with Little Lost Sea Serpent, Baby Ghost, and what were the creative objectives for making these sorts of films?

The simple answer is money. Don began working with a company that sought investor financing for his films. Don knew that if he attempted to sell these investors on making the kind of films he actually wanted to make; i.e. more exploitation based films, they would never invest. So, what he did was to take his own unique vision of comic book based characters and create films, which he felt could be viewed by the younger audience. He did this, while syphoning money from those films, so that he could create the kind of movies that he actually wanted to make.

What was it like working on these films?

All of the films that Don was involved with in his later years, and most of those from his earlier years of filmmaking, were made in the guerilla style of filmmaking. Meaning, Don virtually never rented locations or obtained filming permits to shoot at locations. He simply found places where a movie could be filmed with little concern about the public or police involvement. And, for the most part, he got away with filming his movies for free. The crew on his films were always bare bones.

Filming would begin by Don planning for a location. The cast and crew would meet at our offices in North Hollywood, California, get into their cars, and drive to the location and film. Though he would always be sure to feed his cast and crew, there was never anything like Craft Services, a Costuming or Make-up Department, or anything like that as one may find on the higher budget, more traditional type of film production sets. It was just the get out there and do it approach.

You mentioned in a previous message that these particular films were not really your kind of thing. Can you elaborate further?

During this period of Donald G. Jackson's filmmaking career and, in fact, on virtually every other film he ever made, where I was not directly involved, he based his films around a script. Though he obviously allowed for plenty of room for improv, he felt that he needed a guide for the actors; i.e. a screenplay. As such, I stepped away and simply provided production and post production support.

It is important to note that as a director, Don never really directed his actors. He let them interpret their character any way they wanted to. With a script he was able to step back and concentrate on the cinematography of a film, which was his true love. In some cases, he would become so obsessed with getting a shot right, at least in his own mind, that he would shoot an insane number of takes of a single scene; over and over and over again. I document this practice in the *Zen Documentary, Cinematografia Obsesion*. But, this obsessional mindset is not how he worked with actors. He pretty much allowed them to speak the lines in any way they felt appropriate. So, by working with a script this allowed him to move away from guiding people in what words they would be speaking and the way they would be speaking them.

Did you ever get a sense of what the creative objectives were with films of this type?

Don never actually liked any of the films you are asking about. He used to make the statement, *"Just another piece of shit on the crap pile."*

Don was an obsessional filmmaker. He loved making movies. But, he was willing to make them at any cost. In fact, he was more focused on the process of doing a film than on that of finishing a film. Thus, it was during this period of time, where he was being financed by the aforementioned film finance firm, that he had to hire several people to get these films finished; i.e.: edited, sound tracked, and the like. For, if it were left up to him, none of these movies would have ever been completed. And, finishing them was a requirement of his receiving the financing. This is why when he passed away and left all of his years of random film footage to me that so many more of his films were released than when he was alive. I finished them.

As a filmmaker what is the appeal of creating creatures and scary movies for kids?

If you have seen any of these films, I believe that you would not consider them scary. They are much more, *"Campy,"* than scary. More like *Casper the Friendly Ghost* than a horror flick.

Jumping off that, what are some challenges and, on the flip side, luxuries of creating content for kids? What are the advantages and the disadvantages?

I see no advantages in creating films that are focused on the younger market, as there are far too many limitations about what you can present to the younger audience. The disadvantages go hand-in-hand with this. You have to be so careful of what you, as a filmmaker, expose children to; you are truly limited by the genre.

From your experience can you talk a bit about the logistics behind Don Jackson's films, such as: The types of budgets he was usually working with / how funding was obtained / how casting those films were handled / the distribution of these films / and (on average) how long it took to shoot these films?

No matter how much money Don had in his coffers he always shot a film as if it was a completely independent film with no budget. His films were generally created much more like a backyard film than a film possessing some of the high budgets that some of his films actually possessed. As I have long stated, both when he was alive and after his passing, *"Don was one of the greatest squanderers of money I have ever met."* He would buy an insane amount of personal possessions, always pay for everyone's lunch, dinner, bar tabs, concert tickets, strip club visits, pay the rent for the young actresses who were dependent upon him at any given period of time, pay for boob jobs, you name it... But, any money he had rarely went into his films.

As previously explained, the financing for these films, at least during the period of time you are asking about, came from a film finance company.

In terms of casting, the films were cast via a very traditional Hollywood method used in the indie film community at the time. There was a weekly newspaper called, *Dramalogue*. In this newspaper one would find industry stories, advertisements for photographers and acting classes, and casting notices. Don (and I) cast all of our films via *Dramalogue* at that point in time.

The distribution of these films was spearheaded by Donald G. Jackson himself. Hand-in-hand with the film financing he received he set up a distribution company that would sell these and other films, (including several films I had created without him), to international buyers at film markets such as the yearly, American Film Market.

The actual shooting schedule on these films would vary. As mentioned, Don was an impulsive filmmaker so there was never any formalized shooting schedule. He might go out and shoot what would translate into several minutes of usable footage or he may go out and return with no usable footage whatsoever. Sometimes he wouldn't film at all for weeks or even months on end. So, the actual shoot times of these particular films was all over the place, anywhere from one month to more than a year. So was the filmmaking world of Donald G. Jackson...

Thanks again, Scott!
No Problem.

Donald G. Jackson: Small Town Roots

By Adam Armour

What, if any, influence did Jackson's small town roots have on his filmmaking?

Like many a person hailing from a small town, Don's hopes were always to make it in the big city. Bright Lights, Big City, and all of that... After he completed his second film, which was a documentary based on then thriving wrestling market, he sold the rights to the film which financed his move to Los Angeles where he found employment working for the production company lead by famed independent filmmaker, Roger Corman. There, Don first worked with Jim Cameron whose filmmaking career skyrocketed shortly thereafter. Though Don moved forward to make many of his own films, he was always star struck whenever encountering a famous talent. Thereby showing that the small town boy never truly left him.

As someone who worked closely with Jackson for so long, what do you think drove and/or inspired him as an artist?

Don was an avid fan of comic books and the films and television series that were inspired by them. Don drew influence from the grand feats the characters in that genre were able to perform. Don was also an avid fan of Japanese Samurai Cinema. These two factors formed the inspiration for much of his work.

Jackson's body of work seems really varied. How would you define/describe his work to someone unfamiliar with it?

If I were to be kind, I would use the word, *"Artistic."* Knowing him as I did, however, the one word I would use is, *"Manic."* Don had a million ideas and created as many of them as he could. Filmmaking, particularly filmmaking in the era where Don produced most of his movies, was an expensive process. Thus, not all of his ideas found their way to finalization. The ones that did where either based upon the financial input of a production company, desiring a specific product, or based upon his personal desire to see a specific production find its way to completion. The more formalize of his films were financially instigated by a production company. The more abstract films, those were the ones solely coming from the creative mind of Donald G. Jackson.

What was Jackson like as a director? Was he assertive? Laid back? Why did you enjoy working with him?

Don was an extremely temperamental individual. He was quite prone to shouting and, in fact, breaking equipment and props when he became unhappy with a cast or a crewmember that he felt was behaving in an incompetent manner. To his friends, however, he was a different person; often very giving. As to why we made so many films together, it was simply one of those unique meeting of the minds, where as a team we possess the ability to create many a unique piece of cinema.

I know Jackson never hit mainstream success, but he's developed a kind of cult following over the years. What do you think his legacy will be? How will his work be remembered, and what would he think of the reputation he's gained over the years?

Yes, Don did develop what could be called a cult following. Sadly, as time has gone on, the number of people interested in his work has vastly diminished. Once upon a time, his films were shown on late night TV. This solidified him as a filmmaker and allowed his work to continually be exposed to a new audience. As the internet has taken over the world, I have watched as fewer and fewer people have sought out his work with the exception of a few standout pieces like *The Roller Blade Seven, Hell Comes to Frogtown, Max Hell Frog Warrior,* and *Rollergator* (which was spoofed by Rifftrax). This has predominately been based upon the internet chatter that has taken place regarding these films.

When Don was reaching the final stage of his life he knew I would be the only one who cared enough and had the ability to keep his filmmaking legacy alive. This is why he gave me all of his footage and films instead of bequeathing them to his wife or his daughter. I have tried to keep his name and his films out there. As I've stated elsewhere, and alluded to in the answers to your previous questions, Don was an outrageous guy who had a hard time following projects through to completion. This is why more of his films were released after he passed away then when he was alive. I edited and finished them. Has this helped his legacy? I don't know? But, I have tried. And, for better or for worse, it seems like I am the only one who is trying.

I do not know what his final legacy will be? He was one of those people that if you did not personally know him, you could never really fathom why he created what he created. As I always state, he was a complex, very troubled, individual. But, I guess that is what made him the artist that he was.

It terms of how his work will be remembered, all you have to do is to look around the internet, and as the internet promises, you can immediately see the harshness that many people unleash on his films. Few take the time to understand the artistic foundation that his movies were based upon.

How would he feel about it? He would hate it. He was one of those people who really became upset with bad reviews and negative comments. Like so many artists throughout the ages, he was one of those people that the masses never really understood during their lifetime. At some point will his work be comprehended and have a resurgence? Only time will tell…

Donald G. Jackson and the Demon Lover Diary

Don prepared this list of anticipated questions and passed it out before the press and audience Q & A session at the end of a sold out screening of the Demon Lover Diary held at The Director's Guild of America in 2002. This questionnaire provides a deeper insight into the life, the filmmaking career, and the paradox that was Donald G. Jackson and his movie, THE DEMON LOVER.

Why didn't you fire Jeff Kreines, Joel DeMont, and their assistant Mark as soon as you realized what was going on with THE DEMON LOVER DIARY?

I had no money. Firing them would mean a total failure on my part. They would have taken the camera equipment and there would be no film. Word would have gotten out the film was shut down. I needed to keep the shoot going until we could find local investors. Lucky for me, we found some money and I didn't have to put up with any more crap. I fired them with a vengeance!

Wasn't Jeff Kreines your friend?

I met Jeff in 1974. We got along great until he got hooked up with Joel DeMont who had her own agenda. Also it took so long for the film to start that Jeff was very frustrated by the time we actually started to shoot. Plus, I fired him on the phone several times before he left Boston to come to Michigan. We had plenty of friction before the start of the shoot. He knew I'd talked to other cameramen and also that I wanted to shoot it myself.

What was it about Jeff Kreines that impressed you?

I saw his movie RICKY AND ROCKY at the Ann Arbor Film Festival. It was all shot with a wide angle lens and a moving handheld camera. This is the style I wanted to shoot THE DEMON LOVER. It never occurred to me that our amateur actors wouldn't be able to say but only five or six words without a fumble. We did some long takes, but ended up having to fragment the movie and puppet the actors just like a normal movie.

Does it bother you that all the reviews are in favor of Jeff and Joel and that you get slammed beyond belief?

What can I say? DEMON LOVER DIARY was made twenty-seven years ago. Jeff and Joel were there for six days. How could they live every day with this movie?

I've gone on and made over forty different features plus worked on plenty of others. They've done nothing except promote this DEMON LOVER DIARY and send it to festivals since 1980!

Why do you think the DEMON LOVER DIARY has done so well?

You have to remember. This is before home video; before the internet. There is a lot of BLAIR WITCH type realism in the movie. It is in reality a mixture of real and fake. Many times I was acting for the camera — but try and convince someone of that. People want to believe it is all true. Jeff and Joel were self-righteous brats who were too lazy and low energy to have what it takes to make a real movie.

Do you have any regrets?

I sure wish Joel had focused some of her film on Bob and Dennis Skotak. Bob made the Demon suit. Dennis took over for sound. These guys went on to win three Academy Awards. Also my friend Bryan Greenberg isn't given any coverage. He helped with the sets and became my camera assistant when we fired Jeff and Joel. Everyone on my team moved to California and has been working. I stayed behind a while to make I LIKE TO HURT PEOPLE — a classic wrestling film starring André the Giant. Bryan Greenberg shot a lot of the movie. Dennis Skotak did most of the sound work. Hollywood was calling them. I finished the movie and headed for Roger Corman. Later New World put the wrestling film out on home video.

Did Jeff and Joel miss anyone else who was part of THE DEMON LOVER?

Marvel comic book artist Val Mayerik played the hero. He was on the set and available for interviews. They never once talked to him. We also had Gunnar Hansen — star of the biggest independent movie of all time in 1974-75, THE TEXAS CHAINSAW MASSACRE. Jeff and Joel could have cared less. There is a 10 min sequence where Joel photographs two kids playing on a swing set instead. Those kids are probably 35 years old today!

Any final words on THE DEMON LOVER or DEMON LOVER DIARY?

THE DEMON LOVER was one of the world's first films shot on 16 mm color negative. TEXAS CHAINSAW MASSACRE was filmed on ECO reversal. We were going to be one of the last film shot on 35 mm TECHNISCOPE, but Technicolor discontinued the process a few months before we started the shoot. THE DEMON LOVER was also one of the first movies where a group of kids get together and then get killed off one by one. This later became popular with movies like FRIDAY THE 13TH. Sam Rami and Bruce Campbell came to a midnight show and asked questions. I taped some of their telephone calls to me when they were researching shooting 16 for 35 mm blowups. Fred Olen Ray saw THE DEMON LOVER in a drive-in. He treated it just like a regular movie. Later he called me and I think got more inspired to shoot his own movies. We've been friends since 1977. And I've known The Skotaks and Bryan Greenberg since about 1965.

Where was THE DEMON LOVER shown?
We had seven 35 mm prints. The movie played drive-ins and theaters in Texas, Florida, Alabama, Tennessee, Kentucky, Michigan, Ohio, and New York. When we played the Lyric Theater on 42nd street in New York City, THE DEMON LOVER out grossed CARRIE that had just opened across the street. We had three world premieres and midnight shows. Jerry and I was on the cover of Detroit newspapers and on Detroit TV. We did radio interviews. I got fired from my factory job, but it forced me to find investors and continue as an indie filmmaker.

When did you first see DEMON LOVER DIARY?
John Caldwell showed it to me in a private room when Jeff and Joel entered it in the Ann Arbor Film Festival. DEMON LOVER DIARY wasn't show at the festival because the selection committee

knew it was contrived. Next time I saw it was 1982 at the NuArt Theater in West Los Angeles on a double bill with THE DEMON LOVER. I have pictures of the marque. DEMON LOVER/DEMON LOVER DIARY. L.A. Times critic Kevin Thomas was there and talked to me afterwards. He gave the event a semi-good review. DEMON LOVER DIARY showed at UCLA in 1987 and I answered questions afterwards. The last screening was in Hollywood three years ago. It was a small theater. Sold out. About one-hundred people in the audience. I answered questions for over an hour after the show. The filmmakers loved it!

How did it happen for it to be shown on 22 June 2002 on Saturday night at the DGA on Sunset in Hollywood?

Jeff and Joel are in solid with the IFP. I'm shocked that anyone would care about this 1975 documentary, but I guess the subject is still fascinating. AMERICAN MOVIE came close, but that guy only made a twenty minute film. He was on Leno and Letterman. Got tons of publicity. And there's a lot of BLAIR WITCH type events that go on in the film.

What would you do if you had it to do all over again?

Well, I've had this discussion with my good friend Dr. Scott Shaw. He and I created Zen Filmmaking, a style of filmmaking where we allow spontaneous creativity to be our only guide. He thinks if I hadn't made THE DEMON LOVER, I might still be back in Michigan working in a factory! So, though it was never the film I wanted to make, it did get me out of Michigan and gave me the opportunity of having a filmmaking career.

PART IV
TIDBITS

I'm An Artist, Goddamn It!

"I'm an artist, goddamn it! I don't have to rationalize, justify, explain, or defend anything that I do!" This is a bold statement that my *Zen Filmmaking* brother, Donald G. Jackson and I used to voice whenever we ran into some negativity or controversy about what we were doing. The main thing to know, however, is that this statement was made in fun. We always said it with a smile on our face. I suppose if you read it, this statement comes off as kind of harsh. But, it was not meant to be that way.

It was actually Don who first coined it. But, it became our mutual motto. So, we said it quite often.

Don, more than I, (at least in the early days), received much more criticism for his films and his filmmaking practices. Once he passed away, it became me who was awarded the crown and I became the focus. It is essential to note, however, as has always been the case, there are more people who liked what he and I did than those who did not. But, as also always seems to be the case in life, those who embrace negativity as their primary means of communication, those who look for faults rather than merit, are the most vocal. Wrong, I believe. But, such is life…

Anyway, I believe I put this statement in my book, *Zen Filmmaking*, and I have been told it was quoted a few times, in various places, by people trying to cast shade on me for writing it. I mean come on… Those people who want to base their lives upon criticism always look for something to criticize. This is true in the film game, in the film watcher game, and everywhere else.

Me, I always question, *"Why?"* Why do you, why does anyone, wish to focus their life in seeking out the flaws instead of looking to the perfection of the process? Why??? The world is beautiful, people are beautiful, artistic creations are beautiful, if you just let them be.

Anyway, this statement really goes to the greater whole of anyone who is following the path of creation and/or art; because, as stated, there will be those people out there seeking out your flaws. If you are an artist, you need to be an artist. You need to create your art as you envision your art. That is what true creativity is all about. And, to anyone who wants to criticize it, screw 'em. Let's see what they have created. And then, let's throw some criticism their direction, see how they respond.

In other words, be strong in your art. Do what you do and not care about what others think. If they are so vocal to have the time to waste, simply talking about other people and other things that has nothing to do with them, that means they are not doing anything worthwhile with their own life in the first place.

The Personality of Philosophy

I came upon an interview that this one friend of my longtime *Zen Filmmaking* partner Donald G. Jackson had recently given where he discusses Don. I found it really sad that this guy actually knew Don longer than I did but he simply categorized him as incompetent filmmaker. He totally missed the point…

Now certainly, Don was a psychologically complicated narcissist who, due to his behavior, made a lot of enemies. But, he was far from an incompetent filmmaker. He was a philosophy-based filmmaker. And, that is the point I think many people miss about the man—I know this misunderstanding has occurred to me, as well.

I have spoken about this a lot over the year, but most people view all movies from a place of judgment. Very few people watch simply to see the art. They watch movies with a preconceived notion of what is to come next. They judge and compare any movie that they are currently watching with all of those they have seen before—particularly those with a very high budget where nothing more than the philosophy of making money was employed. But, a true aficionado of film does not frame their basis for judgment on dollars and cents. In fact, they don't judge at all. They simply watch and witness. The fact is, if you want to truly appreciate art, (whatever that art form may be), you need to see any creation for what it is, based upon its own reality of creation, and moreover, on the philosophy that it took to create it.

And… This is where the guy discussing Don completely missed the point. Don made his films based upon a philosophy of actualization. You may like or you may not like this philosophy, and what he created due to it, that is your choice. But, if you do not understand this as the entire basis for the films that Don created than you completely miss the point about the man as a filmmaker. Then, all you become is judge and jury. And, no one should judge art, that is just the wrong way to approach it.

I think this is a very important fact to think about as you pass through life, whenever you find yourself casting judgment. Who are you judging and why? What is the basis for your judgment? Do you know the facts about the person that you are judging? Do you actually understand the motivation for them creating art in the first place? And mostly, do you even comprehend the philosophy they were operating within when they were doing what they were doing—that thing you are casting judgment upon?

People who judge generally do not know, understand, or care about the facts of a person's philosophy. If they did, then there would be no judgment at all.

That's my judgment about judgment. ☺

Everybody Wants Something from Me but Nobody Ever Gives Me Anything

I have long made the semi-joking statement, *"Everybody wants something from me but nobody ever gives me anything."* But, when it comes right down to the reality of it, that is how my life has played out.

Recently, there have been a lot of people asking me if they can distribute Donald G. Jackson's or my films. ...This, at the point in history when distribution is exceedingly easy, anyone can set up a company, and do *print-on-demand*. But, do these people ever ask themselves, *"Why would I want them to make money distributing my films?"* Like the joking statement I have made as an actor in several of my films, *"What's in it for me?"* ...I mean, I own a distribution company, why do I need you? It is not like these people offer me vast amount of money. Then, it may be a different story. But, they do not. They just want what they want for free. ...Do you have any idea the amount of time, energy, creativity, and money it takes to make a movie? And, you expected me to give all that to someone I do not even know?

Here's where we reach one of the philosophic quandaries of life; i.e., people want what they want for free. They want what someone else has. They want what someone else has achieved. They want it, but they do not want to work for it. When they see someone with it, they either want to steal it or, if they have some-what of a conscience, they ask if they can have it.

My answer is, *"No."*

Throughout my life I have always been more than happy to help people. I have always been happy to take people along for the ride. I came of age in a time and a space of doing karma yoga AKA selfless service—doing something and expecting nothing in return. But, that does not mean giving someone my livelihood or letting them make money off of something they had nothing to do with creating.

But, times have changed from the days of caring about the well-being of others and doing karma yoga… People see the vastness of life and cyberspace and how taking what someone else has done and/or flat out stealing it has become easy and, in fact, the norm. But, this is just wrong! If you achieve anything in life by doing this, you have developed exceedingly bad karma. And, then what comes next?

Donald G. Jackson was the last person I can actually put my finger on who went out of his way to help me in a focused manner. But, there was a very high price to pay for that relationship. Yet, I made him a promise to keep his filmmaking legacy alive and I have done my best to do so. So, I hope I have repaid his actions.

Most people are not like that, however. They don't want to help anyone unless there is something in it for them. They want to take; they do not want to make. …And this is where all of the problems of the world arise.

So, how do you encounter life? Are you the point of inception? Or, are you the one trying to make a name for yourself or a dollar off of what someone else has created?

To all the people who thank me as an inspiration and think positive thoughts about me, thank you! To everyone else who wants something from me and offers me nothing in return, you should really rethink your life path.

Zen Filmmaking: The Good, The Bad, and The People That Don't Know What the Fuck They're Talking About

Ever since the inception of *Zen Filmmaking,* that was heralded with the release of *The Roller Blade Seven*, people have contacted me about my method of filmmaking. In the early days, it was largely via letters but soon after that everybody climbed onto the internet and then everybody had a lot to say.

There have been a lot of people, over the years, who have actually contacted me and questioned, how do I do what I do. Those are the people I respect. Love my films or hate my films, they are the ones who cared enough to ask me what was actually going on. They came to the source and inquired. And, going to the source is the only way to gain true knowledge.

Some of these people contacted me because they wanted to follow the path of *Zen Filmmaking.* That's great! Make it your own...

Early in my filmmaking career, (which you have to keep in mind did not begin until I was thirty-two years old so I had a lot of life-experience prior to that), I also began to see people coming to conclusions about what I did, how I did it, and why I did it. These discourses where then mostly entered into magazines that discussed the low budget, no budget, and cult level of filmmaking. In some cases, they got it right. But, in many, (in fact most), cases they were simply wrong. Yet, these people had a pulpit and from that pulpit they broadcasted their thoughts about *Zen Filmmaking, Zen Films,* and me out to the world.

As a professional researcher, I always found this method to be suspect, as these people were simply discussing their feelings that were not based in fact. Yet, they were presenting their opinions, observations, and speculations as if they were fact. This is truly the wrong way to put forward information to the world and this mindset is what has given birth to the whole culture of, *"Fake News,"* we are currently living within—as from these inaccurate depictions further counterfactual statements and misunderstandings are given birth to. People heard, *"This,"* and, thus, they believed, *"That."* But, it is all based on bullshit. It is all based on somebody putting what they think they know out there but they do not have the true facts as they have not done any actual research. I know... I get it... Research is hard to do. It is time-consuming and it often costs money. It is so much easier to just read or hear something and then believe what you want to believe. But, the fact is, if you want to know the truth about a subject, (any subject), research is the only way to arrive at a factual and valid conclusion. And, you must enter into any research gathering with an open mind and not use it as simply a way to justify what you think you already know.

Personally, in virtually all of the aforementioned cases, I found the discourses to be amusing. But, that's just who I am. I easily poke fun at myself. If they weren't flat out defamatory lies or someone making money off of one of my creations when they had no responsibility for its actualization, I was good.

On the larger scale, I have always wondered why do people do this? Why do people want to spread their feelings about something or someone and, moreover, why do they want to transmit something out to the world when what they are saying is not based in fact but is solely based upon personal opinion, second-hand knowledge, and/or speculation? Sure, I understand, most people like something or someone for some nondescript reason but that reason is generally based upon them not possessing a true understanding about anything. Thus, what does that reason for like or dislike truly mean? Do you ever think about that when you form your opinions and from your opinions make your judgments which leads to your statements?

As *Zen Filmmaking* is a defined form of filmmaking, many people have also taken aim at the craft. They have taken aim at it but all they know about it is that in *Zen Filmmaking* we do not use a script. But, there is a lot more to it than that. And no, *Zen Filmmaking* is not just about showing up somewhere and seeing what happens next. So, if you've heard that, if you've believed that, if you've rebroadcast that, YOU ARE WRONG!

Also, there have been a lot of people who have seen *Roller Blade Seven* or some clips from it and decided that was the epitome of *Zen Filmmaking* and all of my films are just like RB7. The fact is, a lot of people don't get what Donald G. Jackson and I were trying to do with *The Roller Blade Seven* and they hate it. I get it! That movie is weird! If you don't like weird movies you probably will hate it. But, think about this, we made that movie over twenty-five years ago—whatever you think about it: love it or hate; we did something right because people are still discussing it.

On a more personal note, occasionally I have seen some people say, *"Scott Shaw makes shitty movies,"* and stuff like that. Okay… That's what you think… But, how many of my movies have you actually seen? Many people make this comment after only seeing maybe *Roller Blade Seven* or *Max Hell Frog Warrior.* I have made a lot of movies! Honestly, how many of them have you seen? Have you seen any of my documentaries? Have you seen any of my music videos? Have you followed my filmmaking evolution and watched any of my *Non-Narrative Zen Films,* my *Zen Film Art Captures,* my *Zen Film Movies in the Moment,* or my *Zen Film Mind Rides?* If you haven't, then you have no idea what I'm doing. Moreover, if you have not read my written words on the subject of filmmaking, if you have not seen my interviews, if you have not met me, again, you are basing your opinion on a preconceived notion that you have no factual bases to possess. Love my movies, hate my movies, I get it… But, if you haven't seen my films, if you don't know my philosophy about filmmaking, if you have not actually spoken to me, then how can you judge anything?

And, this goes to the whole point of this piece… Sure, you're just a screen name out there in the nowhere of cyberspace. You will never have to pay for your cyber crimes. But, no matter what moniker you use, you should be whole enough to know the facts about what you're talking about before you ever spew your misunderstandings out to the world. In other words, BE MORE. For me, that is the key to life. That is how the people who have truly excelled and made a contribution to the world have done it. Care enough to care. Learn the true facts. Go to the source and ask before you speak. Be more than someone who talks about someone else, go out there and create your own something.

The Same Yet Different

As an artist, when you are painting a painting, there is always the question, *"Is it done?"* Sometimes you look at a painting that you are working on and you are just not one hundred percent happy with it. Then the choice must be made, do you go back and rework it or do you let it live in its own perfection?

The thing about this question is—yes you can redo it. In some cases, as an artist, you can redo it over and over and over again. But, at the end of the day, it is still what it was; a painting with paint upon a canvas—the same, yet different.

Life and the way you act in life is very similar to this. There are chances for a redo—most of the time. In other cases there are not. But, one way or the other we are left with our life. It can be seen as having been lived within its own perfection, to the best of our ability, or it can be viewed as if something is missing, something is wrong.

You know, the world has changed a lot over the past two decades in terms of art and creativity. For example, what was once very-very expensive to do, like create a movie, is now relatively cheap due to digital technology. I recently read this piece where Quentin Tarantino stated that digital is the death of cinema. He stated this even though his friend and confidant Robert Rodriguez has used it extensively.

I won't go into this debate because I see both sides of it and I have already written extensively about it. I will say that as one of the first people to ever create a film on video that received international distribution, *Samurai Vampire Bikers from Hell,* that I saw the future early. Years before me, look at Frank

Zappa's, *200 Motels,* if you want to see a really early contribution to the genre.

Anyway, early in the digital game, everybody wanted their movies, that were shot on tape, to look like film. Enter, Film Look. A very expensive process of adding controlled noise to the video movie. Was it film? No. Did it look like film? A little bit. It was the same, yet different.

When Donald G. Jackson and I created, *Guns of El Chupacabra,* we filmed it with a combination of 35mm, 16mm, and digital videotape for the scenes with the reporter, to change the look and feel of the various elements of the film. One day when we were on the set filming with Julie Strain and her then husband Kevin Eastman, we had our videographer along so we had him shoot the scenes on video that we were shooting on film as a backup. When I edited *Guns of El Chupacabra* I used the footage we shot on film. When I did *Guns of El Chupacabra II: The Unseen,* I used the video footage of the same scenes. Did you notice that? Did anybody? It was the same, yet different.

Now, when digital photography came along, I hated it. Just as with video, gone was the depth of field, that myself, as a filmmaker and photographer, loved to work with. But, just like with filmmaking, digital photography made photography insanely cheaper and easier. So, with the changing winds of time, you have to change or be left behind.

Thankfully, now, many of both the new video cameras and still cameras, (which are pretty much one in the same), achieve really nice depth of field. Case in point, I purchased this new Nikon a little while back and was shooting it as digital had been. I expected everything to be in focus, it was not, there was depth of field that I didn't realize until I looked at the shot later. Though I lost the shot I had in mind, I was happy to see the improvement. The same, yet not different.

This is life. It is all about the availability of your options and what you do with that availability and those options. Options are out there, if you want to work with them. Life is out there, if you want to live it. But ultimately, it is you who must decide when what you are doing is done. Are you making it better by working and reworking it? Or are you simply making it the same, yet different?

Honoring People's Wishes and What You Can Do About What You Can Do

For people who create things, they have a specific desire for their creations. For most they hope to get their creations seen, read, heard, or whatever by the worldwide masses. That's why most people create; they have a unique vision or take on a specific art form and thus they want to get what they create exposed to as many people as possible. Though this is the norm, for anyone who creates, they will also understand that there may come a time where you have a different and/or new take on what you have created. At this point, you may no longer wish it to be consumed by the world. You want it to be lost and forgotten. Yet, there are those out there who will not allow this to happen. They refuse to listen to the wishes of the creator(s).

For the creations that the non-creator(s) did not create, this whole mindset becomes a very selfish and/or self-motivated process. They may have liked something (or not) but for whatever reason they want that creation to remain active and alive. They refuse to let it be forgotten, even though that was what the creator wanted.

Case in point; my *Zen Filmmaking* Brother, Donald G. Jackson made a number of movies. As he came closer to his death, he had a change of heart about a few of them. Specifically, those that portrayed violence directed towards women from the male characters. Of which there are two specific examples: *Roller Blade* and *Roller Blade Warriors*.

Don, in his later years, became a very devout Christian. Now, this is not an unusual attitude embraced by a person who knows that their death is eminent. He had leukemia, he knew he was dying. This is a time when many/most people seek a spiritual bedrock. Don's was Christianity.

Ever since I knew Don, he did not like the sexual violence in those two films. He claimed that it was there due to the screenwriter. I don't know if that was true or not. What I do know is that he wished they would fade away as they projected an attitude that he did not ultimately agree with.

For better or for worse, Don assigned all Rights, Title, and Interest to all of his films to me before he passed away. He did this because he knew I would be the best person to keep his legacy alive and to protect his body of work. Though it was not right away after Don's passing but people began to contact me about reissuing some of his films, most notably *Roller Blade* and *Roller Blade Warriors.* Knowing his feelings, I always tried to explain to these people that those titles were not available. In some cases, people did not listen and attempted to release them anyway. Thus, all the legal nonsense began. From this, the only people who befit are the lawyers who make the money. As I explained to a person today, this forced my hand. I had no choice but to release these films so that the unauthorized versions would not flood the market.

I did not want to. I am completely against sexual violence in films. I have never made a film and never will make a film that uses that in its storyline. But, when people have dollar signs in their eyes, they do not care about the way anybody but themselves is feeling.

The thing is, the entire motivation of these people who wanted to release Don's films was money. They wanted to make money off of his creations for free. They didn't create them. They didn't pay for their creation. They just want to copy and sell them and, from a moral standpoint, that is just wrong! And, I am a moral guy.

Today, a man who is doing an event in the near future where a couple of the actresses from *Roller Blade Warriors* will be in attendance, contacted me and asked if he could do a small run of VHS copies of the movie for the signing experience. Wow! I was amazed that anyone would be honorable enough to ask me. And, I told him so. I, of course, said sure he could. I wish him, the actresses, and his event the all the best. But, here is the fact; Don hoped that movie would die. People are not letting it die. Thus, they are not respecting the wishes of its creator.

Do you ever think about this subject when you watch, read, view, listen, or talk about an artistic creation? Do you ever think about the wishes of the creator? If you don't, maybe you should.

Stirring the Pot

There are some people who like to create controversy and disharmony. I believe that we have all met people like this. The say things and do things that are either distorted or not true simply to get people to believe things about life-situations or other people in order to cause them to become angry at that situation or that person. Some call this practice backstabbing but it is actually much deeper than this.

The reason that people commonly behave in this matter is that they hold a low sense of self-worth. Where this comes from can be anybody's guess. But, early in life they have discovered that they can gain a false sense of control over others by guiding them with misinformation and/or lies. The result of this type of behavior causes all kinds of interpersonal disharmonies that can lead to confrontations, arguments, fights, and on a larger scale, wars.

The problem with people who behave in this manner is that the people they are telling their stories to commonly are not aware that they are being lied to and strung along in order for the person to gain a sense of control and self-worth. In other words, people believe the lies.

I believe that most of us want to trust people and believe the things that we are told are true and valid. It is human nature to believe that others are the same as us—speaking the facts, as we know them. It is only after encountering people of the aforementioned type that we then begin to become less trusting and are forced to begin to critically analyze the words of others before we move forward with what we have heard.

From a person perspective, my friend and *Zen Filmmaking* associate, Donald G. Jackson, was notorious for this type of behavior. He would tell people all kinds of things about other people, simply to get a rise out of them. He would, in fact, totally break apart film production teams simply to satisfy his need to gain misguided control. There was several times when I was associated with him that people I considered friends would either shun me or accost me due to false words that Jackson had spoken. It was very strange.

For me, I saw through this character flaw early on and, as such, took his words with a grain of salt. I heard them but I did not allow them to influence me as to my judgment of a person's actual personality. Sadly, other people were not so astute and, as such, he caused our relationships to fall apart.

The causation factor for this type of behavior is rooted in a person's desire for power, dominance, and control. You can commonly see this type of behavior in the workplace when something has gone awry and higher management challenges middle management as to their actual management skills. From this challenge, the person in middle management begins to take out their lack of control on their underlings. They shift the blame, they blame others, they may even make up lies about their coworkers in order to shift responsibility, but the outcome of this style of human interaction is all the same—they have created disharmony due to the fact that they are not whole, confident, responsible for their actions, and complete onto themselves. Thus, they create havoc in order to shift the focus from their own inabilities to manage towards someone else. This type of behavior is commonly titled, *"Saving their own ass."*

Ultimately, (and perhaps sadly), we are all going to be forced to interact with this type of person as we pass through life. There is no way around it. In fact, in the workplace environment, this type of person may actually have a certain amount of control over us. But… We do not have to let this type of person control who we are, how we feel about ourselves, and how we make our life decisions about others.

We must each listen to all that we hear and then make our own choices about the truth and/or validity about what is spoken to us. Then, we must move forward, without judging, and make our own decision about people and this life-place free from the domination and control imparted by the words spoken by others.

Life is full of many people who embrace low human consciousness. In fact, we are more likely to encounter that type of person than one who actually embraces refined higher consciousness. This is life and that's the dilemma. But, by being whole and true onto ourselves, we can exist in a space of peace, knowing that we embrace the truth and are not dominated by the psychological inadequacies of others.

Be silent. Don't try to control or alter the consciousness and understandings of others. Don't desire control or admiration. And, this world becomes such a better place.

Zen Filmmaking: SS vs. DGJ

I am so often asked this question that it used to annoy me, now it makes me smile... The question being, *"What is the difference between your Zen Filmmaking and that of Donald G. Jackson?"* I just got hit with that question again this morning when I was doing a Skype interview for Italy...

So, here we go again... Don, unless he was working with me, virtually always based his filmmaking around a screenplay. Me, I never do. Why did he do this? I do not know, as he was one of the most random, crazy, disorganized, discombobulated people I have ever met. He was a mess! *Zen Filmmaking* was perfect for him. But, he virtually always chose to base his films around a screenplay. Though in the press he rarely revealed this fact.

His mind-mess is what led to him starting so many films but never finishing most of them. It also led to his filming a project and then either losing the film footage or hiding it away somewhere. In some cases, he didn't even know what he did with it. This is why, while he was in the hospitable, shortly before his leaving this world, he had his wife give me all of the film and video footage he and we had filmed. He knew who and what I was, a finisher. The minute I received them, I started editing. This is why so many more films he produced or directed came out after his death than while he was alive. I still a have a few more pieces to put together over a decade since his passing.

The biggest difference between the films Don made, the films he and I made together, and the films that I make, was money. Don would get investors and some of our films had major dollars behind them.

And, Don would freely spend that money. He would buy tons and tons of stuff. He would feed everybody. He would pay for everybody's gas and buy them gifts; especially if they were girls. He paid a lot of rent for a lot of young ladies… He would even pay some people.

My *Zen Films* are just the opposite. I never take money from investors. So, my films are made with no money.

Don and I did, however, follow the same path of spontaneous, spur of the moment production, either when we were working together or apart. We would film like we had no money, even if we did. This is what leads to the fact that it is hard to tell which of our films had a big budget and which did not.

Mostly, Don and I functioned very well as a team. Though we had very different personalities, and he did bring in a large dose of melodrama to every film we ever made together, (something that I trust is absent from my productions), we were friends and from our abstract mindset we did create some interesting pieces of filmmaking.

So, were we different filmmakers? Yes, we were. But, when we made *Zen Films* together the magic did occur.

Again… There, the question is answered. ☺

Knowing What You Don't Know

I always find it very amusing when someone who has no idea about how the independent film industry actually works tells me how I should be doing something or that am I doing something totally wrong.

Over the many years I have been involved in the film industry I have received messages telling me how virtually everything I have done is wrong. These messages generally come from someone who has never made a film and most likely never will.

It all began when Donald G. Jackson and I were making *the Roller Blade Seven*. Don and I knew we wanted to create something very different. We initially hired an editor to help us create our vision when we had completed the filming process of the movie. The man edited the movie for us for a couple of days with Don and I guiding his every action. But, he didn't get it. He took Don off into another room one day and told him, *"You are really pushing the envelope too far."* When Don relayed his message to me with both laughed. We knew exactly what we were doing. And, as I have previously mentioned in my writings on the movie, the mistake this editor made was that he taught me how to use the equipment. We were gone. We rented an editing suit. I became the editor. And, we took the movie to the level we hoped it would reach.

We must have done something right. People are still talking (and criticizing) the film over twenty years later. In fact, most of the people who are criticizing this movie were not even born when we made it.

People also have told me that *Zen Filmmaking* is all-wrong. Wrong? How can anything be wrong when the entire premise of *Zen Filmmaking* is based upon the concept that there are no mistakes? But, I won't get all-philosophical on you here...

People also have contacted me detailing that my story structures are all-wrong. Again, to understand my filmmaking style you must understand that I don't care about stories. The stories have all been told. I care about visional images, with occasional dialogue, taking the viewer on a mind-ride. The fact of the matter is, most people have only seen my most talked about films. They never go and investigate all my other work.

Some of my films actually have defined storylines. Can you believe it?

Also, I have heard random comments about the fact that I don't pay actors. First of all, that is not true. For actors who bring no name value to a film I may not pay them in cash. But, I do pay them in other ways. I give them a chance to be in a film that will be completed and will be distributed—which is not the case of many independent films. During their time on the set they get hone their acting skills for the camera. Plus, they get to have a film, (a calling card), that they can show to their family, friends, agent, and the world.

For only asking a few hours of their life, I think that is quite a nice payment.

Hell, the entire time we were making *the Roller Blade Seven,* which took months-upon-months, I got paid virtually nothing in terms of cash. But, at the end of the day, I was happy to have donated my time. And, in the early stages of my career, I acted in several films where I was not paid.

In fact, this is the case with most of the low-budget, independent film industry. The cast and the crew are not paid in money.

But you see, people don't know these facts. People who watch films, particularly independent films, want to armchair quarterback the production. As has long been the case, my suggestion to everyone is, before you throw in your two cents about something that you know nothing about, why don't you go and make your own movie.

Conclusion

As I have completed this book and read through the final draft, I could not help but realize that though there is a lot of information presented in these pages there are still so many stories left that I could tell about my interactions with Donald G. Jackson. ...Maybe someday they will all get out there. Or not???

What this book is really about is the dreams of one man, who grew up far from Hollywood, but made his way here and succeeded, at least to a small degree, in achieving his vision of becoming a filmmaker.

The man started from nothing but through effort and creative visualization he left his mark on the world of filmmaking.

In the last few months of this life, I would visit Don in his hospitable room quite frequently. There, though I suppose that he knew he was dying, he continued to speak of making more films. In fact, though he looked terrible due to the ravages of leukemia, he insisted that I bring a camera to his room and film him speaking about filmmaking. I have never looked at that footage, however. It would be hard to remember what had become of the once vibrant and feisty man. Plus, I promised his wife I would never show that footage to anyone for she too witnessed the devastation of what leukemia had done to Don.

For me, though Donald G. Jackson and I certainly had our ups and downs throughout the years, he was a true friend. Though I always spoke about the fact and echoed the thought in my mind that there was always a price to pay to be in association with Don, together we were able to make some seminal films. Plus, we had a lot of fun, a lot of good times, and a lot of laughs.

I hope having presented the stories that I have in this book, you, the reader and/or the aspiring filmmaker, will have gained some guidance and possibly some inspiration from the life, the words, and the films of Donald G. Jackson and get out there and carry on the tradition of art-based independent filmmaking.

Though Don was a trouble individual, he was a true artist. ...An artists—there are so few of those people in the world. And, because of this fact, I am happy that I had the chance to know him and to create *Zen Filmmaking* in association with him.

In closing, for the true artist, life is about one thing, art. If you have the dreams of becoming an artist, be like Donald G. Jackson and let nothing stop you. Create art. Live art. Be art. And from this, the world will become a better place.

APPENDIX

Zen Film Documentaries about Donald G. Jackson by Scott Shaw:

DGJ Q and A
Frogtown News
Life in the Aftermath
Preachin' the Gospel
Cinematografia Obsesion
Bluegrass Christmas Party
A Drive with Linnea and Donald
Donald G. Jackson: Confessions
A Little Bit About What Is Going On
Roller Blade Seven: The Unseen Scenes
Diary of a Michigan Migrant Film Worker
Roller Blade 3: The Movie That Never Was
Interview: The Roller Blade Seven Documentary

Documentaries by Other Filmmakers:

Demon Lover Diary

Donald G. Jackson Filmography Overview:

Producer:
2019 Ghost of El Chupacabra
2015 Max Hell Frog Warrior: A Zen Rough Cut
2014 Rock n' Roll Cops Lite
2012 Hawk Warrior of the Wheelzone
2010 El Chupacabra: Las entrevistas perdido
2010 Crimes of Tomorrow
2008 Naked Avenger
2007 Witch's Brew
2007 Yin Yang Insane
2006 One Shot Sam
2005 Interview
2004 Super Hero Central
2004 Legend of the Dead Boyz
2004 Vampire Blvd. (
2003 Rock n' Roll Cops 2: The Adventure Begins
2002 Max Hell Frog Warrior
1999 Blade Sisters
1999/II Ride with the Devil
1999 Vampire Child
1999 Debbie Does Damnation
1999 Guns of El Chupacabra 3: The Lost Interviews
1999 Ghost Taxi
1999 Armageddon Boulevard
1998 Lingerie Kickboxer
1998 Unmaking the Music Video
1998 Crimes of the Chupacabra
1998 Guns of El Chupacabra II: The Unseen
1997 Hollywood Cops
1997 Guns of El Chupacabra
1996 Rollergator
1996 Shotgun Boulevard
1996 Toad Warrior

1996 Frankenblade
1995 Big Sister 2000
1995 Little Lost Sea Serpent
1995 Raw Energy
1995 Baby Ghost
1994 The Devil's Pet
1993 Return of the Roller Blade Seven
1993/II Twisted Fate
1992 Legend of the Roller Blade Seven
1991 The Roller Blade Seven
1990 The Conversation
1988 Hell Comes to Frogtown
1986 UFO: Secret Video
1986 Roller Blade
1985 I Like to Hurt People
1976 The Demon Lover

Director:
2019 Ghost of El Chupacabra
2015 Max Hell Frog Warrior: A Zen Rough Cut
2012 Hawk Warrior of the Wheelzone
2010 Crimes of Tomorrow
2010 Mimes: Silent But Deadly
2008 Angel Blade
2008 Naked Avenger
2007 Witch's Brew
2004 Legend of the Dead Boyz
2002 Max Hell Frog Warrior
1999 Blade Sisters
1999 Ride with the Devil
1999 Guns of El Chupacabra 3: The Lost Interviews
1999 Ghost Taxi
1999 Armageddon Boulevard
1998 Lingerie Kickboxer
1998 Crimes of the Chupacabra
1998 Guns of El Chupacabra II: The Unseen

1997 Guns of El Chupacabra
1996 Rollergator
1996 Shotgun Boulevard
1996 Toad Warrior
1995 Big Sister 2000
1995 Little Lost Sea Serpent
1995 Raw Energy
1995 Baby Ghost
1994 The Devil's Pet
1993 Carjack
1993 It's Showtime
1993 Return of the Roller Blade Seven
1993 Twisted Fate
1992 Frogtown II
1992 Legend of the Roller Blade Seven
1991 The Roller Blade Seven
1989 Roller Blade Warriors: Taken by Force
1988 Hell Comes to Frogtown
1986 UFO: Secret Video
1986 Roller Blade
1985 I Like to Hurt People
1976 The Demon Lover

Writer:
2019 Ghost of El Chupacabra
2015 Max Hell Frog Warrior: A Zen Rough Cut
2012 Hawk Warrior of the Wheelzone
2010 El Chupacabra: Las entrevistas perdido
2010 Crimes of Tomorrow
2010 Mimes: Silent But Deadly
2009 Aliens on Crack
2008 Max Hell in Frogtown
2008 Angel Blade
2008 Naked Avenger
2007 Witch's Brew
2007 Yin Yang Insane

2004 Legend of the Dead Boyz
2003 Rock n' Roll Cops 2: The Adventure Begins
2002 Max Hell Frog Warrior
1999 Blade Sisters
1999 Ride with the Devil
1999 Vampire Child
1999 Ghost Taxi
1999 Armageddon Boulevard
1998 Lingerie Kickboxer
1998 Crimes of the Chupacabra
1998 Guns of El Chupacabra II: The Unseen
1997 Hollywood Cops
1997 Guns of El Chupacabra
1996 Rollergator
1996 Shotgun Boulevard
1996 Toad Warrior
1996 Frankenblade
1995 Big Sister 2000
1995 Raw Energy
1994 The Devil's Pet
1993 Carjack
1993 Return of the Roller Blade Seven
1993 Twisted Fate
1992 Frogtown II
1992 Legend of the Roller Blade Seven
1991 The Roller Blade Seven
1989 Roller Blade Warriors: Taken by Force
1988 Hell Comes to Frogtown
1986 UFO: Secret Video
1986 Roller Blade
1976 The Demon Lover

Cinematographer:
2014 Rock n' Roll Cops Lite
2012 Hawk Warrior of the Wheelzone
2010 Cinematografia Obsesion

2010 El Chupacabra: Las entrevistas perdido
2010 Crimes of Tomorrow
2010 Mimes: Silent But Deadly
2008 Angel Blade
2007 Witch's Brew
2007 Yin Yang Insane
2006 9mm Sunrise
2004 Vampire Blvd.
2003 Rock n' Roll Cops 2: The Adventure Begins
1999 Blade Sisters
1999 Ride with the Devil
1999 Guns of El Chupacabra 3: The Lost Interviews
1999 Ghost Taxi
1998 Lingerie Kickboxer
1998 Crimes of the Chupacabra
1998 Guns of El Chupacabra II: The Unseen
1997 Hollywood Cops
1997 Guns of El Chupacabra
1996 Rollergator
1996 Toad Warrior
1996 Frankenblade
1995 Big Sister 2000
1995 Raw Energy
1994 The Devil's Pet
1993 It's Showtime
1993 Return of the Roller Blade Seven
1993 Kill or Be Killed
1992 Frogtown II
1992 Legend of the Roller Blade Seven
1991 The Roller Blade Seven
1989 Roller Blade Warriors: Taken by Force
1988 Hell Comes to Frogtown
1986 UFO: Secret Video
1986 Roller Blade

Actor:
2019 Ghost of El Chupacabra
2014 Rock n' Roll Cops Lite
2008 The Adventures of Ace X and Kid Velvet
2007 Yin Yang Insane
2006 One Shot Sam
2004 Super Hero Central
2003 Rock n' Roll Cops 2: The Adventure Begins
1999 Guns of El Chupacabra 3: The Lost Interviews
1999 Armageddon Boulevard
1997 Hollywood Cops
1996 Rollergator
1995 Little Lost Sea Serpent
1993 It's Showtime
1993 Return of the Roller Blade Seven
1992 Legend of the Roller Blade Seven
1991 The Roller Blade Seven
1985 Biohazard

Self:
2014 Donald G. Jackson: Confessions
2012 Scott Shaw and Zen Filmmaking
2012 Preachin' the Gospel
2011 Diary of a Michigan Migrant Film Worker
2010 DGJ Q and A
2009 Bluegrass Christmas Party
2008 A Drive with Linnea and Donald
2008 Frogtown News
2005 Interview: The Roller Blade Seven Documentary
1998 Unmaking the Music Video
1998 Strange Universe: Aliens Are Proof
1998 Guns of El Chupacabra II: The Unseen
1997 Guns of El Chupacabra
1996 Strange Universe
1995 Raw Energy

1990 The Conversation
1980 Demon Lover Diary

FADE OUT.

THE ZEN

www.ingramcontent.com/pod-product-compliance
Lightning Source LLC
Chambersburg PA
CBHW071311150426
43191CB00007B/582